Decolonizing images

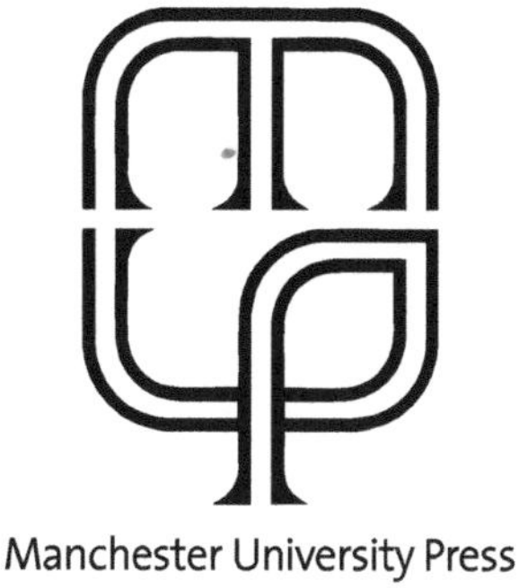

Manchester University Press

Decolonizing images

A new history of photographic cultures in Egypt

Ronnie Close

MANCHESTER UNIVERSITY PRESS

Published by Manchester University Press
Oxford Road, Manchester M13 9PL

www.manchesteruniversitypress.co.uk

British Library Cataloguing-in-Publication Data
A catalogue record for this book is available from the British Library

ISBN 978 1 5261 6595 4 hardback
ISBN 978 1 5261 9473 2 paperback

First published 2024
Paperback published 2026

EU authorised representative for GPSR:
Easy Access System Europe – Mustamäe tee 50,
10621 Tallinn, Estonia
gpsr.requests@easproject.com

Typeset
by New Best-set Typesetters Ltd

Contents

Figures

Acknowledgements

Working within the decoloniality context in relation to Egyptian photographic cultures has proven to be a lengthy research process. I have relied on a number of people whose enormous support helped realize this publication. In particular, I am grateful to those who provided assistance, advice and feedback in the shaping of the manuscript. I would like to thank all those at Manchester University Press who worked on the book at key stages, including the commissioning editor, Alun Richards, who gave me the opportunity to undertake this important project, and Muhammad Ridwaan for the copy-editing, along with the external reviewers who ensured the theoretical orientation of the publication.

I would like to take this opportunity to express gratitude to my colleagues at the American University in Cairo (AUC) for their assistance, especially Dr Mark Deets from the History Department, who collaborated with me on a seminar series in 2020 looking at decolonial issues in relation to Egypt. This research project helped consolidate the ideas for the book and grant support from the institution facilitated my research process and book production. In addition, I thank the Rare Books and Special Collections Library at the AUC for their invaluable experience and consultation, particularly Ola Seif for her expertise in accessing the photographic collections that make up some of the visual materials included in this publication. Other organizations have given immeasurable support by making materials available and hosting interviews during the research period. Tintera's Heba Farid and Zein Khalifa gave their generous assistance and encouragement for the project. I would like to also thank the local artists Ibrahim Ahmed and Nadia Mounier for permissions to reproduce their work and generosity in sharing ideas on their practice for the publication.

I am aware of the omission of many notable Egyptian photographers, artists and photographic works from the book, and this includes images I greatly admire. This book was never intended to be a comprehensive history; rather, it is one of a series of histories of photographic cultures and any omissions should not be seen as a judgement on my part. Due to the focus on decoloniality in the project scope I could not include other local photographic works of merit, and I would like to acknowledge the quality of contemporary photo practices in Egypt. Therefore, it is important to mention some of those whose influential work has had an innovative impact in Egypt: Mohamed Mahdy, Heba Khalifa, Rehab El Dalil, Roger Anis, Rana El Nemr, Maha Maamoun, Amina Kadous, Ravy Shaker, among many others deserving attention. I would encourage future researchers to take up the challenge of writing more inclusively on this remarkable new wave of indigenous photography emerging from Egypt. Where possible I have acknowledged some of the omissions in the chapter endnotes and I apologize in advance to anyone I have left out.

Of course, there are many other people whom I have not been able to mention but I am eternally grateful for their input. I am thankful to Ben Burbridge, Maurice O'Connor and Mark Curran for their encouragement and perspectives on earlier drafts of the manuscript. By no means least, my enduring partner, Yvonne Buchheim, for her unwavering love over the last years in bringing this project to print. Nothing would have been achieved without her ability to listen, ask insightful questions and her endless patience in weathering the upheavals of a writer.

Introduction: Unruly photography

The book you hold in your hands, *Decolonizing images: A new history of photographic cultures in Egypt*, came from an initial awareness about how photographic images function in distinctive ways in local cultures. This was set in motion by a personal decision to move to Cairo in January 2012. As a photographic researcher I encountered a society deeply invested in the currency of the visual and the politics of representation at this time. By attending art exhibitions and events I began to appreciate certain readings, approaches to and diverging roles for photography in Egypt as part of wider visual cultural traditions. The story behind this book comes about from spending over a decade teaching photography and visual media to university students, running public workshops with local arts organizations and, in general, picking up on sensitivities in regard to the visual object. In particular, the photographic draws attention to itself through its public iteration, shareability, while the image remains a personal expression that comes out of an inner, more private world. The idea for decolonizing images in Egypt was the result of an empirical and at times wayward or uneven research process of compiling visual materials from diverse sources, such as Cairo's bookstores, flea markets, arts organization libraries, activist collectives, media archives, online spaces and personal interactions with photographic artists. This book presents an assemblage of diverse visual cultures collected as a way to put forwards not the history of photography but instead a history of photographies in Egypt.

Each of the six themed chapters unfolds a particular critical focus to read bodies of visual materials produced and seen inside Egypt. The book opens with examining decoloniality theory as a lens to consider Egypt's legacies of colonialism and what may be the distinct qualities of its local photographic culture. *Decolonizing images* explores the nineteenth-century encounter between its own cultural traditions and Western-led modernity through photographic technologies of the time, taking place during the rapid colonial expansion across the Arabic-speaking region. From this starting point in history the book looks outwards to examine the role of the visual image in the process of modernity in Egypt, as Walter D. Mignolo theorizes on decoloniality, not to assert that there exists 'alternative modernities but for an alternative to modernity' (Mignolo 2011: xxviii).[1] This involves the process of examining the links to the Western history of photography and to consider other cultural foundations, visual influences and historical drivers in order to appreciate the specific qualities of image production in Egypt. It includes wide-ranging content, such as digital media activism, magazine covers and state censorship, among other relevant materials. Each visual work in this book has been carefully selected to advance the narrative argument on the histories and theoretical approaches to photography in order to provide an in-depth study on the role of the image in the re-envisioning of Egypt from within, spanning the dynamic times of mass nationalism and popular revolt. The visual methodology of the book conceives the photographic-based image as both a documentation device, shaped by social change, alongside one for personal creative expression. The volume has been accessibly written for the reader and is accompanied by lesser-known image works from a range of genres, such as portrait photography, female fashions, digital archives, video documentaries and contemporary photographic art. Such wide-ranging visual works become aesthetic indicators of an indigenous decolonial image culture formed by the internal force of visual sensibilities with their own concerns which do not seek universal validation. The book asks fundamental questions of the medium as a challenge to the dominance of Western-led photographic history to present another genealogy of the image in Egypt:

1. How has this visual heritage constituted its own sensibility of photographic history?
2. In what ways did local photographic practices respond to the impact of Western modernity?
3. In what ways have local traditions shaped indigenous photographic practices and how have cultural forces used the medium?
4. How has popular engagement with and use of the visual brought about an awareness of image politics?

The chapter topics are designed to develop a non-chronological structure on culturally significant image works produced by Egyptian eyes who have, in diverse ways, negotiated the corrosive influence of nationalist-led politics while haunted by the trauma of their colonial past. The radical rupture of the 25 January movement saw digital image technologies become tools of political activism and creative voices for the first time. However, the dolent afterglow of the 2011 Arab uprisings saw such hopes fade away, as has been described by Fahed Al-Sumait in the transition 'from revolution-to-statecraft' (Al-Sumait *et al.* 2014: 27) as Egypt slides into a claustrophobic malaise (Abaza 2020; Paul 2015). Despite the sense of despondency which overshadows the book, reading photographic works may help us rethink the visual as a refuge from the challenges of life in Egypt, both in historical contexts and contemporary spaces, and as 2011 demonstrated there is always hope. Each chapter begins with a framework to mark out the key visual materials connecting important junctures in local history in times of change that ends in the contemporary lacuna of post-2011 Egypt.

Chapter 1, 'Rethinking the histories of photography', starts with a critical theory framing of the book to consider how the camera functions to fragment and transform the world. In this way, specific historical moments are made up of events and the relations between them to constitute what deep-rooted cultural forces can be evident in the image. The photographic moment is specific to a particular situation and environment, but at the same time, it retains the subjectivity of the singular perspective, of its own individual creativity to remain somewhat non-relational. This singularity and specificity can help determine how the image in Egypt is understood because the relationship between being specific and singular deploys these postcolonial concepts in the necessary process of decolonizing the history of photography (Hallward 2002). The book aims to build a premise based on photographic criticism and decoloniality theory in order to form a critical lens to project onto this visual heritage. The local photographic archive of Egypt was informed by the mediation of modernity and this chapter goes on to examine the patina of colonialism.

Chapter 2, 'Decolonizing the lens', discusses the pictorial turn in Egypt's visual history to envision the indigenous uses and potentiality of the medium. Although rarely mentioned by Western photographic historians, Islamic scholars contributed to the invention of the medium and foremost among them was Cairo-based Ibn al-Haytham who wrote the scientifically influential *Kitab al-Manazir* (Book of Optics). In this work he correctly theorized the camera obscura and the process of human vision in eleventh-century Egypt. Subsequently, such scientific discoveries within the Islamic civilization helped form a local image culture which took hold most noticeably during the twentieth century in bustling metropolitan centres, such as Cairo and Alexandria, where a new bourgeoisie embraced photography. In these innovations, the medium became both a subjective lens and psychological space without set boundaries under an age of Ottoman reform and new-found modernity. One intriguing intersection occurred when Orientalist photography met with indigenous visual traditions through the landscape genre of the medium as locals were drawn into an encounter with the external gaze of the camera lens (Golia 2009; Mitchell 1991). Foregrounded in the launch of the daguerreotype image, the French painter Horace Vernet and Daguerreotypist Frédéric Goupil-Fesquet went to Egypt to photograph its ancient antiquity.

However, the lesser-known work by Egyptian photographer Muhammad Sadiq Bey (1822 or 1832–1902) consists of collections of photo albums on the sacred sites of the Islamic world, including the first photographic records of the religious expedition from Cairo to the Kaaba in Mecca as part of the annual hajj pilgrimage. This unique photographic history contradicts the commonly held perception that Islam harbours injunctions against human representation or Muslim restraint in regard to the visual arts. Rather, it could be argued that religious traditions in Egypt may, in fact, have inspired photography to become a cultural tool at a formative time of rapid change. European colonial eyes often desired landscape images depicting ancient Pharaonic history at the centre of Orientalist photography (Woodward 2003). However, local photographers did much to redress the Eurocentric colonial lens to produce, instead, other representations of the landscape that emerge out of different social concerns and aesthetic traditions to transcend dominant visual frameworks.

Chapter 3, 'National images', considers how the use of photography was popularized through the illustrated magazine media industry to shape collective belonging and influence the cultural imagination of an emergent nation-state. Various types of visual magazines flourished in the early twentieth century and these collections recorded and shaped the transformation of everyday life under modernity. Illustrated magazines, like *al-Musawwar* (The Photographer's Studio), used photographs in graphic ways to report on news, culture and celebrities in order to reflect the interests of its middle-class readers. Hence, the photograph in print takes on a persuasive role in mediating new social values and the nationalist politics of a country moving from colonial to decolonial self-rule. Later, in the Nasserist Arab Republic, the press was nationalized and the state inherited various photographic collections while struggling to set up institutions that could safeguard the medium, resulting in decades of slow decay of valuable historical materials. These surviving magazine archives help position the role of the photograph in the popular press, but are often poorly archived in government-run institutions or by independent organisations (Ryzova 2014). The preservation of image materials has become contentious as the housing in archives brings into question the maintenance of cultural memory, autonomy of knowledge and the unlearning of colonial legacies.

Chapter 4, 'Histories of the street', looks at how the street activism during the 2011 period has been archived through online digital platform projects. These vernacular images enabled, in a fundamental way, new understandings of cultural politics and social transformation to visualize the revolutionary hope of emergent grassroots movements. Two such activist projects, 858: Archive of Resistance and Filming Revolution, are unconventional and innovative online media 'anarchives' (Snowdon 2020: 64) which corroborate the historic visual legacy of street struggles and collectivist thinking in an unconventional way. These media projects set out to counter the best efforts of the military regime to detract from the popular memory of political dissent and civil disobedience during this revolutionary time. Cairo video collective group Mosireen (Determined) were indicative of this activist spirit and formed within the visceral street atmosphere, becoming a seminal part of digital media projects Tahrir Media Tent and Tahrir Cinema. A second project, Filming Revolution, is a multi-layered, meta-documentary media work developed by filmmaker and academic Alisa Lebow and published by Stanford University Press in 2015. This interactive website uses a graphical interface and non-linear design to arrange the contents drawn from interviews, films, artworks and other digital materials. Both archival projects, in contrasting ways, seek to preserve the digital image history of this time to offer a counter-narrative to the governmental propaganda disseminated on mainstream media networks in Egypt (Snowdon 2020).[2] These online works contextualize the recent memory of citizenry and emancipation during times of revolution and call into question the values, codes and ethics of the digital image in the documentation of struggle. These projects warrant careful consideration because they move beyond chronotropic readings of the digital image alone to embody the activist potential of photography and represent the marginal in the reproduction of new knowledge in this non-linear treatment of history.

Chapter 5, 'Censorship gazes on female portraiture', deals with female representation as subjects operating under the heteronormative lens that polices Egyptian public space. This includes cultural censorship and the problematic role the Egyptian state continues to play as the patriarchal arbiter of behavioural and moral values set against pervasive contemporary visual media technologies. Three diverse image-based works involve the regulation of female bodies in the public sphere which have triggered remarkable responses that tell us much about the logic of censorship. The first involves the digital self-portrait of activist Aliaa al-Mahdy, who took much of Egypt by storm when she posted a nude self-portrait on her personal blog, Diary of a Rebel. The image went viral within hours resulting in over 1.5 million visits to the website and sparked radical reactions that ranged from praise to death threats. The second visual work for consideration consists of doctored fashion photographs on the Adlat website, a female-orientated online community which offers users tips on a range of gender roles aligned to conservative Muslim values. The last visual case history in this chapter examines international book compendiums of photography stocked in Cairo bookstores. Such anthologies often include nude art images as part of the canon of Western art history and this presents a dilemma for the regime. In these editions a process of state censorship has been carried out that entails hand-painting each photographic image to deny the full erotic impact of the body for the public viewer. These three visual case studies map out differing reactions to female photographic representation as the globalized nature of contemporary image culture encounters Egyptian censorship. These mediated visual works, in certain ways, are indicative of the entangled expression of gender which appears to refute the objectification of Westernized female representation and conform to traditional conservative societal codes. Such expressive tensions, between public and private behaviours, are often part of the stresses many feel within contemporary Egypt which are regularly negotiated through photographic representation.

The final chapter, 'Contemporary lenses within Egypt', looks at the visual approaches of innovative photographic art practices in Egypt. These art photographers remain marginal, if not rather eclipsed by the volume of content produced by the mainstream media under the tentacles of governmental control. The dubious nature of the state's interference in visual culture has altered, if not impeded, the development of a sustainable ecosystem of creative contemporary art practices and, in broad terms, an appreciation of the photographic image which often challenges clichéd visual narratives about the medium. Many photographic artists operate with nuanced forms of personal expression, manipulating images and thinking beyond the direct image object itself to instil a subjective vision and poetic truth about their position within Egypt. Moreover, the photographic artists in the chapter share something of an interest in the imaginary to transcend the everyday and adopt an indirect approach to social or political issues in a visual representation of subjective realism. This generation of photographic artists has emerged in the aftermath of the 2011 uprisings, and aims to create dialogue on cultural representation, identity and photographic aesthetics. The selection of art photography projects examined in this chapter consists of the work of two practitioners, Nadia Mounier and Ibrahim Ahmed, who express the indigenous imagining of Egyptian visual culture. These creative photographic practices use the image to mediate a number of positions involving the state, the wider conservative society and globalization by inscribing themselves within specific contexts. This generation has much to say about the state of the nation and patriarchal power, as the personal can become political. These artists constitute a contemporary wave of Egyptian image-makers who are rethinking Western narratives on the medium to look both outwards and inwards, capturing life among Egypt's sprawling cities. This contemporary vision turns the personal inner space towards the social world to explore the self-image, represent the marginalized and offer psychological lenses to complicate national narratives. Such art photography projects in this final chapter reflect on earlier themes, historical phases and theories addressed in the book to revisit key issues of specificity and singularity in Egypt's photographic cultures. These present-day photographic artists hold a mirror to the globalized nature of modernity, colonial pasts and the emancipatory potential of image cultures vividly felt during 2011.

Decolonizing images looks at the role the visual has played in knowledge-making of a different genealogy of thoughts, needs and effects. Through the invention of photography Egypt encountered Western modernity head on but went on to reclaim it in its own terms, most visibly in 2011, by using the digital image and mediating it into the technological twenty-first century. However, Egypt has never lost sight of its own culture to ensure its visual traditions endure in the contemporary world and beneath a cursory glance remains independent of the full force of external cultural capitalism. This book opens up a richer understanding for the reader to appreciate the rare and often misunderstood visual materials and responses to the photograph that constitutes this particular archaeology of the medium; seen beyond the commonly held image of Egypt as a land of ancient Pharaonic pasts. Outside of the stereotypical lens, Egypt and the photographic enjoy an invaluable connection to other values, rhythms and rhymes rarely included in the dominant revisions of the medium. The heady days of 2011 still ask fundamental questions of the digital image to disseminate diverse political views, accommodate deep-rooted religious sensibilities and address the need for social change in a complex vision of this culturally influential Arab state. This volume is an opportunity to re-imagine Egypt from within, circumvent the visual cliché of historical wonders alongside the ghostly spectre of colonialism and appreciate its own photographic image culture anew.

The picture of Egypt has been fiercely contested and often mythologized within its own nationalist notions for far too long. Moreover, the meaning of photographs cannot be anchored down easily or pigeonholed into uncomplicated and, arguably, unrepresentative narratives. *Decolonizing images* sets out to develop a vision on the local, indigenous genealogy of the photographic heritage of Egypt and, in doing so, continues the essential practice of edifying the history of photography. The events of 25 January 2011 placed Egypt at the front and centre of discussions around radical transformations taking place in photographic cultures at the time. The widely circulated digital image of Khaled Said, a victim of police brutality, became archetypal of photographic agency integrated into networked computational systems and political activism.[3] This book seeks to provide a deeper understanding of the cultural role of photography in Egypt and to unpack its ability to disrupt stereotypical visions and challenge Western narratives in the history of photography, in order to do the urgent labour of delinking knowledge. The connection between photography and colonial power structures is evidenced in the aforementioned introduction of the daguerreotype process in 1839. Politician and scientist Dominique François Arago launched the new technology in Paris for the members of the Institut d'Égypte, and as part of his speech, Arago reflected on earlier French colonial expeditions to Egypt to lament that the Pharaonic monuments had not been captured by the daguerreotype photographic process in the past because 'the learned world is forever deprived of it by the greed of the Arabs' (Grigsby 2013: 115).[4] Egypt's photographic heritage is as much a psychological space as a geographical one, based in the realities of the everyday life as experienced in its metropolitan areas and vast desert landscapes. This book posits the photographic image in a new light as a mediation between colonial legacies, nationalist strategies and decolonializing aesthetics to frame the image as part of a homegrown culture. Moreover, Egypt's visual culture is a creative expression of its own value codes in the contemporary paradigm, on its own terms, and can authenticate a non-Western visual history which refutes Orientalist trajectories. The following chapter will discuss the critical debates on decoloniality theory to rethink local cultural sensibilities in regard to the photographic image.

Notes

1 Walter D. Mignolo's theory on three aspects to modernity is of particular relevance here, and in his *Darker Side of Western Modernity: Global Futures, Decolonial Options*, he defines his critique. He writes, 'One type is internal to the history of Europe itself and in that sense these premises are a Eurocentered critique of modernity (for example, psychoanalysis, Marxism, poststructuralism, postmodernity), and the other two types emerged from non-European histories entangled with western modernity. One of them focuses on the idea of western civilization (for example, dewesternization, Occidentosis), and the other on coloniality (such as postcoloniality, decoloniality)' (Mignolo 2011: xi).

2 Peter Snowdon uses the term 'anarchive' in his *People Are Not an Image* (2020) as a portmanteau definition that blends anarchy with the archive to deliberately distance his scholarship from dominant Western narrative understanding of the archive as being representative of static repositories of the past. The vernacular anarchive, then, operates as a living or performing archive of the people as well as the people as an archive that exists in a symbiotic relationship.

3 Khaled Said died in police custody in 2010 over six months before the 2011 uprising erupted. His mother took his photo in the morgue with her phone and then released this disturbing digital image of his badly disfigured face on social media platforms and to local journalists. The image sparked a widespread public reaction on Facebook as Google executive Wael Ghonim moderated a group, 'We Are All Khaled Said', that was to grow to prominence during the 25 January protests.

4 On 7 January 1839, members of the Académie des Sciences first viewed examples
  of Daguerreotypes invented by Louise-Jacques Daguerre. On 3 July 1839, French
  mathematician, physicist, astronomer and politician Dominique François Arago
  made the first brief scientific announcement and explanation of Daguerre's process
  to the Chambre des députés. Daguerre's method of fixing an image on a metal
  plate became the first commonly used photographic process. It produced a single
  positive image on a highly polished silver-plated sheet of copper.

1

Rethinking the histories of photography

Unlearning photographic modernity

Decolonizing images involves examining the meaning, function and aesthetics of locally produced photographic works circulated in the context of visual traditions and cultures mostly within Egypt. The approach is an interdisciplinary one, informed by photographic criticism and postcolonial theories, and, in particular, decoloniality is deployed as a framework to examine the visual material histories as a means to understand the camera image as a discursive episteme. By this decolonizing, the image can counter marginalization and contribute to a richer debate on the histories of photography rather than the Western-dominated narrative of the medium. This proposes the photographic image is both specific to its conditions of cultural production, yet it is not only specified by its origin alone. In this way, decolonizing photography reflects how an indigenous culture visually communicates and becomes constituted; resolute in its own environment while existing in a network of historical markers and aesthetic concerns that can transcend geographical boundaries. In this sense, the decolonized image occupies a space as an object of knowledge that is neither simply delinked from the Westernized conventions of photography nor a rejection of Western knowledge systems per se. Rather it is aware of other non-Western economies of knowledge beyond 'epistemological subordination' (Connell 2016: 3) that in many regards have been overlooked by mainstream photographic history. Raewyn Connell advocates decolonizing Western knowledge so as to enrich epistemological debate and endorse other universalisms in an alternative knowledge history, such as the Golden Age of Islam as an exemplar of alternative knowledge structures (Connell 2016). For Connell this is a substantive system which did not emerge solely from within the Western canon and remains significantly autonomous.[1] Broadly speaking, decolonizing the photographic image disconnects from the prevalent lens of Western art history to enjoy a degree of autonomous agency from its judgement values and the room to rethink the cultural encounter with imperialism, modernity and, later, neoliberalist forces. Moreover, it remains informed by and embedded within its own visual aesthetic traditions which have been supressed and unacknowledged in an asymmetrical relationship with the ideological *Weltanschauung* of Western knowledge systems. Nevertheless, within the goals of decoloniality measures of Western thought itself can be useful critical tools to further its own cause because the ambition of autonomous thought is more intersectional than mere outright rejection. Achille Mbembe continues to be a reference point on this decoloniality issue, as he comments:

> The western archive is singularly complex. It contains within itself the resources of its own refutation. It is neither monolithic nor the exclusive property of the West. Africa and its diaspora decisively contributed to its making and should legitimately make foundational claims on it. Decolonizing knowledge is therefore not simply about de-westernization. (Mbembe 2015: 24)

In this sense critical theory includes the means to challenge hierarchies of knowledge and delinking of decoloniality does not necessarily involve dismissing the entire intellectual canon of the West. From a historical perspective, modernity itself is a somewhat capricious term created by imperial cultures with photography a mischievous partner to its conceptual hierarchy. Modernity, shaped by the Enlightenment project, is not solely a phenomenon, unlike industrialization or modernization, and modernity has a cultural framework often thought of as Eurocentric. This is part of the schism of the modernity project which separates out the natural and social worlds to place the subject in an anthropomorphic centre. Part of the uncertainty of modernity emerges from the fixed-point perspective of the subject that frames the world under the appearance of progress and advancement because the modern age has never really existed and every different age can be thought of as modern (Latour 1993). Cartesian perspectivalism is the subjective rationality of a single-point viewpoint, in the photographic through the scopic lens of the camera, as it appears to bring into focus a vision of the world as a field of spatio-temporal certainty. Colonialism was bound up with such certainties rooted in hierarchy as the invention of photography was a chronotropic regime that fixed subjects and objects within set relationships. As has been noted, identities can become entombed in the photographic process and this contact zone of representation establishes an exterior to existence, a mediation of life through the camera image that is an inseparable character of modernity (Mitchell 1991; Pinney and Peterson 2003). Martin Heidegger's lecture in 1938, *Die Zeit des Weltbildes* (The Age of the Worldview), appears to call into question this organizational gaze of modernity as the world becomes an image in the distinction of the modern age (Mitchell 1991). This separation of the image and the world through modernity was taken up by critical theorists when discussing photography who pointed towards photographic images as particularly potent because they simulate and seem to reproduce the world to thus intrude on human perception (Flusser 2000; Mitchell 1992; Sontag 2001). As Susan Sontag suggests, 'Notions of image and reality are complementary. When the notion of reality changes, so does that of the image, and vice versa' (Sontag 2001: 160). In other words, the image can become an impression, resemblance or mimesis of reality as an object or as a mental process, and in turn, reality can be conflated with the image. In this Western philosophical tradition, as Sontag implies through her use of Plato's *Allegory of the Cave*, arguably there is a closed ontological loop between reality and the image as both are viewing experiences and mental processes tied up in the perception of the world (Sontag 2001).

Decoloniality in African studies repudiates some of the orthodox understandings and deployments of modernity as the term in visual technologies is often narrated as a dichotomy between localization and globalization. Henry Drewal challenges set notions on cultural modernity as he points out that Western art movements, such as Cubism, arguably took aesthetic influence from African artistic practices: 'Modernity is not a European invention. It is the result of the interactions and exchanges of diverse peoples across the planet over a long period of time' (Drewal 2013: 23). Decoloniality theorist Walter Mignolo outlines three distinct forms in the critique of modernity; first, from within the Western traditions and found in psychoanalysis, Marxism and postmodernity, among other analytical tools. From this he goes on to suggest the two others were formed externally in non-European historical contexts and can be found in, second, de-Westernisation movements (e.g. Islamic Republic of Iran) and, third, in the field of decoloniality studies originating in postcolonial studies (Mignolo 2011). However, these last two potentially intersecting trajectories of knowledge with similar goals of autonomous thought and socio-political transformation have both become entangled with and complicated by the first decoloniality category of critical tools of Western modernity. Nevertheless, the contemporary denunciation of modernity is still timely as the concerns of the Global South knowledge-making can have another heritage of thoughts, affects and problems, as Mignolo writes, 'Coloniality, in other words, is constitutive of modernity – there is no modernity without coloniality' (Mignolo 2011: 3). In a similar way, Prita Meier expresses concern about the appropriateness of modernity when discussing Swahili visual culture:

> But I suggest the very interpretative framework of modernity cannot fully account for the ways Africans co-created cultures and aesthetic practices in and outside the African continent during the age of colonialism and global capitalism. (Meier 2013: 96)

Postcolonial writer Paul Gilroy adds to the debate to envisage a nuanced, plural modernity composed of multiple histories to reject dominant narratives which try to reproduce and placate modernity as a collision between the imperial and the local, or the Western and the Other, Occidentalism and Orientalism (Al-Saidi 2014; Gilroy 1993). Such scholars set out to challenge the prevailing idea of modernity comprising dominant core narratives alongside ancillary and ultimately inferior ones (Mignolo 2011). In the Global South marginalized modernity orbits differently in the knowledge economy to be often rendered secondary to Western modes of knowledge. According to Mignolo, modernity's historical roots were formed as a result of three main phases of Western imperialism: first, the Iberian of Spanish and Portuguese power; second, the rise of Northern Europe in the nineteenth century; and last, North American control over the twentieth century. Each had a period of global influence which generated wealth exploitation under the guise of technological advancement and inserted modern values to the so-called under-developed. In the contemporary setting the new world order has consisted of dispersed global capital in 'a polycentric world interconnected by the same type of economy' (Mignolo 2011: 7).[2] Therefore, the introduction of photography in the nineteenth century was bound up with the expansion of European modernity in all its modes and the operation of colonial empire. Under this phase of world rule the colonial exploitation of Egypt included the cultural production of photographic images and brought about an awareness of the world in the production of an image of the world, containing external ideological concerns and foreign frameworks. Decoloniality seeks to disconnect from the logic of Eurocentric modernity which can be constitutive beyond the rhetoric of modernization and industrial development. In historical terms decoloniality has been blurred with decolonization which relates to a third option of non-aligned nations; the twentieth-century Cold War forces of capitalism and communism as first materialized in the Bandung Conference in 1955.[3]

Western value coding can privilege the indexical depth of the photograph at the price of other approaches, such as the surface materiality in what visual anthropologist Christopher Pinney defines as 'surfacism' in reference to everyday Indian photography as a sign of 'vernacular modernism' (Pinney 2003: 202). Moreover, in discussing the photography work by Nigerian artist Olu Oguibe, Pinney goes on to suggest that the importance of surface aesthetics lies in the haptic form of the senses that is part of a decolonial aesthetic. This emphasis on image touch can be understood as disconnecting from vertical depth in the photographic which has often been representative of colonial regimes (Pinney 2003). This perspective reiterates the surface as the location of meaning in the visual object to suggest this is a decolonializing act that delinks from indexical and other more cerebral ways in the Western approaches to reading images. As Arjun Appadurai suggests this is part of the labour of decolonization and adds that the postcolonial stays within the subject and object relationship of the social sciences, while decoloniality questions more broadly the entire representational framework itself and those relationships embedded within it (Appadurai 1997). The representation of the world is mediated as someone represents it, articulated through thought, ideology and the senses. But such expressions are enunciations not only of the world but also of earlier enunciations that form representational regimes. Therefore, enunciation is performed and framed by other disciplines and systems of ideas like liberalism or Marxism, or even artistic conventions (Mignolo 2011). To the casual reader such distinctions may seem inconsequential or pedantic even, but it comes into play here because decolonializing images relates to the knowledge present in marginalized epistemologies. Moreover, despite the useful ways postcolonialism and decoloniality absorb each other in research fields, some differences remain; however, to rank such variations would be a short-sighted venture (Appadurai 1997). Therefore, photographic cultures in Egypt can be read from a non-Western perspective of the medium that strives to circumvent the tendency towards fixed-view positions that often sets up hierarchical knowledge.

As stated, challenging the primacy of the indexical in reading photographic images could be useful to rethink aesthetic values and visual materiality in a decolonial context. However, it may also be prudent to retain historical depth because it remains a key part of a photograph's specificity. This vertical axis brings together time and space of the exposure moment that can anchor intersecting cultural and political contexts in the image production to exhibit social relations and power dynamics. In order to counter the history of photography the shutter of time needs to be paused so as to make the viewer work to see the inversion of colonial gazes. Like the negative–positive relationship in layers of analogue film, the decolonial can expose contemporary social relations and imperial powers bound together in the photographic moment. Visual culture theorist Ariella Azoulay argues for reparations to address long-standing legacies of colonial injustice and inequality as social hierarchies can be mediated through image politics. Azoulay has written on the imperial violence in the case of plantation slave Renty Taylor's portrait held by Harvard University:

> Unlearning is a way to reverse the role of the normalized milestones that structure the phenomenological field out of which modern history is still conceived and narrated, such as those of progress and democratization in the place of (for example) destruction, appropriation, and deprivation, followed (as if in later phases) by the imperial "generosity" of providing for those dispossessed by imperialist policies. (Azoulay 2019: 15)

Azoulay makes a powerful case for the historical inequality of photography through its means of production and coercion at the time of exposure. Moreover, such collections of photographs have been housed in academic archives for decades of scholarly silence over the injustices documented in the images that served the interests of Western knowledge. The issue of how photographic collections are preserved and hosted plagues the visual heritage of Egypt. Colonial contexts, nationalism and digital image activism, among others, have all struggled to maintain a functional visual archive to embody a collective memory and as this book shows this is no simple matter in the case of Egypt.

Decolonial aesthetics in Egypt's visual heritage is a fluid process full of uncertainty in haptic senses and latent readings of the photograph in a chronotropic world. Image archelogy is in constant flux to better understand the photographic as an object that can move between surface to depth to indexical concerns, to reveal past and present histories, seen and unseen motifs and local cultural meanings. Reading images through decoloniality yields new insights for the viewer to undo the passivity of spectatorship and the excessive lethargy of image consumption most evident in globalized social media cultures. This is not simply about the labour of de-Westernizing the history of photography because such knowledge was never the exclusive property or construct of the West alone. Rather it is the realization that Egypt, like other places in the Global South, played its own role to develop a specific photographic heritage with the critical tools to determine itself within its own traditions. Decoloniality becomes pertinent to consider earlier formations of visual knowledge generated by Islamic thinkers who fore-shadowed the ocular in Europe through theological investigation and scientific discoveries.

Reification, representation and meaning-making of photographic images in the Egyptian context requires consideration of Islamic jurisprudence that is part of its cultural genealogy. This affects the reading of the visual in this specificity as there is a fixed stability of the sacred and divine which retains some level of epistemic and ritualistic resoluteness. Photographic ontology is complicated for Islam by the mimetic quality of the image that can be seen to add a level of separation between the individual and direct experience. As noted by Christiane Gruber, when researching the visual representation of the Prophet Muhammad, 'depictions of the Prophet developed from naturalism to abstraction, that is, from figural presence to physical absence' (Gruber 2019: 17).[4] In the contemporary situation two Egyptian sheikhs, Yusuf al-Qaradawi and Taha Jaber al-Alwani, appeared to harbour similar concerns as Plato over mimesis in Western philosophical traditions. In the sheikhs' lectures they sought to differentiate between the world and the world of images in order to remedy Islamic beliefs with contemporary culture.[5] Photographic values, histories and processes have drawn on non-Western belief systems and need to be understood as an encounter between Islamic thought and the photographic modernity. A particular example of the intersectionality lies in the Nile Delta area that holds a long-standing tradition of regional Sufism through *tariqa*s (orders), founded in the city of Tanta by al-Sayyid Ahmad al-Badawi in the thirteenth century. Sufi beliefs embody intellectual, emotional and psychological dimensions to life, such as *hal* (spiritual state) and *maqam* (stage on the path), among others. This local religious sensibility of the Delta region embodies a spiritual geneal-ogy that goes beyond any Sufi order to be aligned to a broader Muslim perspective which states the universe constitutes both visible and invisible properties. The components of the visible consist of natural materials and geography, whereas the invisible involves the unseen spiritual dimension of the unknowable and imperceptible presence of God (el-Aswad 2006). This spiritual realm is made of important entities and forces active in the world of 'angels, soul (*ruh,* as being eternal), holy persons (prophets and *wali*s, friends of God), holy places, and *baraka* (divine grace or blessing) intermediate between the two worlds' (el-Aswad 2006: 503). The spiritual and cultural heritage interconnects with elements of religious dogma to become a socially constructed knowledge specific to Egypt and is shaped by the use of and reception towards photographic images. Visual methodologies must include this social dimension that involves the viewer as a key part in the production of collective narrative meaning. As visual culture theorist Gillian Rose states, 'what is important about images is not simply the image itself, but how it is seen by particular spectators who look in particular ways' (Rose 2001: 11–12).

New aesthetic regimes

The dominant narrative of the history of photography begins during the nineteenth century to mostly view Egypt as a colourful backdrop for European adventurers, a sun-soaked location of Pharaonic splendours with an ancient alluring beauty. Such a constructed vision suggests photographic culture was mostly dominated by foreign producers who focused their colonial gaze on ancient monuments and, despite some merited exceptions, only included the local population as extras in the performance of Egyptomania. For the casually informed reader this view of nineteenth-century photographic history ignores the key role local Egyptians played in the evolution of the medium as both a science and an art form. In time, Egyptians redressed this representational imbalance by moving from in front to behind the camera

(Golia 2009) to become active participants in constructing photographic cultures, thereby shaping their own specific visual sensibility from within their own visual traditions to mediate photography as a tool of modernity. Maria Golia describes this process in her book *Egypt and Photography* as a transformation in local photographic culture, 'when Egyptians [are] no longer only the subjects of photographs, but photographers' (Golia 2009: 7). Egyptian sociologist Mona Abaza in her *Cairo Collages: Everyday Life Practices after the Event* discusses the motivation of European photographers who favoured elevated perspectives to distance themselves from Egyptian life and in an Orientalist manner, 'dominate the city from above, and to try to comprehend the logic behind the labyrinthine, visually chaotic, and opaque oriental cities' (Abaza 2020: 54).

This legacy of early photographic history was forcefully eclipsed in the twenty-first-century setting by digital communication technologies that became critical parts of the 2011 protest movements as the camera phone became a subversive voice of the citizenry in a time of revolution. As part of this political process through photography the digital image became an instrument for personal voice and collective expression as well as propelling the public demands for political reforms and social change. However, such an apotheosis for digital technologies throws up other questions of what technological protocols, social codes and meanings exist in regard to the use of the visual in Egypt. Furthermore, this raises the issue of whether digital image production and dissemination can truly empower citizens in meaningful ways. The camera fragments and transforms the world in three distinct ways of what is involved in the photographic act: as the shutter records in time the image taken; in space as the lens frames what is before it; and finally, in the political as those who operate the apparatus go on to control value and produce meaning. As the photographic act slices up this chronotropic world, at times in the violent reproduction of colonial power, the camera's shutter can be understood as not only a metaphor for the operation of power, but in the materialization of colonial technologies of control in the 'intolerable gaze of conflict' (Carville 2010: 345). Azoulay goes on to discuss image politics in a forthright manner to state that the categorical problem is that 'photography developed with imperialism; the camera made visible and acceptable imperial world destruction and legitimated the world's reconstruction on empire's terms' (Azoulay 2019: 6).

Specific historical moments are made up of events and the relations between them constitute what is specified in the acumen of cultural meanings. The decolonizing image seeks to unlearn the ideological currents running through the dominant narratives of photographic cultures, one mostly a Western version of the medium underwritten by European white males involved in the reproduction of cultural, political and technological privilege (Azoulay

2019). The photographic moment is thus created in a specific historical and geographical situation but is not determined fully by its environment alone as it retains a subjective element of its own creative singularity to remain, to a degree, non-relational. The absolutely decolonized image can manage to account for its own specific qualities beyond debates on cultural authenticity and fidelity to societal norms. Decoloniality looks beyond temporal and spatial qualities of the image and such a critical undertaking is not a straightforward task in Egypt because the state is unaccustomed to probing visual criticism that can expose the shortcomings. The contemporary is contentious and, in many ways, it is less complicated to do research work on the ancient Pharaonic past than on more recent visual culture.

The narrative of local image production within the photographic heritage of Egypt continues the urgent process of decolonizing the history of photography. Photography was a dynamic communication medium for a new age in the nineteenth century as colonial powers developed visual themes, genres and uses of the technology emerging through diverse practices complemented by academic disciplines. Early image-making processes helped usher in the photographic age with the daguerreotype technology developed in France in 1839 and the slower release of the calotype process in Britain at the same time. Soon after other photographic image innovations advanced quickly in the following decades as the widespread use of ways to visualize the world led up to the amateur camera, known as Kodak's Brownie, in 1888. This new technology heralded the age of social photography in the hands of legions of 'Kodak fiends' (Berkley 2015: 375) that enriched the aesthetic with vernacular approaches to the medium. Much of this type of outline forms a heritage comprising well-known historical developments that can seem authoritative on the nineteenth-century timeline in the cultural history of photography. However, such a narrative omits the contribution of those from the Arabic Middle East and North African (MENA) region themselves and fails to significantly acknowledge the role of local populations in the creation of the medium in technological or creative terms. In the contemporary setting, the 25 January protest movements of 2011 appeared to intersect with twenty-first-century digital image discourses occurring at the time. A key part of this democratization of the photographic medium included the widely circulated digital image of Khaled Said who became archetypal of photography's integration into networked computational systems and political activism on the streets. Indeed, the photograph released by Said's mother of his mutilated face drew iconic resonance with earlier iterations in the history of photography, such as Emmett Till's photograph circulated in the media decades earlier.[6]

In broad terms, the early history of photography comes across as a Eurocentric one, a lens onto the world, as the medium became a visualizing discourse tainted by the construction of empire (Edwards 2006). Despite the body of contemporary literature which has set out to readdress this asymmetry in the canon of photography by putting forwards other visual practices and image narratives beyond the prevailing discourses, the medium remains, principally, underpinned by Western concerns and cultural values.[7] Furthermore, such a disequilibrium of interests in nineteenth-century photographic work of the Arabic MENA region, arguably, has become overly formulaic by leaning on Orientalism too heavily in the evaluation of archives which are over-referenced image sources. Bodies of well-known nineteenth-century photographic work, such as the Pascal Sébah collection in the Getty Images archive, prevail in research and are presented as prominent photo studio work reflective of the region and read as ciphers of local visual sensibilities or even non-Western visual traditions. The over reliance on Orientalism as theory framework itself in relation to photography has been debated by some critical voices; however, others suggest it remains the most authoritative framework available in the examination of visual representation. In certain terms, this viewpoint proposes that all local practices of the medium cannot be disconnected from Western modernity and no genuine cultural autonomy is truly possible for photography made within the Arabic MENA context. Indicative of this, the photographic historian Ali Behdad writes, 'Indigenous photography in and of itself, I maintain, does not constitute an oppositional locus or resistant iconography, for it too belongs to the Orientalist network that mediates its vocabulary and thematics of representation' (Behdad 2016: 8). This suggests photographic production was infused by Orientalism in light of modernity's historical impact and that no camera-based productions can be truly autonomous or wholly delinked from the legacy of Western colonial imperialism. Such a viewpoint can easily become overly determined itself because when looking back at historical materials colonialism and photography's acquiescence to imperial concerns is clearly evident but this is not the whole picture either. Other contemporary writers suggest the term Orientalism itself has been overstated in photographic histories and rejects the basic binary of imperial dominance met by local resistance; in that respect the colonial gaze meets with the defiance of indigenous cultures. Scholars suggest Orientalism has been a critical lens which can, at times, be crudely applied as it tends to overlook the subtlety of the specified works or narrative deviations in the individual identity of nativist photographic practices. For instance, photographer Pascal Sébah was born in Turkey and moved to work in Cairo in addition to different parts of the Arabic MENA region expanding the family business. Photographic historian Michele Woodward discusses Sébah's legacy and states that Orientalism 'has been used too broadly, obscuring nuances and inconsistencies, not only between different photographers' bodies of work but also within them' (Woodward

2003: 363). This position typically aims to revise Orientalism's impact on the region to explore the complex contours of postcoloniality in relation to Egypt's photographic heritage.[8] Much of the contemporary writing and scholarship on nineteenth- and early twentieth-century photography has examined the imaginary Orient by administering a degree of Saidian theory in order to show how European powers intersected with and exploited cultural politics (Behdad 2016). Commenting on this, Nissan N. Perez writes, 'Literature, painting and photography fit the real Orient into the imaginary or mental mould existing in the western's mind' (Perez 1988: 50). However, issues arise on what constitutes the notion of the local because it may not be entirely indigenous. Harder to resolve is the debate on the veracity of the image which haunts the visual materials in representational terms. In this regard, the photographic image is particularly prone to controversy in the struggle to constitute image politics, as James Clifford states, 'to displace any transcendent regime of [cultural] authenticity or purity' (Clifford 1988: 338). Late nineteenth-century photography conforms to certain technological limitations of the time and social conventions of the age that produced a type of recognizable monochrome look and aesthetic approach. This sense of visual uniformity was added to through the production process itself which had to use cumbersome camera equipment, unstable darkroom kits and long exposure times to make images; coupled with immobile and unwieldy props such as painted studio backdrops often used in portraiture work of the time.

Part of the attraction to the Arabic MENA region lay with the volumes of sunlight required to make photographic exposures in this period as Egypt became a media hub. Within this Europeans depended on unacknowledged local labour in the photographic process that over time resulted in a gradual decolonializing of the colonial gaze as skills and technical knowledge was appropriated. Despite impediments many photographers of mixed backgrounds excelled, such as Abdullah Frères and the aforementioned Sébah, who opened successful studios in Cairo and across the Ottoman region to establish an early visual narrative that muddles Orientalist debates. These early practitioners adapted Eurocentric aesthetic models to cater for various local photographic markets, going on to produce significant archives documenting the unfolding of modernity at this time.[9] Hence, Egypt, like many similar colonialized states, developed its own distinctive photographic culture to contribute in a meaningful way to global histories of the medium. Moreover, this criteria does raise a number of supplementary points about the value of these photo studios, namely, are such image forms derivative of European work or do they stand alone as authoritative forms of visual culture production, free of colonial influence? What constitutes indigenous value and what should local Egyptian photography practices possess in order to remain sufficiently distinct from other practices of the time or even as a singular form of expression?[10] Pinney succinctly frames this question of cultural autonomy in *Photography's Other Histories* when he writes, 'How do local visual traditions mediate modernity in ways that are independent from and critical of European modernity?' (Pinney 2003: 202). Amid the indisputable power asymmetries between European colonial photographers, their Ottoman counterparts, local elites and wider population, a process of imperialist expansion and industrial transformation was underway which influenced the course of photography in Egypt. Local photographic practices were bound up in the spirit of this new age and operated within a closed system of powerful elites who mostly employed the photographic medium as a tool of capitalism and signifier of modernization to further impoverish the marginalized. This type of uneven and disproportionate progression under Ottoman rule did little to improve the lives of the wider populace as access to the medium was mostly restricted beyond the reach of the average citizen. Therefore, the asymmetry in image politics at the core of the Orientalist framework between the colonial and the colonized was, in turn, refracted through local class politics and power relations to place Egypt's photographic heritage as a contentious part of such a visual culture discourse. In this sense, modernity is underpinned by colonial contexts and class struggles. Theorist Neil Lazarus noted that debates on culture and progress can be insensitive to the systematic inequality of capitalism because it is 'of practical significance only to foreign elite and indigenous comprador classes: to the overwhelming masses of local people, they merely spell out exploitation in new letters' (Lazarus 2011: 99). Other scholars question the usefulness of leftist political viewpoints as Mignolo proposes decoloniality could be more appropriate to the Global South because it questions the universality that Marxism upholds, which he views as just another Western code to be delinked from. He goes on to state, 'The decolonial confronts all of western civilization, which includes liberal capitalism and Marxism' (Mignolo 2011: xviii).

The nineteenth-century photography produced in Egypt was bound up in the reproduction of a colonial modernity and under Ottoman rule studios were established to re-imagine and stabilize the status quo through a new socio-economic class. Shaden Tageldin argues for continued Orientalist readings, drawing on Said's writings, to examine cultural imperialism in *Disarming Words, Empire and the Seductions of Translations in Egypt*, as he states, 'culture is a discursive armament that colonizers almost always impose and the colonized almost always oppose' (Tageldin 2011: 17). The influence of postcolonial tendencies on photographic criticism gravitates between two opposing polarities: Orientalism's critical framework on the visual and disproportionate claims of cultural hybridity and resistance in response to dominant colonial gazes. But schemas fall short in attempting to truly define the uneven photographic heritage of Egypt as this lens is fractured in accommodating the diversity of cultural traditions. Philosopher Peter Hallward states more is required to look 'beyond a recourse to the criteria of the *authentic* (as measured by fidelity to cultural norm or origin)' (Hallward 2002: 39). Arguably in the case of Egypt and in other parts of the Global South new lenses are necessary to display the trauma of colonial pasts and modernity itself in order to account for the specific organic qualities of place combined with the singular creativity of Egypt in the decolonized image.

Ocular specificity and singularity

The visual formations of Egypt made by local nineteenth-century photographers establish a valuable contribution to the debate on subjectivity in history-making and affirm a self-vision of a time under rapid transformation. Photographic production and visual culture during the Khedivial Egypt period (1867–1914) was concerned with more than artistic experimentation and auteurship alone, so it should not be thought of alongside other more formalist-led Western movements in the medium's history. Notably, this is a visual heritage which functions within its own terms to encompass a social imagination that can be defined within its particular specific historical context. Egypt's photographers worked with certain technological limits of equipment, economic controls and authoritarian politics that influenced the means of photographic production that was managed by elite networks of distribution. In broad terms, something can also be shared with the wider history of photography beyond Egypt as photography itself was evolving as a discipline with emerging uses, styles and expressions taking shape. Therefore, it would be ill-conceived to consider late nineteenth-century photography as a stable and homogeneous unit of analysis as it functioned, like many periods of new media invention, in a time of flux before representational categories and set practices took shape.[11]

Photography in Egypt became a space for the social imagination in response to the lure of 'Nahda image-screen' (Sheehi 2016: 27); Nahda was the nineteenth-century cultural renaissance immersed in the process of Ottoman modernization and the Tanzimat (New Ordering) reforms. This awakening is found in the writings by prominent Egyptian and regional intellectuals of the time. One such figure, Yusuf al-Jalkh, in 1869 delivered the first ever public lecture in Arabic on the subject of photography, entitled *Fi Nabdha min 'ilm al-tabi'iyyat wa fi al-taswir al-shamsi* (A Treatise on Physical Science and Photography).[12] This lecture presented photography as an important practice essential to broader concepts of social progress and regional modernity. Local photography produced in Egypt in the nineteenth century can be understood, in part, as embedded in the political agency of Nahda ideology that formed new types of citizens, among them the Effendi classes, during Ottoman rule. Under the influences of social purpose and political agendas photographic images held their cultural value with a passing similarity to European photography of the time. Arguably Orientalism may not be the only reliable framework to disseminate image production of the time and attitudes towards political and social transformation shaped photography as a catalyst, signifier and after-image of local modernity (Pinney and Peterson 2003; Woodward 2003). One indicator of these cultural changes was the School of Fine Arts Cairo, founded in 1908, that produced a new generation of local artists known as *al-ruwwad* (pioneers).[13] Through this creative process and cultural awakening a door is left ajar to allow the local imagination and visual traditions to enter, which shape the immanence of twentieth-century visual cultures.

This time of transition formed a contemporary-minded intellectual class who attached Egypt in cultural terms to Europe and envisioned a democratic, if not secular vision of the future. The Nahda movement materialized in various forms to counter the full force of European colonialism which began to wield a growing influence and control in the region. Paradoxically, a certain self-validation was sought out and projected onto the European cultural forms as colonial coercion increased, in particular through the translation of Western texts into Arabic. There is an element of Edward Said's 'contrapunctual' at play as developed in his *Culture and Imperialism* (1994) that involves the intersectionality between parallel narratives, one obviously dominant and the other marginal. This notion of counterpoint, borrowed from musical composition, is not only an original reading of the text in what it includes but through what has been overlooked in the terrain of imperialism (Said 1994). Part of the response to modernity and photography in Egypt, for some, heralded an internalization of aspects of cultural colonialism which became merged into a national self-image. Whereas Orientalism has been debated from various standpoints (Ahmad 1995; Clifford 1988), the asymmetry of the contrapunctual can acknowledge more nuanced complexities in cultural entanglement. This occurred in part through the use of seduction in cultural imperialism to coerce, subdue and assimilate; first evident with Napoleon's invasion of Egypt in 1798. On arrival the French colonial forces circulated a proclamation, in Arabic mimicking Quranic style, which stated that they were, like the majority of the Egyptians, 'sincere Muslims' (Tageldin 2011: 10).[14] Napoleon's translation into Arabic beguiled some Egyptians on the cusp of momentous change because it appeared to affirm the survival of the pre-colonial self through colonial submission, to exist as an entity still sovereign and not yet trapped in the language of the Other.

Orientalism and the contrapunctual can be useful ways to decipher the cultural forces in circulation in photography in Egypt during the nineteenth century as both local photo studios and European productions framed the Arab Islamic world. In general terms, Said's theories can be reduced to dualisms or interlinked opposites of colonial domination met with local resistance, and through the dominant narrative versus the marginal in cultural representation. However, such binaries can require a degree of discretion in the case of Egyptian photography in order to avoid overly determined readings of contingent visual cultures. In broad terms, this suggests that what becomes lauded as a universal principle is formed in a particular environment by particular subjects and there can certainly be no normativity in relation to photographic histories. It is important to desist from the tendency to universalize what has been rejected by postcolonial theorists, as Gayatri Chakravorty Spivak categorically stated, 'there can be no universalist claims in the human sciences' (Spivak 1993: 53). In some regards, photographic readings of nineteenth-century images produced in Egypt can be insensitive as they are, on occasion, underwritten by a white Western gaze.

Decolonizing photography would suggest it is necessary to decentre and delink to reveal the local image of Egypt to move beyond resistance as a response to colonial gazes. Culturally deep-rooted image works also possess singular attributes that are not only specific to the situation but are equally not specified by particular circumstances alone. Creative expression is unseen and singular to its setting; therefore, it should not be read as overly determined by the wider environment because the singular transforms what it describes (Hallward 2002). The idea of the specific must not be mixed up with what is specified, nor with notions of the universal. As Hallward comments when he discusses a subjective approach to postcoloniality, 'The singular creates whereas the universal prescribes' (Hallward 2002: 4). Therefore, the singular can be the key distinctive attributes which have been formed from an inner realm, individual and personal, and it does not account for the cultural, social and political operations of a particular situation and time. Accordingly, the decolonized photograph is self-constituted, internal to its culture, somewhat non-relational, while at the same time existing in the specificness of the historical moment where it has arisen. Moreover, the singular is not specified to nor bound by its environment of origin; in this way, it is crucially more than the sum of its parts. The photographic places the visual as an arbiter between the creative qualities of the singular which can transcend the specified, without resorting to arguments over cultural contingency nor authenticity alone.

This photographic heritage of Egypt sits between the subjective, inner domain of singular creativity to become specific to but not specified by the particular situation alone. Subsequently, decolonized images occur within their own local environment but as a disobedient entity to circumvent local regulatory forces and the pressures of cultural imperialism. The photographic can disrupt rather than depict in order to call into question prevailing forms of representation. The building blocks of discursive properties in regard to the local image can often involve lags and disjunctors in the tension between 'cultural homogenization and cultural heterogenization' (Appadurai 1997: 30). This is an interplay between the appearance-image of reality and how appearance-image proceeds from imagination to symbolization to form one's sense of objective reality. The photographic image can be part of a 'fantasmatic screen' (Smecker 2014: 92) where human desire is projected by ideology and, in turn, layered on to the world's external reality.

The process of decolonizing images in the context of Egypt is rooted in the local visual culture to create an awareness of subjective realism. A dominant part of the nation's cultural foundation is located in religion, specifically Islam and to a lesser extent in Coptic Christianity. Throughout centuries diverse populations with regional identities have shaped modern Egypt and the first encounters with photography came about at a time of European imperialism. Its rational form of modernity used the image to compel and subjugate the local cultural lens comprising different religious beliefs. The quality of light which attracted early European photographic pioneers and colonial adventurers to Egypt at the height of nineteenth-century exploitation was also ontologically religious. Islamic beliefs in the divine light of God's absolute knowledge have been brought into the postcolonial debate by Hallward, who goes on to suggest a connection when he refers to the mystical side of Islam. He writes, 'we are born at a distance from the light' (Hallward 2002: 9), and what is available to the human subject is the opacity only of knowledge and its true presence because a perception gap obscures the purity of light. Knowledge can only be known through God, as opposed to mere image representation, and knowledge can only exist through God, not through rationality alone as it is he who thinks and acts through human subjects. A photographic image is an expression of an intimate religious singularity that meets with physical light to reproduce visual representation; in the Egyptian setting this has often been imagined through the motif of veils. Optical cones in the camera lens refract light and this process has its roots in Islam because light physics originated with the medieval scholar Ibn al-Haytham. Islam's rejection of iconography informs the role of photography in the local setting as the Egyptian state acts as the patriarchal arbiter of cultural matters through its system of official bureaucracy underpinned by military force.

Through this cultural context decolonial aesthetics incorporates the interplay between the transforming creativity of the singular and the specificity of place. In subsequent chapters the intersectionality between religion and the image, metaphysical realms and rationality, are examined further through the production and consumption of the photographic in Egypt. A spiritual genealogy pervades the social frameworks of society to become deeply intimate sources of personal expression for some and, through this, form one of the ideological pillars of modern Egypt. Chapter 2 sets out to explore these non-Western image sensibilities, often intersecting with this religious heritage, more extensively through the long history of visual traditions in Egypt. This involved the encounter with European modernity in a series of asymmetrical relationships that detracted from other possibilities and sensibilities under an unforgiving colonial gaze.

Notes

1 Connell writes of three possible definitions of non-Western knowledge production and describes the second one as 'alternative universalisms, that are knowledge systems intended to have general and not just local application, whose logic and authority do not derive from the Eurocentric knowledge economy' (Connell 2016: 3).

2 Mignolo writes on phases of modernity in history to state that 'during the time span 1500 to 2000 three cumulative (and not successive) faces of modernity are discernible: the Iberian and Catholic face, led by Spain and Portugal (1500–1750, approximately); the "heart of Europe" (Hegel) face, led by England, France, and Germany (1750–1945); and the U.S. American face, led by the United States (1945–2000). Since then, a new global order has begun to unfold: a polycentric world interconnected by the same type of economy' (Mignolo 2011: 7).

3 The first large-scale Asian–African Bandung Conference was a meeting of newly independent states which took place on 18–24 April 1955 in Bandung, West Java, Indonesia. This anti-colonial alliance allowed them to link Islam and the Indian cause with the struggle for decolonization across the Global South.

4 While earlier depictions showed the Prophet's face, later medieval depictions began blotting out his face or showing it covered with a white veil. Gruber hypothesizes that the increasing unease with figural imagery of the Prophet can partially be attributed to images being more widely available in the public sphere, via the reprographic arts and mass media. One recent controversy arose when Muslim groups objected to the US Supreme Court chamber including a marble image of the Prophet Muhammad, sculpted in the frieze. In the statue he carries a sword and the Quran and stands in the company of more than a dozen other historical figures from Moses to Confucius to Napoleon.

5 In part this can exist because the word is superior to the image; the latter considered without the former is incomprehensible. In their rulings while one

can have words without definitive images attached to them, one cannot have comprehensible images without words. The culture of the word is thus the ultimate culture of abstraction, comprehension, transcendence and limitless possibilities, 'yet, the word remains accessible to its students of all nations, and is abundantly available for everyone's use in a diversity of contexts' (al-Alwani 2001: 4). Al-Alwani's point is that the culture of the word is democratizing, because, the image, on the other hand, is restricted to those with artistic skill and elites.

6 The vernacular digital image of Khaled Said resonates with earlier events in visual history. For instance, the 1955 image of Emmett Till, a fourteen-year-old boy, who was lynched in Mississippi shocked the United States. His mother posed for the media beside the open coffin of her son and the images of his beaten face and body changed public opinion.

7 The resilient Eurocentric narrative of the history of photography has been challenged forcefully in the last two decades with critical interventions originating from the field of visual anthropology. Scholars such as Elizabeth Edwards, Christopher Pinney, Deborah Poole or Karen Strassler have contributed to fresh conceptual approaches and paradigm-shifting insights. Other notable pioneering scholars such as Issam Nassar, Nancy Micklewright, Zeynep Çelik and Edhem Eldem have attempted to link Middle Eastern photography to broader realities of the medium in the Arab context.

8 Postcolonialism has exposed doubts on the claims of cultural authenticity and Marxist discourse has assembled coherent assaults on aspects of postcolonial theory itself by challenging the primacy of cultural hybridity.

9 Abdullah Frère and Pascal Sébah were the most celebrated photographers in the Ottoman period with studios in Cairo. Prince Edward, the German Empress Augusta, French Empress Eugenie, Mark Twain and Khedive Tawfiq and his family were some of their famous sitters.

10 An example of an indigenous visual practice is Iranian filmmaker Abbas Kiarostami's works, which are distinctive from other film histories and embody a cultural specificity but are not specified only by the environment.

11 Jacques Rancière distinguishes between three different values for art. Firstly, the 'ethical regime of images' designates the attempt to subordinate images, whether plastic, literary or auditory, to the ethos of community. The 'representative regime of art' refers to the artistic canons to define a separation between art and life to give rise to a series of hierarchies, movements and criticism. In philosophy, if the ethical consideration found inspiration in the writings of Plato, the representative regime is derived from Aristotelian poetics. The final definition, 'aesthetic regime of art', is the most daring of all the regimes and abolishes hierarchies and forms of subordination to which the other two regimes give rise. This regime creates an ambiguous sensorium in which art and life dissolve into each other. In his books Rancière uses the notion of the aesthetic regime to re-narrate the history of nineteenth- and twentieth-century art histories.

12 Stephen Sheehi has written on Yusuf al-Jalkh and other Arab intellectuals in his *Arab Imago*. Al-Jalkh was the author of the first treatise on photography in

Arabic and Sheehi quotes him thus, 'The rays of light' captured by the camera '*admihlal* [illuminate] the darkness of the ignorance from our *absarina* [vision]' and provide our 'daily realities' and inner feelings with 'scientific *barahin* [proofs]' (Sheehi 2016: 266).

13 The School of Fine Arts Cairo was founded in 1908 by Prince Youssef Kamal and became influential in local aesthetic cultures. Figures like sculptor Mahmoud Mokhtar and painters Ragheb Ayad and Mohamed Hassan, among others, emerged from the school and offered free classes to Egyptians.

14 Evelyn Baring, first Earl of Cromer, who effectively ruled Egypt as British consul-general from 1882 to 1907, drew lessons from the French strategy. In *Modern Egypt* (1908), Cromer hints that England must shed its matronly respectability and become an 'attractive damsel' like France, manipulating the appearance of intimacy.

2

Decolonizing the lens

Transcending the image

This chapter discusses the pictorial turn in Egypt to look at the historical origins of the photographic medium as many Islamic scholars contributed to the invention of photography centuries before the daguerreotype process and other European image-making technologies were developed. The local photographic heritage is often excluded from Orientalist readings of Egypt which can even view the Arabic-speaking world as unsettled by the visual representation of the human form. Moreover, this can fallaciously suggest Egyptians, as predominately Muslim in cultural identity, oppose the visual image as proscribed by Islamic statutes. However, the historical reality differs as aniconism in Islamic societies was restricted in modern times and to specific religious contexts and theocratic positions. This type of misleading impression was created in part by figures such as Egypt's Muslim Brotherhood founder Hassan al-Banna, who wrote a homily in 1945 entitled *Nahw al-nur* (Towards the Light). In this commentary he expounded on different entertainment technologies of the twentieth century (cinema, illustrated magazines, etc.) that were in need of pious supervision if not full-blown censorship. Similarly, the popular Egyptian Sheikh Yusuf al-Qaradawi viewed photographs as a necessary part of secular life in certain cases, like passport ID photos, but at best perceived images to be not meaningful and essentially frivolous in character. This is representative of how conservative Islamic thinkers define a moral world of *halal* (permissible) or *haram* (illicit) behaviours and through photographic performance and reproduction sentient beings with souls can be represented as close to idolatry. The Quran does not forbid the representation of a human form as an image per se; rather, it is sceptical of photography because the creation of living forms is God's prerogative alone. Therefore, anthropomorphic images as part of photographic cultures may distract one or even encourage transgression or immorality through its attendant aesthetic forms.

Nonetheless, during the Golden Age of Islam (622–1258) there existed a scientific foundation in image technologies that later enabled European discoveries in light physics, such as the camera, to become part of the colonial apparatus; often to subjugate local populations in the nineteenth century. Ottoman viceroy Muhammad 'Ali Pasha (1769–1849) was attentive to technological developments in Europe and his curiosity helped establish a local development of photographic culture. The most rapid advancement of the medium took place during the early twentieth century in bustling metropolitan centres, like Cairo and Alexandria, as a new bourgeoisie notably embraced the genre of studio portrait photography. Indeed, despite Islamic religious doctrine even al-Azhar scholars in Cairo could not resist the lure of the photographic and commissioned studio portraits of religious leaders with the new process to embrace the image mania of the time. But Egypt and photography in many ways share a longer, richer history rarely addressed through the lens of the local by Western institutions and its art historians. This chapter disputes the Orientalist assumptions that perpetuate and reproduce stereotypical visions of Egypt, and through this provides a deeper understanding of the histories of photography.

In the nineteenth century the colonial impact of early photography was in the hands of Europeans and was felt sharply in Egypt when it became a popular destination for photographic enthusiasts drawn by the regular sunlight and lure of ancient Pharaonic wonders. In October 1839, Frédéric Goupil-Fesquet and Horace Vernet made daguerreotypes of ancient monuments in Egypt. Their photographs were reproduced in a travel album publication, *Excursions Daguerriennes* (1841–1842) and also in Hector Horeau's *Panorama d'Egypte et de Nubie* (1841). Both publications catered for a well-established Orientalist travel album format for the European market that had developed rapidly since the late eighteenth century. The glare of Orientalist depictions in the nineteenth century and subsequent criticism has tended to overlook local visual heritages of the region that endeavoured to gain a cultural foothold and unseat hackneyed representations. The dominant lens of the history of photography gravitates towards Western concerns about the medium to situate local visual practices of Egypt in an ancillary category or even within the secondary, if not patronizing subgenre of world photography. Such a history of photography can contrast with the histories of photography as marginal photographic heritages move in a more distant orbit to intersect with the dominant narrative at certain points of cultural specificity or geographical importance become sought after.[1] Moreover, the commonly applied notion of encounter infers a state of not knowing, on one side, and knowledge, on the other, of a placelessness that presupposes the convention of a starting point, of the normalized, in what Dipesh Chakrabarty termed the 'silent referent' (Chakrabarty

1992: 337). The Western art history version of photography upholds a hierarchy of aesthetic innovation and is underwritten by the conventions of its own visual literacy. The local visual traditions of Egypt met with the Eurocentricity of photography which presumed no significant visual heritage had existed before the introduction of the medium by Europeans. Foreign photographers at the time gave in to an obsession with the ancient Pharaonic past rather than the actual living local cultures of the time. Regardless of how postcolonial discourses in recent decades have brought an awareness and sensibility about marginality, a separation can still occur, a fragmentation of subject position. This disequilibrium can contribute to what Ahmet A. Ersoy defines as 'a vibrant and commanding master narrative on the one hand, and multiple subsidiary histories on the other' (Ersoy 2017: 311).

Egypt rapidly transformed in industrial and technological ways during the nineteenth century as the photographic medium intruded into representational politics with the camera becoming, mostly, part of the colonial apparatus. However, the origins of visual cultures have many earlier precedents and rich influences to contest the prevailing chronology. Islamic scholars contributed to the invention of photography centuries before the daguerreotype and other processes took hold in Europe. The Islamic civilization of the medieval ages, in which Egypt was a key intellectual centre, produced scientific method and cultural knowledge on optics, translating between cultures, art and science to generate critical scholarship independent of the orbit of the West at this time and delinked from European thought. It is, accordingly, prudent to look back at earlier histories and significant points in time where developments of the image in Egypt decolonized the visual and new encounters brought forth the specific qualities of this extraordinary, singular photographic heritage. The foundation of thought and knowledge generated by medieval Islamic scholars helped shape the decolonial aesthetic concerns, values and scientific methods of camera technologies. When the subsequent encounter with colonial powers came about in the nineteenth century this new photographic technology was understood through a local lens consisting of Egypt's own visual traditions.

Pre-colonial singularity

Islamic scholars contributed scientific knowledge on light physics and optics centuries before experiments with image-making resulted in the invention of photography in Europe. The Abbasid caliphate supported scientific research and one notable eleventh-century scholar, Abu 'Ali al-Hasan Ibn al-Haytham (965–1040), based in Cairo, wrote the *Kitab al-Manazir* (Book of Optics), which has been later translated into Latin as *De Aspectibus*[2] to form the intellectual foundation of light physics centuries later. Ibn al-Haytham's significant work theorized the camera obscura and the process of human vision during this time of discovery in Islamic civilization. This book depended on an earlier period of invention that began with the transfer of the capital of the Islamic world from Damascus to Baghdad under Abbasid rulers. The establishment of the intellectual centre Bayt al-Hikma (House of Wisdom) was significant because both Muslim and non-Muslim scholars sought to gather all the world's knowledge to be translated into Arabic.[3] During this period the Muslim world was a hub for science and philosophy which collected, synthesized and substantially advanced knowledge gained from earlier civilizations. Like Ibn al-Haytham, polymath al-Kindi (801–873) was an early Arab philosopher who translated Aristotle and Plato and, among other wide-ranging discoveries, researched light optics to become a dominant figure in Baghdad.

The body of research that evolved during the Islamic renaissance impacted on the development of ocular knowledge. Part of Egypt's heritage began with Alexandria-born Claudius Ptolemy's (100–170) book *Optica*, which was an initial investigation of the properties of visual perception and became known in the Arab world when translated from ancient Greek to Arabic by Baghdad-based Ibn Sahl (940–1000). Ibn al-Haytham's key contributions in his treatise, *Kitab al-Manazir*, concerned a rebuttal of Ptolemy's hypotheses on the nature of human vision. Ibn al-Haytham correctly distinguished that vision and perception occurred because light rays enter the eye, not the opposite way around, as was commonly believed up until then based on Ptolemy's theories. In addition, Ibn al-Haytham was to further define the physical nature of the light rays in mathematical formulas laying down a foundation for the scientific method in light physics. Such discoveries on refraction and human perception were crucial elements that enabled significant scholarly discoveries in Europe. His writings impacted beyond the confines of medieval Islam to become part of Latin scholarship, read by René Descartes and Isaac Newton, among others, and it was through the discoveries by these eminent scientific figures that Ibn al-Haytham's contribution to knowledge can be recognized. Part of his research addressed how the mental image is formed in the mind and went on to outline the distinction between two types of human vision (El-Bizri 2005). His hypothesis puts forwards that there exists a shorter, glance-like way of looking and a longer, contemplative way of seeing. This discovery reveals manifest properties of an object when perceived to allow sight itself to ascertain and influence the true form of the object. Contemporary philosopher Nader El-Bizri discusses Ibn al-Haytham's (Lat. Alhazen's) research on phenomenology:

The thrust of Alhazen's theory of visual perception implicitly points to the possibilities of grasping optics not merely as a discipline that inquires about the conditions of sight and light in terms of an epistemology of photosensitive surfaces, but moreover as an eidetic inquiry about the geometric constitution of forms in their essential ordering structures that is grounded by experiential verifications. If one were to endeavour to elucidate the question of being based on Alhazen's geometric optics, the resulting discipline will not readily be that of a surface-ontology but more likely a line of inquiry that elucidates the presencing of beings. (El-Bizri 2005: 207)

Here, El-Bizri guides one to consider Ibn al-Haytham's significance lies with his reading of the intrinsic properties of forms beyond the pictorial materiality or visual perception of the world. Rather, it is his development of scientific method in the study of optics that truly opens up the latent structures and being of the world within the process of vision and light refraction.

The renaissance across the medieval Muslim world involved Quranic injunctions and hadiths that often stressed the value of pure knowledge in geometric forms rather than the image object and appearance itself. Islamic prohibition of idolatry stems from the belief that the creation of sentient life forms is God's exclusive prerogative alone and contrasts with photographic representation.[4] Although the Quran does not forbid visual representation of any living being, it does use the word *musawwir*, meaning forms or designer or photographer, as one of the ninety-nine epithets for God (Q. 59:24). With the introduction of the photographic medium into the Arabic-speaking world, *musawwir* was applied to describe the properties of photographic technologies and differs, for instance, from the word for artist, *fannan*, which implies a different visual role for the fine arts over photography. Moreover, the light studied by Ibn al-Haytham and other Islamic scholars was for them a divine light that illuminates the world of creatures and objects unified under God's absolute knowledge; often represented and understood through geometry. The purity of God's light is blinding to the subject and as such, illumination can only be experienced in a refracted way. This indirect veiling refers to the state of ignorance one is born into to begin the religious journey of life towards an awareness of God's full presence. The sacred sunlight is ontologically singular and we remain separate from its real source of insight on a path towards its transformative power. Sufi philosopher Ibn al-'Arabi (1165–1240) explains how living things are not simply given this light because access is contingent on the subject's readiness. He writes in *al-Futuhat al-Makkiyya* (Meccan Openings), 'The sun spreads its rays over the existent things. It is not miserly with its light toward anything. The loci receive the light in the measure of their preparedness' (Corbin 1998: 337).

In the more mystical realms of Islam the opacity that stands between the subject and God's illuminating light, the human body and soul, strives for the achievement of a singular vision of the knower and the known, as when perception is realized one becomes closer to God's own perception. This divinity is only present on a contingent basis to the subject who remains in an opaque state, blind to the purity of divine light. Accordingly, certain shades of opacity arise indirectly through and because of this potential awakening. In the tenth-century book *Kitab al-Mawaqif* (Book of Standings) Sufi scholar al-Niffari describes how a veil acts as a mirror that the mystic must discover in a process towards full self-knowledge that brings forth God's wisdom. Knowledge on light physics is more than scientific, and refraction and human perception are conceptualized within religious singularity to remain inflected by the metaphysical and, therefore, not only born in rational processes. This differs markedly from the European Age of Reason that led to the invention of photography in the nineteenth century and such differences signify a division between these intersecting traditions in regard to knowledge of the visual. The fundamental difference of Islamic thought means the image remains another entity, intertwined but disconnected in key ways from modernity that would emerge in Europe centuries later.

Within Islam there are considerable variations between religious schools and movements as each marks out differences in reference to the anthropomorphic image. Therefore, aniconism tendencies are more pronounced among fundamentalist Sunni sects, such as Salafis and Wahhabis, whereas Sufi mystical orders have less fixed views on the ontology of the image. Islamic artistic expression has been typically characterized by the absence of material representation of the world and human figures, favouring the extensive use of calligraphic, geometric and abstract forms in the composition of images. In contrast to the use of the visual in Christian traditions, this under-use of the anthropomorphic image in Islam is evident in the infrequency of representations of the Prophet Muhammad. When represented in the figurative form at all he is sometimes seen with his face veiled or blanked out. Manuscripts found in India and more recently on a public mural in Tehran have depicted Muhammad riding on the mystical Burad creature with his face obscured to the viewer. Christiane Gruber and Avinoam Shalem have written on Islamic art history, 'Visual evidence clearly undermines the premise that images of Muhammad are banned in Islamic law and practice, thereby providing us with a less ideologically divisive and more fact-based way to speak about a subject' (Gruber and Shalem 2014: 3).

When Muhammad's representation was used in Islam it usually served to illustrate his *sira* (biographical story) so as not to infringe on the Islamic prohibition of idolatry; despite some virile objections from some more orthodox movements. Broadly speaking, outside of Persian, India and certain Ottoman contexts, Muhammad has more commonly been depicted in symbolic forms only, such as a rose flower, a flame or in calligraphy or lengthy written descriptions.[5] Anthropomorphic visual representation is historically evident but often significantly altered; for instance, with a stroke line drawn over the neck and this curious mark symbolizes the severing of the soul from the body. This drawn line in the image clarifies that this visual object is a representation only, not something alive or sentient but a pictorial record only that lacks the properties of a soul. Prohibition on the visual representation of God has remained absolute because God made the world ex nihilo. Islamic scholar Titus Burckhardt outlines this hesitancy to depict the human form or the figurative because 'the absence of icons in Islam has not merely a negative but a positive role. By excluding all anthropomorphic images, at least within the religious realm, Islamic Art aids man to be entirely himself. Instead of projecting his soul outside himself, he can remain in his ontological centre where he is both the vicegerent (*khalîfa*) and slave (*'abd*) of God' (Burckhardt 1987: 223).

Here the visual intersects with religious beliefs as Islamic sensibilities value more than mere representation. Alternatively, the focus on the figurative in Western art history made it a more straightforward process to accede to the mimetic qualities of the photographic medium. The photograph involves light bouncing off objects and through this process the direct representation and impression of the physical world. The theocratic lens of Islam, arguably, favours a disruption of direct transference to the image with specific attributes found in the Egyptian cultural context. The frozenness of time in still photography is unlike the narrative and diegetic sound qualities of film which shares something with the oral tradition of storytelling in Egypt; photography has never been as highly valued in cultural terms as cinema. In this context the photographic medium takes on an inimical role, essentially mimetic in character and somewhat enigmatic or obstruse in narrative terms. In part, such differences may be affirmed by phenomenological distinctions of vision established by Ibn al-Haytham in the divergence between the glance-like look of cinema versus more contemplative slow forms of seeing in photography. At its most affecting the photographic image arrests fast-moving vision to be a contemplative pause and a pensive act, rather than the fleeting visual process of cinema. The frames of the cinema camera combine with audio to produce a sensorial experience in movement with sound and narrative engulfing the viewer in an aesthetic experience. This is as opposed to the long-pause still silence of the frozen photographic moment which invites deeper study of what is represented, a crucial facet of the anthropomorphic object. As Burckhardt suggested in religious terms the anthropomorphic inner core remains unavailable to the probing camera eye and its direct form of idolatrous mimesis. Islamic religious beliefs distinguish between the image as surface appearance and the photograph is a representational object only and not the real object itself. In these terms, to do so would confuse or divide the self, mix ontologies with the inner being linked to the divine human soul. The sacred light physics of Ibn al-Haytham illuminates the core human being to see beyond the concerns of mimesis or anthropomorphic representation to reveal the background in the hidden structures of the world. His mathematical formulas and scientific methods were combined with Islamic belief systems of the time to offer up a nuanced but religiously inflected form of vision onto the world attempting to incorporate the divine in everyday life.

Crisis in Cairo

In a forewarning of the nineteenth-century European colonialism to come the Armée d'Orient arrived in Alexandria in 1789 led by Napoleon Bonaparte. They quickly took control of Egypt, defeating the Mamluk forces in Imbaba outside Cairo in what the French mythologized as the Battle of the Pyramids. The French established control over Cairo by exploiting divisions in the political caste, pursuing Mamluk renegade troops and crushing sporadic uprisings with decisive military force. Egypt at this time was, arguably, no longer the scholarly centre it once was in the eleventh century during the Fatimid caliphate and had been in decline since the Islamic civilization. The relatively small population of the country, around four million at the time, lived off the land as Egypt had become the breadbasket for the Ottoman Empire. However, the natural riches were not shared uniformly and poor administration coupled with tax burdens imposed by Mamluk rulers meant that sometimes Egyptians starved despite the country's agricultural abundances.

To the French eyes the fabled city of Cairo had faded, there were just twenty schools compared to seventy-five in the fifteenth century, and as historian Christopher de Bellaigue has written, 'the citadel of the Egyptian intellect, the squalid, arcaded school of al-Azhar, suspected science, despised philosophy and hadn't had an original thought in years' (de Bellaigue 2017: 95). However, de Bellaigue's damning comments, despite the undisputed decline in the fortunes of Egypt, do tend to reaffirm the colonial lens, thereby ushering in the prejudice of nineteenth-century Europeans. In the context of the French, an exemplar can be read in the preface to *Description de l'Égypte*, written by Jean-Baptiste Joseph Fourier. This extensive academic study was produced by the French to rationalize their colonial occupation and puts forwards a well-worn narrative to suggest Egypt has been destroyed by the 'ancient doctrine' (Fourier 1809: 8) of the Arabs (see also Godlewska

1995). This colonialist scholarship of the time suggests Egyptians needed modern industries and required European expertise to progress, as the French author Louis Bréhier described it in the early twentieth century, '[Egypt] ceased to be part of the civilized world' (Bréhier 2018: x). The force of the Napoleonic invasion came not only through its military advantage but also in the revolutionary spirit of a retinue of scholars who formed a vital part of this colonial campaign. French forces took control of Egypt in a month and set up a *diwan* (council) of local elites to co-administer rule. Despite merited resistance in these years by some Egyptian groups, such as the Cairo Revolt in October 1798, French colonial rule divided the populace in the name of modernity and economic development.

In one neighbourhood of Cairo, Azbakeya, the French expropriated a palace from Hassan Kashif and Silvestre de Sacy became director of the Institut d'Égypte. This research establishment predates the invention of photography itself but did include visual representation through engravings with artists suppling drawings of Egypt for metal plates and lithographic print reproductions. In addition, the centre included an aviary, botanical garden, sky observatory, museums, as well as workshops to produce scientific tools, microscopic lenses and other scopic-precision instruments. The French military expedition was complemented by a research group, the Scientific and Artistic Commission, consisting of 165 engineers, cartographers, scholars and artists. This part of the invasion force used coercive tactics and the lure of new technology and knowledge to gain the support of the ulema (Islamic scholars, lit. 'learned ones'), therein propagating the upper hand of the French invaders. This research institution found no contradiction in the radical politics of French republicanism alongside the subjugation of the Egyptian populace to set the stage for a calamitous cultural encounter. Within the comfortable confines of the institute palace intellectuals demonstrated and discussed contemporary European discoveries with the al-Azhar scholars, to mixed results.

By a long-standing tradition, the ulema had been educated in madrasas to be oral transmitters and interpreters of the knowledge in Islam, including doctrine and law. Among the prominent delegation of local intellectuals to visit the French foundation was ʿAbd al-Rahman al-Jabarti (1753–1825), one of the leading scholars in Egypt at the time. Like many of his compatriots al-Jabarti was mostly unaware of the scientific work taking place in Europe and believed in the hand of the divine in all human history. However, the spirit of the age had served up the alternative of European knowledge production to separate the divine from the worldly, and this intellectual difference compelled al-Jabarti to chronicle closely the activities of the French. His subsequent publication, *Tarikh muddat al-Franasis bi-Masr* (Chronology of the French Occupation in Egypt), was intended for the elite class of

Egyptian readers at the time and spans the first seven months of the occupation from July to December 1789. Al-Jabarti was an al-Azhar cleric who remained unimpressed if not deeply perplexed by the foreigners. He rebukes the French promotion of liberty and equality: 'How can this be? When God has made some superior to others as is testified by the dwellers in Heavens and on the Earth' (Moreh 2004: 189). He observed troops ransacking at will in Cairo, describing one such pillage in al-Azhar mosque, 'Furthermore, they soiled the mosque, blowing their spit in it, pissing, and defecating in it. They guzzled wine and smashed the bottles in the central court and other parts' (Moreh 2004: 93). Such disrespect for the sacrosanct and personal hygiene disturbed al-Jabarti greatly and many of his contemporaries, who could not fathom how the French could be so lewd and lack sophistication yet be so dynamic in scientific knowledge and military affairs. However, local intellectuals faced few options against this French colonial force with its technological prowess. A sense of despair and *kufr* (disbelief) took hold at the realization of Islam's apparent impotence to deal with the French invaders at this time. In some ways the medieval Islamic civilization in Cairo had stagnated over centuries as the cultural diversity and spirit of invention of the Golden Age waned to be supplanted by two contrasting but interconnected visions that tended to stifle political organization and scientific advancement: on the one hand, the doctrines with literal interpretations of God through the Quran, hadiths and Sunna to narrow the world, while on the other, more mystical forms of Islamic beliefs which induced an escape from the contemporary world.[6] These contrasting visions offered no respite from the impact of the French revolutionary ardour, with its rational approach to knowledge, to be built on later by other European powers. Al-Jabarti in his book despaired at the situation and resorted to calling for divine intervention to expel these Europeans from Egypt, as he pleaded, 'May God hurry misfortune and punishment upon them, may he strike their tongues with dumbness, may he scatter their hosts, and disperse them, confound their intelligence, and cause their breath to cease' (Moreh 2004: 33).

Al-Jabarti's book on the French was the first publication to chronical the magnitude of this early wave of European colonialism about to alter the course of the Islamic world. Over these seven months al-Jabarti observed the invaders with curiosity and bewilderment as he described the savants working in the chemical laboratory, hosting demonstrations of electricity and presentations on the human anatomy that were subjects that played no significant part in Cairene life at this time. The French challenge to the status quo, the order of the world as the ulema perceived it, was a fundamental reconfiguration of existing values in Egypt. For the French knowledge was not a gift to humankind from the divine but one where humans, through their own intellect and reason, generated deeper insights and truths. The revolutionary turmoil in France was, for al-Jabarti, another anathema to the preservation of natural order. However, the occupiers' concept of liberty (*hurriyya*) and emancipation from the rule of God was antagonistic to al-Jabarti's ideals for a civilized society. He was not the only one to be unimpressed by French behaviour and al-Azhar's Islamic council agreed. Sheikh ʿAbdullah al-Sharqawi castigated the invaders, 'They deny the Resurrection, and the afterlife, and … the prophets' (Cole 2008: 159).

The incursion of Napoleonic France had a detrimental effect on Egypt and seemed to present stark choices between engaging with Western modernity and, if possible, adapting to this new situation, or simply looking away to ignore this belligerent external force. The question of choice for the Islamic world to emulate or not colonial dictates was, in fact, a falsehood as Europe was never interested in consulting the wishes of Egyptians or to afford the Islamic world a choice to forestall their perfidious ambitions. Despite the crisis presented by the French invasion other voices emerged from within the local intelligentsia, some had even been students of al-Jabarti, and they were more susceptible to this encounter with modernity. Debates emerged between progressive and conservative strands of the ulema, between those looking into the future and those afraid of letting go of the past.

Hasan al-ʿAttar (1776–1835) was one of the more progressive figures to emerge at this time and developed a relationship with French scholars in Cairo. However, he was left out of any official ulema delegations and had to visit the institute of his own accord. This contemporary thinker began his journey where al-Jabarti's ended, at the crucible of the French knowledge in the Institut d'Égypte. Al-ʿAttar was from a relatively humble background and, although he rose to the position of Grand Imam of al-Azhar for the last five years of his life, he remained a maligned figurehead as vendettas reigned against him until his death. The liberal atmosphere of the French base in Azbakeya appeared to have had a deep effect on al-ʿAttar with its curious polymath savants as the young Muslim scholar became infatuated with their attitude to learning. Moreover, he was impressed by their knowledge of Arabic language and literature in this soft power colonialism, as he described one of the French scholars, 'his Arabic to be free from ungrammatical usages and from barren phraseology and other defects' (Gran 1998: 79).

There was little intellectual interaction between the Coptic and Islamic religions at this time and the French openness to gathering ideas from any source matched the young scholar's curiosity. His engagement with the institute was controversial in Cairo as he became so attached to the colonialists that he even contemplated living with this foreign community. However, his career might have been salvaged when the French imperial occupation ended somewhat prematurely after three years as the Armée d'Orient left and the Institut d'Égypte was forced to close. This sudden departure meant the savants took their research materials and discoveries with them as the Treaty of Amiens returned Egypt to Ottoman rule. Lacking patronage al-'Attar was exiled to Istanbul as an atmosphere of recrimination took hold in Cairo among vengeful sheikhs who sought out anyone who appeared to advocate modernity. Regardless, even for the conservative al-Azhar clerical classes the equilibrium of Egyptian intellectual life had been irrevocably changed and European modernity had left a mark on the nation. For the French the impact of their invasion can be read through the controversial compendium *Description de l'Égypte*,[7] a series of twenty-two extensive academic publications. In the preface mathematician Fourier suggests that 'the Muslim religion would on no account permit the development of the mind' (Fourier 1809: 516) and the lasting legacy of the French incursion cannot be redeemed from the operation of European imperialism as Egypt would never return the status quo ante. In the name of modernity and progress an asymmetrical relationship was imposed on Egypt and the photographic image would soon become part of social tensions between long-held beliefs and new schools of thought. The short-lived Napoleonic invasion established a narrative, excluding other possibilities, to debase Egypt under an unforgiving colonial gaze and trace the connection between imperialism and culture.

Pasha modernity

Muhammad 'Ali Pasha (1769–1849) was a coercive modernizer who took control of Egypt as Ottoman viceroy soon after the withdrawal of French forces. 'Ali was to rule for almost half a century and set about to redirect the country towards a contemporary nation-state; feasibly in part to avoid further foreign subjugation. His intuitive grasp of political opportunity helped manoeuvre between what was left of the Mamluk regime, the Ottoman Empire and the interests of other external colonial powers vying for control of the region. Under 'Ali's rule Egypt established a type of new regime with an *au courant* military, imported new technologies, encouraged scholarly research and expanded the centralized state to control most aspects of the citizenry; therein setting up a blueprint for future authoritarian rulers of Egypt. As the country's coffers swelled the government grew in size and wealth as the prestige of the clerical class diminished proportionately. In one technological development, despite the concerns of the ulema and Islamic scribes, the Quran was set in type for the first time on the new printing presses in the Bulaq area of Cairo; reproducing cheap book editions available beyond the supervision of the al-Azhar-led clergy. It was into this period that early photography became one of a range of new technologies to change the course of visual culture and 'Ali was equally curious about the medium.

The British sent John Bowring to Egypt to investigate ʿAli's economic policies, about which the British Foreign Minister Palmerston had received interest from merchants and consuls. This brought Bowring to the attention of the Pasha and his *Report on Egypt 1823–1838: Under the Reign of Mohamed Ali* was published in 1840. The Ottoman viceroy and the English colonialist opened up a dialogue on disciplinary methods or what Bowring termed 'the productive powers' in the country under the Pasha's rule' (Mitchel 1991: 9). Through Bowring, a correspondence started between the founder of utilitarianism Jeremy Bentham and the Egyptian ruler as they discussed the merits of, among other concepts, the panopticon system. In this new political climate European modernity became internalized to play a key role in the externalizing power through the new structures of the state formed by ʿAli in this period. The rebirth of the military is an example of how this approach to modernity saw groups of men transformed into a systemized machine, and how the individual finds him or herself embodied and expressed within such state-run frameworks.

This form of modern domination uses coercion through the gaze to control a population by the partitioning of space and the isolation of individuals within the system. Such disciplinary methods are modern forms of power relations that do not depend on sheer blunt violence alone but instead on the ability to infiltrate, rearrange and colonize individual psychologically from within. New organizations became spaces to test such approaches; Egypt was one of many other colonial frontiers where so-called political reformers, like Bowring and Bentham, could advocate the introduction of the panoptic principle and other new control techniques in order to test methods of state power. As historian Timothy Mitchel writes in *Colonialising Egypt*, 'For many Europeans – military officers, Saint-Simonist engineers, educationalists, physicians, and others – a place like nineteenth-century Cairo provided the opportunity to help establish a modern state based on the new methods of disciplinary power' (Mitchel 1991: 9).

Part of this new ordering can be found in the creation of a new Egyptian army and the establishment of a public school system where the principle of systemic order was propagated. Disciplining the population was a political process to accompany the capitalist transformation of Egypt and surveillance serves as a motif for this kind of colonial intervention. Bentham reminds us of the ocular power of photography, of what is seen and surveilled, and can therefore bring order to the world as though it were an image to be focused, framed and arranged. The point of view of the camera gaze is a place set apart, outside the world or often above it. Also, it was an ideal position from where, like the authority at the centre of the panopticon system, one could not be seen but still observe. Optical experiments in vision and the presence of the divine articulated by earlier scholars in the

Islamic world were replaced by a disciplinary logic as light changed from the divine or sacred to state power and control. The schema of the panopticon imposes codification onto the gaze that enforces the latent power of regulation to become the defining vision of modernity.

Muhammad 'Ali Pasha modernized in the manner of an autocrat, though at the same time, he did authorize and endorse the intellectual vigour of peripatetic Egyptian scholars, such as the aforementioned Hasan al-'Attar and the anti-colonialist Muhammad Abduh (1849–1905)[8] among others. Such intellectuals became influential in rethinking Islamic knowledge, institutional reforms and how to mediate European modernity. After studying in the libraries and scholarly communities of Istanbul and Damascus for over a decade al-'Attar returned to Cairo with a store of knowledge and an appreciation of the versatility of knowledge itself.[9] He was also a wary reformer, as the situation had become so precarious at al-Azhar that he conducted most of his teaching with students in his home. Beyond his peers this cautious metropolitan shaped a significant cultural legacy and formed a new generation of scholars, among them Rifa'a al-Tahtawi (1801–1873) who was to take many of his radical ideas to their logical conclusion. He shaped an important pedagogic and decolonial culture in Egypt where new knowledge was embraced but also remained critical of Western values linked to the operations of colonial power. In many ways the domination at the heart of Orientalism proposes the opposite is the case and such progressive nineteenth-century Egyptian thinkers demonstrated how Islamic culture was amenable to modern developments. Orientalism was mistakenly seen to have overshadowed the Orient as a system of thought and to diminish the influential legacy of many progressive local reformers.

When al-Tahtawi entered al-Azhar he was soon invited to study abroad as part of 'Ali's reforms in educational programmes which enabled him to act as an imam for forty-three other Egyptian scholars who moved to France. Al-Tahtawi was able to study ethics, social law, political philosophy, mathematics and geometry in Paris and he read broadly the works of Rousseau and Voltaire; particularly taken with Montesquieu's *Espirit de Lois* (Spirit of the Law). The young scholar wrote the first comprehensive description of contemporary France in Arabic, *al-Rihla al-Pariziyya* (The Parisian Journey), which was soon translated into Turkish to be widely distributed across the Ottoman Empire. Written for a Muslim audience with no note of dejection, this travelogue describes his impressions of the city of light. Despite the disequilibrium between France and Egypt at this time the bias of European colonialism appears to have not taken hold in al-Tahtawi's mind. Rather, he is curious about aspects of French life and notes without pleasure that Christianity has been replaced by secular knowledge because, as a religion, it was too irrational to last. His five years in France convinced him of the need to integrate modern sciences and technologies into Egypt as he absorbed the emerging knowledge of this time. The radical atmosphere in France was triggered by the tensions between revolutionary republican politics and the return of the Bourbon monarchy. In contrast, for al-Tahtawi the production of knowledge does not solely emerge from the process of human reason alone; rather, all knowledge is underwritten by God in natural law. Therefore, according to this doctrine, reason may foster intellectual achievement but it was not the preserve of the West alone. His writings suggest that the most accomplished notions of contemporary Europe – liberty, equality, pluralism – were in fact familiar features in early Islam as 'precursors of modern values' albeit in a more uncorrupted form (de Bellaigue 2017: 111). He perceived the influence of foreigners to be mostly benign for the Islamic world; he had missed the shock force of Napoleon's occupation and died before the British invasion in 1842. Under the influence of 'Ali's modernizing reign Egypt's interest in France was a deft inversion of France's interest in ancient Egypt.

When al-Tahtawi returned from France he embarked on his most important project through the newly founded Madrasat al-Alsun (School of Languages); this remained part of Ain Shams University, Cairo, until 1973. This institution became one of the most meaningful intellectual projects in Arabic thought since the Abbasid caliphate centuries earlier. Unfamiliar concepts flooded into Egypt through this organization as this intellectual milieu heralded a formative metamorphosis of ideas. Over the nine years of the bureau, he and his colleagues produced translations in Arabic of 2,000 European and Turkish works.[10] Books were translated to Arabic from various European languages on wide-ranging academic disciplines (Hourani 1983). This centre was a hub for much more than language translation with an independent curriculum which introduced a local audience to Enlightenment ideas, even if with a tinge of *de haut en bas* scepticism towards secular influence of libertarian politics. Al-Tahtawi's translations were more interpretations in some cases as he incorporated his own original ideas into the publications. In later life al-Tahtawi became editor-in-chief of the first official national newspaper, *al-Waqa'i' al-Misriyya* (Egyptian Affairs), and introduced the term *watan* (nation) to popular discourse leading the way for nationalist politics to emerge in the early twentieth century. In little over fifty years since the French invasion, Egypt had transformed from a nation run by Mamluk rulers to a type of new modern state.

Reformers like al-Tahtawi facilitated the photographic medium to take hold in Egypt and Muhammad 'Ali Pasha was himself an enthusiast for the daguerreotype invention. When Frédéric Goupil-Fesquet and Horace Vernet travelled to Egypt in the autumn of 1839 'Ali requested a demonstration of this technology. On 7 November the Frenchmen made a daguerreotype

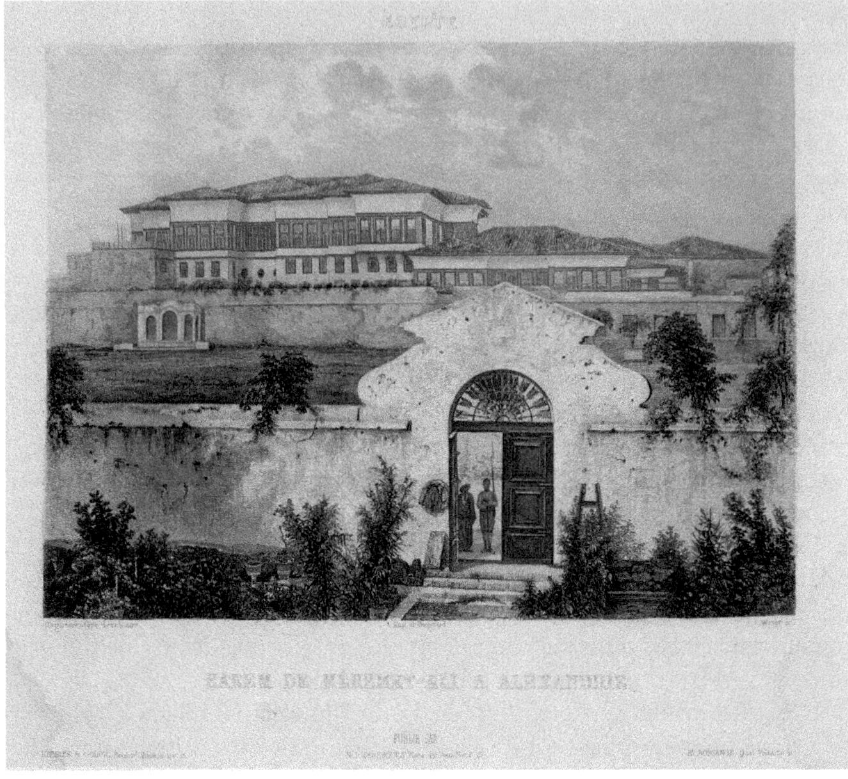

Figure 2.1 *Le Daguerréotype au harem*, Egypt, 1839

image, entitled *Le Daguerréotype au harem* (Figure 2.1), which was a view
of the ruler's harem from outside the walls, the camera placed at a distance
pointing towards the wing of the palace containing the female apartments
only. According to Goupil-Fesquet, they first showed ʿAli and his entourage
the internal camera view consisting of a faint upside-down image on the
focusing screen inside the camera body, viewed under a light cover hood.
The daguerreotype metal plate was then exposed to light inside the camera
before plunging it into the mysterious mercury bath for immediate chemical
development. The resulting image composition recorded the view overlooking
the building wing and a gate wall manned by two army sentries. According
to the accounts of the French visitors, the internal camera view on the screen
intrigued the local onlookers more than the final daguerreotype photograph
did, as the Pasha exclaimed, 'It's the work of the devil' (Hannoosh 2016:
33). French accounts emphasize the locals were mostly curious about the
lens image inside the camera of the palace, essentially a manifestation of

Ibn al-Haytham's scientific camera obscura, and the palace guards appeared to defy gravity as they were visible upside-down, marching in real time, across the camera viewing screen. ʿAli's exclamation on the Devil should not be taken too seriously as an injunction against photography; he would, in fact, sit for painters using cameras and engravings were made of his self-image. Even a lithograph of the Pasha from this time has been accredited to Vernet as Maria Golia has written, 'He [ʿAli] had probably considered photography's import for posterity; indeed, he was soon posing for the camera himself' (Golia 2009: 15).

The original daguerreotype plates of Egypt's first encounter with the camera have been lost, though it is known that Goupil-Fesquet and Vernet made around thirty successful photographic exposures of ancient monuments and historical sites on their trip. They finally produced the travel album *Excursions Daguerriennes. Vues et monuments les plus remarquables du globe* (1841–1842) and only eight original views from the thirty made were selected for reproduction in the work and the photographic plates were used only as part of the engraving process for high-quality reproduction. This is due to the main technological limitation of the daguerreotype process itself, namely, that it is a one-off, a single metal plate image which cannot be copied or photographically printed from; unlike other paper-based processes in early photography, such as the calotype that used a negative paper image to enable printing multiple positive copies. However, the popular use of the daguerreotype system was based in its sharper image resolution which was superior in this early phase of the medium. Moreover, in this experimental photographic art culture of the time, the medium was unstable and unreliable, as art historian Michèle Hannoosh writes:

> Early photographic practice was a struggle between an infinitely variable, unstable reality – the object depicted, the conditions under which it was taken, the materials of the process – and the photographer's limited ability to manipulate these so as to produce a 'fine image'. Always retaining something beyond the control of the artist, the daguerreotype harboured no pretensions of mastery over its subject. (Hannoosh 2016: 432)

Excursions Daguerriennes contains the first photographic-based images made of Egypt and happened despite the volatile nature of the technology and everyday challenges even to produce photographic images at this time (Hannoosh 2016). However, notwithstanding technological challenges in producing this travel album it could be seen as a series of rather misleading representations and inaccurate depictions of scenes in Egypt at this time. The daguerreotype plates were used as the foundation only, a base layer, for engraving plates with various details drawn in later by the hands of the French artists; for instance, details such as human figures and camels were added in post-production. Goupil-Fesquet justifies such image manipulation of the photographic reality by suggesting in his own published account of the trip, *Voyage d'Horace Vernet en Orient* (1843), that placing human figures and details was done to add scale to the ancient monuments (Hannoosh 2016).

Such image enhancements in this early period set out to heighten the exotic embellishments of the picturesque Orient as the images would be competing with other Orientalist fine art depictions for the attention of European eyes. Part of the explanation sits with photography's potential to create something more real or even too real, and thus less mesmerizing for the Western vision of this imaginary Orient. As fine artists, Vernet and Goupil-Fesquet could have sensed the limits of the photographic aesthetic of the medium at this time and were frustrated by its ability to undermine Orientalist representation by revealing realism, or perhaps a new kind of aura. In this way, more by technology than human intent, photography can seem to deconstruct or frustrate the alchemy of the engraving process needing to become infused with the imaginary in order to reassert Orientalist readings of the scene. Vernet and Goupil-Fesquet were undoubtably pioneers who produced the first photographs in Egypt to remind one of the limitations of camera technology in projecting the Orientalist lens. In addition, their methods made sense from a fine art perspective as artists had used image technologies to enhance art production since the camera obscura. However, this brought about little understanding of cultural differences or new awareness of Egypt as is evident in the underlying biases which guided the photographer's eye; Goupil-Fesquet's account of the trip, *Voyage d'Horace Vernet en Orient*, exposes the common colonial gaze of many Europeans at the time. In his commentary he wrote, 'The Arabs are bad-faith rascals, liars and deceivers who take pride in fleecing Christians' (Hannoosh 2016: 460). Indeed, the nineteenth-century colonial travellers preferred to see through the majority of Egyptians, as if invisible, and aggrandize themselves in the ancient grandeur of Pharaonic artefacts and monuments that, for them, echoed Greco-Roman splendours and, in turn, their own cultural heritage in Europe.

Refracting the colonial gaze

Topographical and anthropological photography converge to foreground some key issues about the intermittent nature of homegrown photographic production in Egypt. Within these genres the camera lens first looked towards Egypt in the mid-nineteenth century in the work created by Vernet and Goupil-Fesquet in their aforementioned expedition. This is hardly surprising given the convergence of aesthetic, cultural and technological concerns in Egypt; the abundance of natural light was also a key advantage in early photographic production, and this was matched by the array of ancient historical sites that had attracted European colonial travellers. In the landscape image there is a tangible sense of intention as the photographic eye projects subjectivity in the selecting and framing of the subject matter in the image composition. Such early nineteenth-century colonial photographers were calculating the interests of the viewer in the reproduction of Pharaonic history set in eternal desert landscape scenes. Moreover, photographic tropes are culturally significant as they are understood as the layering of history and engagement emerges through the passing of time in the residue of events. In this way, the photographic landscape image can be a discursive document in a slow illumination of the place portrayed as unchanging over time.

There is a crucial connection between the invention of photography and colonial systems, famously foregrounded in the launch of the daguerreotype process in Paris by the republican politician and scientist Domonique François Arago. Announcing the new camera apparatus in his speech, he recommended the Institut d'égypte be equipped with this new technology to further imperial research. Egypt may have overreacted to this modernizing force in the second half of the nineteenth century through grandiose national projects, dependent on financial support and technical expertise from Western industrialists. Amongst the most impressive projects was the construction of a train network from Alexandria to Sudan and the opening of the Suez Canal in 1869, marking some of the prodigious undertakings of the time to usher in a new technological age of modernity in Egypt. The Suez Canal was imagined by the French, built by Egyptians in a decade between 1859 and 1869 and was subsequently subsumed by the British as part of their global network in 1875. Ruler Khedive Ismail Pasha (1830–1895) was the then Ottoman viceroy to Egypt who initiated monumental ventures and followed in the footsteps of earlier impatient modernizers. Buoyed up by a temporary boom in cotton prices, due to the American Civil War, he had large sums at his disposal as he set about borrowing from foreign lenders to construct these, and other, colossal projects of suitable ambition to his plutocratic ego as he spared no expense in constructing the nation. The building of a new metropolitan capital adjacent to medieval Cairo was styled on Georges-Eugène Haussmann's renovation of Paris and this cutting-edge project alone would become a pauperizing mania. A year before he was dethroned, he famously declared, 'My country is no longer in Africa, we are now part of Europe. It is, therefore, natural for us to abandon our former ways and to adopt a new system' (Robinson-Dunn 2006: 9). Under his rule debt rose from £3 million to £91 million and enabled Britain to purchase 45 per cent of the shares in the Suez Canal for £4 million only, therein allowing this imperial power effective control of the canal and the country. In this reckless episode of modernization Egypt became a costly and superficial imitation of the earlier, more innate concepts of al-Azhar scholars, such as al-ʿAttar and al-Tahtawi, who embraced newness with sustainable approaches and curious minds. Under Khedive Ismail's misplaced rule rapid changes enfeebled sovereignty as Egypt fell into the entrapment of European colonial exploitation.

Britain began its invasion of Egypt in the summer of 1882 with a heavy bombardment of Alexandria by the Royal Navy. The British military incursion was triggered by the nationalist revolt led by Egyptian army officer Ahmed Urabi, which threatened imperial financial investments incurred under the Khedive regime. The popularity of the uprising even enabled Urabi to obtain a fatwa from al-Azhar which condemned the young successor to Khedive Ismail, Pasha Tawfiq, as a traitor to Egypt and Islam. Through a number of decisive battles with the nationalist forces Britain seized back control of the Suez Canal and Egypt, thereby ousting the Ottoman regime permanently as they became the dominant power in the country. Khedive Ismail Pasha was exiled as his son, Tawfiq, was installed as a puppet ruler to serve the interests of British powers. Colonial persecution would alter the modernization project again to take on a more a strident nationalist direction as independence movements emerged from the Nahda cultural renaissance.

The introduction of the camera in Egypt had been fundamental to the modernization processes of imperialism and this colonial apparatus coerced and seduced in equal measure, to become a non-partisan tool which enthralled local populations.[11] Despite Islamic injunctions on human representation in visual form it could be argued that religion may have inspired photography to become a cultural tool during this formative late nineteenth century. Regardless of theological concerns about photography the medium has held a central role in the public imagination in Egypt and prospered through various social and cultural contexts in public life and space.

A form of indigenous image culture became visible, most clearly in the boom in studio photography which arose in bustling metropolitan centres, like Cairo and Alexandria, as a bourgeoisie embraced portrait photography and in broader terms through other types of visual culture. New monthly magazines appeared, such as *al-Muqtataf al-Fotograf* (Digest of Photography) and *al-Funun wa-l-Tawsir al-Shamsi* (Art and Photography), to offer spaces for public intervention and education, in particular via readers' question-and-answer sections. According to Stephen Sheehi, the lack of articles on how to read a photograph or what makes a 'good photograph' (Sheehi 2016: 92) indicates that visual literacy was already legible, at least for the journals' target of middle-class readers. Nahda writing related to the field of visual culture helped to establish a knowledge base for photographic practitioners in the Arabic MENA region who were aware of what scholars have labelled as the 'technomateriality' of the medium (Pinney and Peterson 2003; Sheehi 2016). In this sense they were not merely passive consumers of photography, but instead instructed themselves in its origins, styles and scientific technologies in order to participate in the development of their own photographic cultures on their own terms. A cross-section of middle-class Egyptians became edified in visual culture and mirrored their European counterparts to produce similar types of editorial content for an eager amateur readership.[12]

Beyond the cultural activity in the cosmopolitan hubs of Cairo, Alexandria and other regional cities a ground-breaking Egyptian photographer, Muhammad Sadiq Bey (1822 or 1832–1902), made the first photographic albums of sacred Islamic sites, producing the earliest known topographical anthropology work on the hajj pilgrimage to the Kaaba.[13] Born in Cairo he was educated in Paris where he trained as an engineer at the École Polytechnique and was first exposed to photography. As a colonel in the Egyptian army he began working as an engineer and travelled numerous times in the Arabian Peninsula. In 1861 as part of a survey trip Sadiq Bey took photographs with the wet-plate collodion technique using glass plate negatives.[14] As part of this image production process he took photographs of al-Madina al-Munawwara (The Enlightened City), creating the first images of the pilgrims to the Prophet's Mosque and its dome, and then capturing striking panoramic views from outside the city walls. This was achieved by taking two separate camera exposures and later joining them in such a fashion that it looked as though the photographic print had come from a single plate. Sadiq Bey noted the cultural and historical importance of the photography in his diary of the trip to state, 'No one before me has ever taken such photographs' (de St. Jorre 1999: 40).

Although the survey and his photographs were not published for the public until 1876 his accomplishments were widely reported on and this unique early photographic work was well-regarded.[15] Soon after the success of his first photographic trip he returned to Saudi Arabia to produce more extensive sets of visual documentation of the interior sanctuaries in Mecca and Medina, as well as other key ritual locations on the hajj while including panoramic images of the cities. He was, by then, assigned as treasurer to the annual Mahmal caravan train transporting the *kiswa*, the large traditional embroidered textile cover for the Kaaba, by land from Cairo to Mecca. He photographed the hajj to include the pilgrims as they camped along the journey to document the people involved in this Islamic ritual. In Mecca he took photographs of Muslims in the circumambulation of the Kaaba, and used walls and mosque roofs to offer an elevated view onto this sacred site. Sadiq Bey even made portraits of Sheikh Umar al-Shaibi, the guardian of the key of the Kaaba, and over the next decades he built up an exhaustive record of visual documentation of this pilgrimage taking in sites such as Mina, where pilgrims camp and perform the stoning of the Devil ritual, and in Mount Arafat, where pilgrims must be present to conclude the hajj. In addition to Sadiq Bey's photographic pilgrimage of the holy cities of Islam he recorded written descriptions and poems associated with the sacred sites. He amusingly writes in a poem about photographing one of the custodians, Sheikh al-Shaibi in Mecca, 'In Ka'aba's grace and radiance, Your parting burns my heart, Yet aren't photographers destined to burn in fire?' (de St. Jorre 1999: 42).

Sadiq Bey's achievements were widely acknowledged during his lifetime; his earliest photographs of Medina were exhibited in the Egyptian pavilion at the Philadelphia Exhibition of 1876, followed by the gold medal at the Third International Congress of Geographers in Venice in 1881, and he was also elected to the Khedival Geographic Society in Cairo with the honorific award Bey bestowed to his name. His work was widely disseminated in prints, photo albums and journals, and he produced a number of significant publications including *Mash 'al al-Mahmal* (Torch of the Caravan). His final work included a retrospective of photographs and commentaries, *Dalil al-hajj* (Guide to the Hajj), which became his compilation from various trips in the region in 1886.

Sadiq Bey's photographic work was a precursor to further extensive visual records of the hajj made by other Egyptian photographers and in the early twentieth century Ibrahim Rif'at Pasha was similarly assigned to the official Mahmal caravan. He published a detailed visual narrative using photographs from four pilgrimages to Mecca and Medina, designing a lavish book with over 500 photographs, *Mir'at al-Haramayn aw al-Rihla al-Hijaziyya wa-l-hajj wa-masha'iruhu al-diniyya* (The Mirror of the Two Holy Sanctuaries, or Travels in the Hejaz and the Hajj and Its Religious Rites), published in Cairo. Rif'at Pasha was accompanied twice by another photographic pioneer, Muhammad 'Ali Effendi Sa'udi (1865–1955), a civil servant who proved to be a more accomplished photographer than his senior. Sa'udi's images offered spectacular 3D views of this Islamic culture at a time of change in the hajj ritual. In his two journeys he combined his images with his own astute observations as a devout Muslim addressing the hardships, health hazards and other dangers facing pilgrims. For instance, he abstained from many religious rituals of the hajj for health reasons, such as drinking the blessed water from the well of Zamzam or even touching the Black Stone on the Kaaba to avoid infection, cholera being one such risk at the time. Sa'udi's literary flair and visual content are highly accomplished narratives and he even used the German-made Dresden Stereo-Palmos camera to produce his distinctive stereoscopic images of the holy cities of Islam.

Sadiq Bey's photographic achievements in the nineteenth century picked up a thread of Egyptian visual culture and scientific research stretching back to Ibn al-Haytham's treatise on how an inverted image could be made in a darkened chamber, a camera obscura. Italian Renaissance architects used a device based on this research to help them with their drawings, leading into the nineteenth-century European developments of Daguerre and Fox Talbot, among others, in photographic production and camera technology. These early pioneers experimented with the lens focus and refraction of light to, ultimately, fix the photographic image for the first time. Ibn al-Haytham's theories were the foundation for the study of optics that resulted in the invention of photography in Europe in the nineteenth century. Much of the early photography produced in and of Egypt at the time was bound to the reproduction of empire, be it Ottoman or European, as images and documents stabilize particular values for an upper-middle elite class. Principally this occurred with the spread of portrait photography, often associated with this *Osmanlilik* modernity of the late Ottoman period in the enactment of 'ideas of *Nahda* ideology' (Barouti 2017: 2). In this way, photography adopts a key role in the expression of social relations and new cultural behaviours. Part of the lure was the medium's promise of modernity as the boldness of representation and identification with a space beyond the self. The visual heritage of the indigenous topographic photographers, Saʿudi, Sadiq Bey, among others, represents a generation of Egyptian pioneers with another perspective beyond the dominant Orientalist readings of photography in the region. Furthermore, the non-metropolitan and religious inflection of their visual frame calls into question the over-emphasized research on prominent photo studios in Cairo, Beirut, Damascus or Istanbul, made under the gaze of rulers. The cartographic vision of photographers like Sadiq Bey and Saʿudi challenges the assumption that modernity and photography are inherently urbane, Western and were imported into the region. In turn, this points towards other sensibilities of decolonizing images beyond the internalization of external cultural forces in shaping the new self as part of modernity. Part of the seduction of photography for local elites was this attachment to the coercive qualities of modernity and reinvention that signified social progress, mechanization and rationalization of world order. This pushed up against more indigenous cultural beliefs and religious traditions based in the rural to indicate the 'materialist and ideological nature of photography' (Sheehi 2016: 192). The non-secular image works of hajj photographers are cases where the cosmopolitan vision of modernity has been destabilized and is no longer in the hands of modernizing Effendi classes of Egyptian society alone. Arguably, this type of latent image, influenced by the Nahda intellectual movement and fusing with other preceding traditions, deployed photography in a new context. This visual heritage is not only bound by the connection to modernity as seen through cosmopolitan eyes but via image technologies extends the medium to become more than the sum of these parts. Tageldin suggests that often the intellectual classes overlook the violence of modernity itself towards those less privileged in Egypt and modernity's reform project attests to a reinvention of the self and nationhood: 'The elite Egyptian intellectual positions both himself and the European on the inside and casts the lack attached to him onto a "bad" Oriental alter ego who no longer can count in the mainstream nation's self-fashioning' (Tageldin 2011: 24).

When the nineteenth century gave way to the twentieth, the despotic rule of monarchs and colonial powers was about to encounter new nationalist fervour emerging from within public space as the politics of self-determination and militant anti-colonial awareness ignited in Egypt. Photography began to accrue a new-found popularity in this dynamic cultural phase as visual media became part of the experience of everyday life. Photographic technologies jostled to influence the imagined sovereign state as European colonial powers shifted under the geopolitical order. The following chapter explores how the photographic took on its role as an ideological device in the service of the state that led to new forms of visual censorship.

Notes

1 Britain, France or the United States are authoritative in the photographic canon and scholars rarely discuss French photography as indigenous despite the importance of specific political, social and cultural contexts in respect to these heritages.

2 The *Book of Optics* presents arguments against the extramission theory of vision and proposed the modern intromission theory; the accepted model that vision takes place by light entering the eye. Using the scientific method, its description of the camera obscura, the book extensively affected the development of optics, physics and mathematics in Europe between the thirteenth and seventeenth centuries.

3 The House of Wisdom in Baghdad included scientists and academics, a translation department and a library that preserved the knowledge acquired by the Abbasids over the centuries. Institutionalized by Caliph al-Ma'mun, the academy encouraged the transcription of Greek philosophical and scientific efforts.

4 Aniconism is the absence of material representations of both the natural and supernatural world's various cultures, particularly in the monotheistic Abrahamic religions.

5 Christiane Gruber has authored articles and books which include the role of the image and figural representation in Islamic art history over centuries. Largely rebutting the assumption that Islam has been an aniconic faith she points to specific images produced in Sunni and Shia traditions which are different.

6 Both of these visions of Islam can be found in the division between philosophy and fundamentalism established in the ninth century. An example of a more progressionist sect of Islam can be seen in the Mu'tazila who believed in free will and were influential in the eighth century as they relied on a synthesis between reason and revelation. But this rationalism operated in the service of scripture and Islamic theological framework.

7 The *Description de l'Égypte* was a series of publications, appearing first in 1809 and continuing until the final volume appeared in 1829, which aimed to comprehensively catalogue aspects of ancient and modern Egypt, as well as its natural history. The collaborative work consists of about 160 scholars and scientists, as well as about 2,000 artists and technicians, including 400 engravers. The cartographic section, *Carte de l'Égypte*, had approximately 50 plates of maps, was the first triangulation-based map of Egypt, Syria and Palestine and was used as the basis for most maps of the region for much of the nineteenth century. Through the eyes of the French expedition, Egypt was a land full of resources and colonial potential to be exploited. As discussed by Edward Said those who experienced the 'non-Western' exhibits of world fairs received a Western representation of timeless, primitive exoticism in the Cairo Street live exhibition from Chicago's World Exposition of 1893, as well as the Universal Exposition of 1867 in Paris, among others.

8 Muhammad Abduh (1849–1905) was an al-Azhar theologian, scholar and writer who spent time in Europe. He argued for Egypt and the Arab world to emulate the visual practices of Europe in order to strengthen and preserve the language, literature and sciences of the Umma. Abduh's student, Rashid Rida (1865–1935), became an editor of the journal *al-Manar*, and responded to readers' concerns over the capture and display of photographic images.

9 Key to education was the dissection of bodies but Muslim belief scorned any incision upon the deceased. The Prophet had forbidden the cutting open of the dead body and even the anatomical drawing of the human form was, to some, a violation, even though dissection was indispensable to modern medicine. Defying mainstream clerical opinion al-'Attar supported the gradual breakdown of prejudice against dissection winning a key battle with the conservative majority of the ulema. The first official autopsy was carried out under the instruction of French surgeon Antoine Barthélémy Clot in 1827 but without the knowledge of the public.

10 Among them Greek philosophy and Enlightenment thinkers as these translations had a lasting impact on many professions and disciplines helping to form a new elite and middle class that would dominate public life for the next two centuries in Egypt.

11 Some Egyptians were less enthusiastic and continued to perceive the medium as somewhat estranged from a more devout vision of Muslim identity because of conservative religion. The influence of non-secular movements, such as al-Ikhwan al-Muslimun (Muslim Brotherhood), appeared to be inimical towards the visual representation of the human form and even suggested Islamic doctrine backed up such beliefs.

12 For instance, the *British Journal of Photography* (1854) or the *Photographic Journal* (1853).

13 Sadiq Bey published three important works: *Mash 'al al-Mahmal* (Torch of the Caravan) in 1881, *Kawkab al-Hajj fi Sayr al-Mahmal Bahran wa-Sayrihi Barran* (The Star of the Hajj along the Travels of the Caravan by Sea and Land) in 1886 and *Dalil al-Hajj li-l-Warid min Makka wa-l-Madina* (Guide to the Hajj for Those Arriving in Mecca and Medina) in 1896, all of which included his detailed observations of his journeys. *Mash 'al al-Mahmal* contains his collection of photographs, a history of the Mahmal and the *kiswa* cloth which covered the Kaaba and his observations of Mecca and Medina. *Dalil al-Hajj* is a distillation of his earlier journeys. Later publications on the holy cities often used Sadiq Bey's photographs, including Muhammad al-Batanuni's *Journey to the Hejaz* and Saleh Soubhy's *Pèlerinage à la Mecque et à Médine*.

14 The collodion method used a glass plate rather than paper as a support for the light-sensitive salts, and it had only been invented a decade earlier by Frederick Scott Archer.

15 Sadiq Bey presented a report to his military superiors, but he did not publish anything until 1877, when his account appeared initially in *The Egyptian Military Gazette*. Shortly afterwards he produced the *Summary of the Exploration of the Wajh-Madina Hejaz Route and Its Military Cadastral Map*. The book contained the details of the journey, a long description of Medina and the pilgrimage, four photographs, a map of the route and the plan of the Prophet's Mosque. After his photographic exhibitions in Philadelphia in 1876 and Venice in 1881, he had a circular stamp made which read: 'Sadic Bey, Colonel d'Etat-Major Egyptien. Photographe Diplomé a L'Exp. de Philie 1876 Medaille d'Or a L'Exp. de Venise 1881' (de St. Jorre 1999: 43).

3

National images

Photography and the archival narrative

This chapter sets out to consider how photography was popularized to become part of the social fabric and, in turn, go on to influence the cultural imagination in Egypt. This happened mostly through illustrated magazines, popular press and later in vernacular photographic practices as the photographic image shaped the collective memory of the nation. Various types of print magazines flourished in the first half of the twentieth century and these publications recorded and impacted on the transformations taking place in everyday life. The early part of the century saw an upsurge of magazine publications which deployed the photographic image as a new visual communication tool. Hence, the photograph in print takes on a persuasive role in mediating modernity in all its guises and the new social values permitted within the nationalist narrative of a country moving from the colonial rule to decolonialized independence. In the second half of the century, during the Nasserist Arab Republic, the local press was nationalized and censored by the regime as it inherited various photographic archives. However, the state-run media has struggled to set up institutions to safeguard the medium, resulting in decades of the slow decay of valuable visual materials. This chapter draws from what documents remain to look back at the value of the photograph in the popular setting, which is often stored in government-run institutions, independent cultural organizations, university libraries or as part of private collections. This image heritage in Egypt can demonstrate how the social integration of camera practices and visual literacy came into everyday life from an intimate, ground-level viewpoint to iterate decolonial aims. Photographs in the illustrated press and media can function in similar ways to the idea of 'vernacular modernism' of amateur photography (Pinney 2003: 202) as the visual informs us of the symbolic values of the pictorial in the collective imagination. Over the course of the century Egypt transformed Pan-Arabism as Cairo became a hub for anti-colonial movements from Africa and Asia during the Cold War. At the same time state censorship of the local media and control of photographic materials has meant that Egypt's visual heritage is too often in external spaces despite the best efforts of some organizations to address a culture of indifference in the preservation and curation of visual memory. In a way, the labour of image decoloniality is not only directed at the colonial system, but, in turn, towards the negligence of Egyptian statehood as manifested in the twentieth century along with new calls for reparations.

Despite the odds well-resourced archives endured to care for pictorial documents in Egypt, among them the Rare Books Collection in the American University in Cairo, the Bibliotheca Alexandrina and the Middle East Photographic Preservation Initiative.[1] Dedicated social media groups also disseminate content or other initiatives, such as the Internet Archive, synergizing library collections across the world for online research. Regrettably, some of Egypt's visual history remains housed in archives outside the nation; for instance, in the Harvard University Fine Arts Library or the Getty Research Institute, among other renowned specialized foundations based in Western countries. Well-organized institutional archives are invaluable resources for visual history and the illustrated magazine history contextualizes the photographic legacies of Egypt while remaining problematic when one considers ethnical arguments over the ownership of 'potential history' (Azoulay 2019: 9). Western modes of archival representation can appear to fill in the gap in critical knowledge while, at the same time, such repositories can sustain a disequilibrium in intertextual relationships between photography and history. In broad terms, some photographic historians edify the overuse of Orientalism in cultural politics or to even prefer the privileging of purely aesthetic arguments.

John MacKenzie and Ken Jacobson are suspicious of critical theory per se preferring to propose a return to the prior usage of unproblematic aesthetics in art historical contexts without critical baggage. As MacKenzie naively states, 'there is little evidence of a necessary coherence between the imposition of direct imperial rule and the visual arts' (MacKenzie 1995: 51). Scholars on the critical side of the decolonial spectrum (Pinney and Peterson 2003; Woodward 2003) have suggested to revise the binary of colonialism met with indigenous resistance because in cultural matters subtle influences can be significant in the exchange of gazes. They suggest simple duality can easily overlook the scope of local visual practices and the nuances of the colonial lens in photographic production. Others propose too much energy has already been spent in addressing how inadequate Orientalism may have become over decades to propose another position of a 'network theory' (Behdad 2013: 11). Here, Ali Behdad states that relationships should be considered between photographic production, specific individuals and groups in an imaginary construct of 'exotic signifiers' (Behdad 2013: 11). By this he means indigenous photography can be seen as another constituent of the Orientalist system, indebted to its ideological and aesthetic values. When considering the ownership rights and preservation of photographic archive materials, Behdad's network, in the contemporary context has become viable through cross-national museums, international collectors and wide-ranging producers. However, this belies a concern about the asymmetrical power relations in such knowledge archipelagos as the assemblages are still uneven. Moreover, networked archival knowledge and institutional intersections can seem to undermine the reparations argument that has proven necessary to readdress legacies of exploitation.

In the vernacular context Egypt hosts dozens of social media accounts which are dedicated to collections of local magazine culture (Vintage Egypt or Antique Cairo) and function as practical solutions for many in accessing a wider range of visual culture materials. A review of Maria Golia's *Photography and Egypt* in *Bidoun* magazine noted the problem of authoritative local institutions in the region and outlines how 'archives have been destroyed by indifference as well as disasters natural and manmade, but the end result is the same: a whole lot of material is missing' (Wilson-Goldie 2010). However, the true nature of the situation may be more pessimistic than suggested as even when photographic materials survive decades of neglect there is little regard for the physical materiality of the object, be it the photograph, negative, magazine or some other surviving visual relic. Part of the reason why there exists such large quantities of nostalgic photography and visual materials on social media platforms, in contrast to access to well-managed physical archive collections, comes through the deregulation of the market. Commercial and amateur dealers have digitized old photographs and magazines at the expense of preserving correctly the original image objects. A dematerialization has taken place in the digital realm at the expense of the worsening condition of original analogue negatives and images that are discarded, traded or lost in Egypt. Historic content dispensed with contrasts with the ease of the digital copy which appears to be preferred by the public over the analogue version. Therefore, the digital image is seen to retain the same level of aura status or even increased value over the analogue object because of the fragility of the original photograph as this position holds an indexical equivalence between the archival object and the digital copy. Historian Lucie Ryzova in her research on archives in Egypt in *Photo Archives and the Idea of Nation* states:

> The conflation between photographs (or other cultural artifacts) as material objects and their digital copies is leading sometimes to market valuations of digital scans of historical photographs on a par with that of their material referents. (Ryzova 2015a: 303)

Accordingly, a number of forces of destruction converge on this photographic heritage driven by neoliberal interests of collectors, state indifference and through the blurring of image indexicality in regard to analogue versus digital ontologies. The public setting appears to privilege the reuse and re-materialization of the digital image online rather than the potential of slower vertical excavation work in analogue image archelogies, digging deep into the patina of history encased around the physical materiality of the document. The cumulative effect is to create an alternative regime of visual culture that privileges the digital copy, in contrast to the Western criterion of photographic value, and results in the fragility of twentieth-century photograph and illustrated magazine materials.

Visual magazine modernity

The early twentieth century saw an upsurge of magazines in Egypt with some key influential publications using photography as the primary communication tool, predating the advent of more immersive screen media technologies in the latter phase of the century. Illustrated magazines were, at the time, diverse pictorial periodicals which used photographs in inventive ways to report on news events, reflect commercial interests and comment on social trends across print pages. This period of magazine production can be defined by the contested forces at play, in broad terms, ranging from political Islam and nationalist movements under the watchful eyes of colonial powers. From the Ottoman Empire in World War I to the successful anti-colonial *coup d'état* spearheaded by Gamal Abdel Nasser in the decade after World War II, Egypt enjoyed a prominent role as a political and cultural hub in the Arabic MENA region. However, the popularism of the new republic fought for by the Young Officers group in 1952 led to pragmatic understandings of photography and uses of the image, to typically become unilateral if not outwardly propagandist application. Such a military regime seemed intent on impeding the development of a vibrant visual culture and resulted in a restrictive control of the medium and the broader field of the arts. Through the nationalization of resources this new sovereign state inherited various photographic materials from collections, taken from colonial legacies in local media outlets, photographic studios and private family archives. The Nasserist state struggled to set up institutions to safeguard this visual history, resulting in decades of gradual deterioration and neglect of this cultural repository. As Maria Golia writes in *Photography and Egypt*:

> An authoritarian state by definition controls information, hoarding, destroying, or preventing its gathering, and photographs are information of a powerful

kind. Paradoxically the intricate bureaucratic processes devised to protect state-owned records have resulted in their neglect. Whether through cupidity, contempt or a conditioned loss of interest, the archives of many state-owned publications have been sold or decimated and others only partly or haphazardly digitalized, difficult to access and therefore to study and prize. (Golia 2009: 8)

The use of photography in popular magazines of the 1920s and 1930s helped to determine the nature of visual literacy and contours of the cultural imagination in Egypt throughout the political turbulence of the century. In addition, the preservation of visual materials helps define how such a photographic history is situated and understood in the contemporary setting from its role in the propagation of nationalist nostalgia. Such indigenous magazine cultural productions vividly demonstrated how photography was integrated into the socio-cultural framework to visualize social change in a 'contact zone with modernity' (Pratt 1991: 33).[2] Neglecting such a past renders Egypt's visual heritage mostly in a nostalgic setting, and in a narrative sense is often overseen by international institutions, despite the efforts in recent years of local and regional organizations to establish valuable cultural resources. The photographic images used in the magazine publications of the twentieth century can apprise us of the symbolic role of photography in the popular imagination and the development of other value codes in visual culture.

Various types of popular magazines flourished, in particular during the interwar years, and contemporary photographic collections and archives preserved documents which map out the transformation of the everyday as a form of nostalgia for the modern (Ryzova 2015b). Egypt gained conditional independence from the British Empire in 1932 under the imposition of a constitutional monarch, King Farouk, and included the establishment of a national parliament and constitution. Such steps did not appease the situation as tensions in society went on to expose various political factions manoeuvring to take advantage of the democratic opportunity at hand. This fraught time was underpinned by the continued military presence of British forces in Egypt as full-blown sovereignty remained a nationalist aspiration. In part because of these political tensions and the atmosphere of radical social change, Egypt experienced a period of dynamic cultural revival and new magazines reflected the broad range of new-found interests of the readership under the changing political climate. A survey of media productions in 1937 estimated that there existed over '250 Arabic newspapers and 65 English language papers in circulation' (Ayalon 1995: 75). Many of them were aligned to nationalist sentiments with anti-British leanings and some were produced privately by groups seeking to gain a political foothold for publicity or profit. As the national struggle for autonomy intensified more established print media owners, often headed by Syrian and Lebanese émigrés, were aware of the nationalist feelings and by the early 1920s generations of émigrés could have found themselves easily on the wrong side of political trends. As a result, some withdrew from mainstream journalism altogether to diversify and specialize in the printing industry or other related technologies. There were, also, renowned figures who survived in editorial contexts, notable among them was the Syrian-owned *al-Ahram* (Pyramid) newspaper, which dominated the daily news market due to its high quality of journalism that expressed popular concerns. Another exception was the monthly *al-Hilal* (Crescent Moon), which mediated the nationalist position by including Muslim Egyptian writers and secured their hold in the market as one of the most influential media groups, Dar al-Hilal.

In the congested print media environment of the early twentieth century political parties launched their own newspapers rather than depend on existing publications to propagate their political visions.[3] Within this intense phase of nationalist struggle the publishing houses diversified to produce less overtly political periodicals for the Effendi bourgeoisie who were drawn equally to cultural topics in the arts and lifestyle pages as well as current affairs. Effendi is an honouree title derived from Turkish and these were an educated class who had prospered under the Ottoman regime. The new illustrated magazines went on to become popular with large circulations of loyal readers and some publications stand out for their innovative use of photography combined with eye-catching graphic design. One of the most notable periodicals was the weekly *Rose al-Yusuf* founded by and named after the well-known actor Fatima al-Yusuf. In this early phase the magazine mostly focused on popular culture and entertainment subjects; however, two years later the magazine changed editorship under Mohammed al-Tabiʻi. He shifted *Rose al-Yusuf* towards a nationalist agenda in line with the political Hizb al-Wafd (Delegation Party)[4] and this new editorial line, from cultural topics to popular nationalist politics, enabled the current affairs weekly to become the country's best-selling periodical with a circulation of 20,000 by the end of the decade. Later, editor al-Tabiʻi left to set up his own satirical weekly, *Akhir Saʻa* (Latest Hour), which gained prominence in the media during the interwar years.

Many publications were influential on the Egyptian political and cultural landscape over much of the twentieth century but most of them limited the use of photography to a descriptive or illustrative role. However, a key proponent of new visuality in current affairs was the weekly *al-Musawwar* (Illustrated) and it is significant in terms of photographic narratives in Egypt. Dar al-Hilal launched this weekly magazine in 1924 and through the 1920s *al-Musawwar* printed on average thirty photographs per thirty-six-page edition, a minimum of 1,500 per year (Ryzova 2015b). Dar al-Hilal's image archives have expanded over the decades to over seven million items, stored in a rundown building archive under poor conditions with only a fraction of images available, mostly in low-resolution digital formats.

Only two publishing houses, Dar al-Hilal and Dar al-Lata'if al-Musawwara, specialized in the use of photography in their magazines. The first ever illustrated magazine in Egypt, *al-Lata'if al-Musawwara* (Illustrated Witticisms), launched in 1915 and in the 1920s, publishers went on to produce different types of illustrated press which were both political and entertainment orientated, and commonly to exploit the popularity of Egyptian cinema. Titles such as *al-Masrah* (Theatre), *al-Tamthil* (Acting), *al-Sabah* (Morning) and *al-Malahi al-Musawwara* (Nightclubs Illustrated) featured a repertory of celebrity actors, dancers and performers in a veneration of celebrity culture.[5] The popularity of cinema meant illustrated magazines could hardly afford to keep film stars, and by extension, Egyptian women, off their pages. New styles of magazines emerged which impacted on mainstream periodicals. Dar al-Hilal launched a quality fan magazine, *al-Kawakib* (Stars), which two years later in 1934 was combined with *al-Fukaha* (Humour) to become *al-Ithnayn* (Two). The release of this magazine indicates how the Dar al-Hilal company transformed the format over earlier incarnations of illustrated magazines. Previously photographs had been used in an auxiliary sense to highlight the editorial content in the weekly magazine much of which was often already known from the daily newspapers. *Al-Ithnayn*, by contrast, broke this mould and set out to use photography as a bold, primary form of visual communication. Influenced by avant-garde movements and modernist trends through photomontage juxtapositions of imagery this weekly produced striking graphic designs for an eager readership. These approaches to illustrated magazines ushered in a transformation in the modes of reading the visual and shifted from reading text to interpreting images. Throughout the following decades reading contexts changed in the Egyptian illustrated press who redefined entertainment, social commentary and current affairs rather than simply promote political movements. Moreover, *al-Ithnayn* was the first truly family-orientated variety magazine available in Egypt, appealing to different tastes and interests of the typical middle-class household. The weekly edition included political events of the past week, serialized novels, highlighted fashion spreads and popular entertainment features on cinema spread out evenly throughout the magazine. Articles in *al-Ithnayn* varied in appeal not just to different tastes, but to the senses with a heavy reliance on visual literacy. One reoccurring feature in the magazine routinely used photographic reportage stories from beaches or exclusive clubs, often on the North Mediterranean coast, where Egyptian women were commonly portrayed in social interactions, as well as in bathing suits, to challenge orthodox cultural norms.

Egypt's strident anti-colonial movements of the early twentieth century changed the nature of the press media as popular magazines with an emphasis on photography as a modernizing force in society. Publishers used subscriptions and extensive networks to promote new titles and distributed the magazines in provincial cities across Egypt and internationally to the diaspora.[6] The propagation of photographs used in the illustrated press at the time included a diverse range of topics: protests, crime stories, charity events, sports, ceremonies, celebrations and even political funerals. Egyptian nationalism coincided neatly with new innovations in printing technologies as the camera lens enabled magazines to reproduce large numbers of photographs in decent quality on periodical pages. Images were made available to the public of current affairs events, like the German air attacks in Cairo and protests and meetings led by iconic nationalist leaders, and the publication was monitored by British military censors. Indeed, scenes of violence, executions and battlefields were made available from Arab territories under French rule rather than British military violence in the mandates. The readers and viewers of the illustrated periodicals grew accustomed to presume images of local and regional political events would be seen in print pages on a regular basis as a type of witnessing real news through the photographic image. British colonial rule made the local camera take on a nationalist frame in the public eye as Egyptians became keen to participate in the social construction of an 'imagined political community' (Anderson 2016: 6) as narrated by the Wafd Party.

The visual portrayal of this national community in the illustrated press was subjective as the Egyptian press focused mostly on people. In this way, the illustrated magazine edition served as a collective scrapbook, a series of communal photographs, cartoons and images of the national family, to constitute the boundaries and strengthen collective bonds. New middle-class professionals formed the core of the nationalist movement to include government workers, lawyers, students, journalists, industrialists and others who posed for the camera. Extensive captions would even list names of those depicted and this naming function helped to bring people into the communal circle (Baron 2005). The illustrated press of the time covered protests, nationalist leaders and other forms of political agitation along with depictions of sporting events and heroes, youth movements, such as the Girl Guides, in a nationalist representation of a dynamic new nation on the move. Vigour would be important to building the new nation and discipline, loyalty and duty socialized young people into the idea of national service and opened the way for the celebration of militarism that would define the Egyptian state in later decades. Ideology was extended to both sexes and promoted body discipline and group solidarity through various outings at iconic locations, such as the Pyramids, in order to connect the ancient past with the new emergent nation. Sporting success, travel and technology, Egypt Air was founded in 1932, and other state developments signified an independence movement that could not be stilled or held back; progress of nation awoke and was animated by the contemporary force of nationalism. However, this powerful representational lens mostly omitted the working class from the frame, who were seen as lacking the same kind of kinetic energy. When the poor where depicted they were often seen as idle and apathic in a negative inversion of the national self-image. In the press ordinary people were seen sitting around, motionless and disordered, awaiting on charity for some calamity, like a collapsed building or as survivors of fires and typically as perpetrators or victims of crime. This unsophisticated poor class was now seen as passive and dispossessed of good citizenry despite the fact that they keenly wanted to participate in the new imagination of the national family, while the working classes showed up on the political stage by attending large demonstrations and cheering leaders in support of an independence agenda. This unity of the nation, as the individual subject becomes part of something greater, encapsulates the concept of the nation itself and in this new era cameras became omnipresent as the illustrated press formed a popular expression of cultural imagination. The medium of photography appealed in other ways as interest grew in the practical applications of photography and appreciation of images. *Al-Lata'if al-Musawwara* (Illustrated Witticisms) founder Iskandar Makarius wrote on how to develop photographs and other practical tips in magazine editions. Illustrated magazines regularly included advertisements from professional photographers, editorial features on photography, readers competitions and other solicitations for those interested in the medium who could easily find instruction in Arabic on various aspects of the discipline.[7]

The illustrated press marked a distinct phase of popular visual literacy skills to aid the public in reading photographs by interpreting the ocular information and signifiers of a particular image. Readers of *al-Lata'if al-Musawwara* and *al-Musawwar* in the 1920s may have yet to be fully habituated in such a decoding process but by the emergence of another generation of journals a literate audience was found and the curious readership was ready to appreciate the visual, dynamic juxtapositions in graphic design. Specialized periodicals flourished, like *al-Masrah*,[8] as well as the mixed variety magazine *al-Ithnayn*, which had a circulation of 120,000 by this time (Ayalon 1995). Photographs in the illustrated press transformed the modes of reading to bring forth visual literacy as part of a new lens through which the whole context of the print media was altered. Reading a magazine was reformulated to interact between the textual and the visual, thereby introducing entertainment and emotion as reading experiences alongside preceding values of erudition and self-education. The illustrated magazine became a space for an unregulated mode of learning without subordinating to the discipline of formal educational systems.

Modernist social trends in illustrated magazines included photographs of women in swimming suits, which became a common visual trope, and publications pushed moral boundaries to market magazines through semi-clad female bodies. Low-budget magazines appeared at the vanguard of pushing cultural norms and one example, *al-Riyada al-Badaniyya* (Physical Culture), was launched in 1930. At first glance, it seems to extend the benefits of physical fitness for the youth but upon closer inspection of a 1931 edition, the various photographic illustrations of exercise poses are combined with suggestive texts to titillate for its time in the local press, hidden under the cover of sport and healthy lifestyles.[9] Low-cost pulp content suited the tastes of new urban working-class readers and dubious content circulated easily through networks of street vendors to compel the illustrated magazine industry to accommodate differing social trends in sports, cinema, fashion genres and romantic novels. However, magazine culture was rooted in the interests of comprador elites who regarded class and gender equality as topics to be carefully controlled. Therefore, the majority of photographs used in the magazines at the time featured Egyptian males performing important public functions and political duties while women are objectified in different ways. The aforementioned features on seaside resorts permitted images of women in swimsuits to be used openly alongside with editorials on cinema actors, iconic starlets and glamours singers as the Egyptian female body becomes a visual selling point of the magazine under the male gaze. Working-class *baladi* women were rarely visible on magazine pages and are only present photographically when seen as illustrations for sensationalist crime reports and dramatic narratives; for instance, reports about scheming runaway brides.[10] Indeed, the non-urban classes and regional cities are seldom part of the illustrated magazine lens as news stories and cultural events of what was happening in Western countries were more likely to be considered of value to the readership.

Spiritual genealogy of the image

Three illustrated magazines stand out in the genealogy of visual culture in Egypt in this time and symbolize shifts in visual literacy in public space. *Al-Lata'if al-Musawwara* was the first publication to use photography as a visual communication tool to illustrate current affairs topics. This was followed by Dar al-Hilal, who launched its own flagship magazine, *al-Musawwar*, and then in the early 1930s advanced the illustrated press format with the introduction of *al-Ithnayn* to the market. Despite many other notable illustrated publications in circulation the quality, duration and dissemination of these three magazines above others lay claims to further examination of how the photographic image became interwoven with new social trends and political movements. In order to establish the centrality of photography to forms of modern life certain visual signifiers in photographs, textual content and magazine design became synergized in these illustrated publications to explore the ways modernity intersects with gender roles and other political concerns over the course of the twentieth century. In this sense, images used in the Egyptian illustrated press have become visual prompts and historical drivers from non-Western sources to say something key about the histories of photography. *Al-Lata'if al-Musawwara* deployed photographs, drawings, cartoons plus other visual materials to add new graphics to current affairs reporting. Published on a weekly basis the cover page set out to have a direct visual impact by using a large photographic image as a leading news item of the week in order to catch the eye of the readers. Other photographs would be included in the edition across the magazine spreads but, at this stage, photographs were still relatively expensive to print which limited the image resolution and quantity of images per edition. However, the appeal of the visual spoke to the aspirations and expectations of Egyptians from different social backgrounds at this historical juncture. Photographs represented nationalist politics, largely concerning male leaders, to enable modern subjects to constitute themselves as part of an imagined nation. Much of the surviving magazine materials in archives show the ways photography became a reflection of the nationalist movement as it jostled for attention with other regular features on the constitutional monarchy, celebrity entertainment, sporting heroes and advertisements.[11] Intriguingly the shape of modern selfhood was played out on this stage as female citizens often endeavoured to push boundaries and assert their political visibility both on the streets and, in turn, on magazine pages.[12]

One of the most significant examples of images affecting perception can be seen in a series of photographs (Figure 3.1) initially printed in *al-Lata'if al-Musawwara* on 21 April 1919 at the height of anti-colonial resistance (Baron 2005). The photographs comprise small groups of female nationalists during this historic spring uprising and these images have become emblematic of Egyptian nationhood. In one remarkable photograph, dated 8 April, a group of four face-veiled women are in a carriage, two sitting and two standing, as one looks defiantly towards the camera with an arm raised aloft in mid-speech. The second woman stands to the side of her holding the nationalist flag; although not clearly legible in the black-and-white photograph, it was green with a crescent moon and cross to symbolize the unity of Muslim and Christian traditions in Egypt. Two others are seated

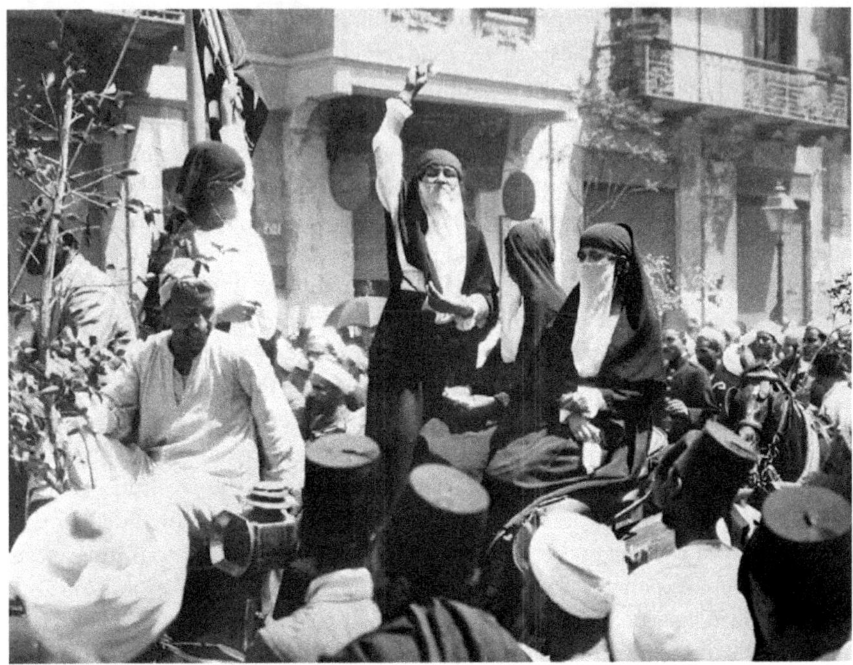

Figure 3.1 Group of Egyptian women assemble in public to make a speech
during nationalist protests, 8 April 1919

in the carriage, one faces forwards, the other has her back to the camera.
In the composition the photographer placed the upright woman with the
arm raised in the frame centre as the point of focus, who addresses a crowd
of men gathered below her wearing tarbush hats and turbans. On the far-left
side of the carriage two drivers sit dressed in long-flowing galabiyas indicating
their working-class status; one holds a tree branch in lieu of a nationalist
flag and the other turns towards the crowd. The standing female figure
looks towards the lens and faces the camera gaze as all the other subjects
appear to be unaware of the photographer who has been credited as R. Co.
(Ramses Company). Like the women in the carriage, the camera lens enjoys
an elevated viewpoint, higher than street level to overlook the crowd, and
is positioned at a distance away from the female group. The photographer
was, mostly likely, in another carriage or a car considering the cumbersome
technical equipment used in this time. The four women are dressed uniformly,
in black clothing with light white face veils that denote their elite privilege;
at the time working-class women wore a heavier black face veil in public.
The dominant woman in the middle of the frame has been captured mid-
sentence and one can observe how her veil has lowered slightly to just below

the nose, perhaps to aid her enunciation, and a breeze blows against her face giving a strong impression of facial features. Such public exposure challenges the gender roles of the time as this face veil becomes part of the negotiation to assert female agency.[13] Furthermore, she stands above the crowd of men gathered below her, listening to her speak, her arm raised, her fist holding a white handkerchief while her other hand is held open in a consolatory gesture of support or care to combine into a powerful rendering of feminist potentiality within Egypt. However, the true motivations behind the attention of the male crowd and their attentive presence in front of the female speaker remain unknown; behind the carriage another street crowd moves freely and they appear unaware of her public enunciation and protest stance. Furthermore, her carriage driver at the front seems to undermine some of the authority in her performance by chatting with the audience despite his role in the event. Descriptively a caption underneath the photograph in *al-Lata'if al-Musawwara* declares, 'An Egyptian lady standing in her carriage raises her hand to greet the people and to acclaim the nation and Egypt' (Baron 2005: 124). This image is one of a few visual records of female protesters that were part of a wider feminist agenda included in the nationalist politics of the time. Eminent figures such as Huda Sha'arawi and Saad Zaghoul's wife, Safiya Khanum, demanded a public role for women in the new vision of Egypt's shaping up. The self-determination movement resisted British rule but its egalitarian spirit was undermined by misogyny and, in many ways, was akin to other anti-colonial movements of the time across the globe.

This well-known image is hosted licence free online but is also part of the Getty Images archive but here it has been incorrectly listed as dating from 24 May 1919 with no photographic source listed, adding to inaccurate use of these historic images.[14] This photograph is part of a series of pictures taken by local photo agencies for publications over this revolutionary spring and the other female activists photographed were dressed in a similar uniform fashion. *Al-Lata'if al-Musawwara* published the image as part of a two-page spread entitled 'Long Live the Egyptian Ladies' (Baron 2005: 124). The additional photographs consist of nine images which document the public celebrations held in April when the Wafd nationalist leaders returned to Egypt after their release from captivity in Malta.[15] The other images from this magazine edition are similar in camera compositions and *mise en scène*; the women are dressed the same, some holding banners and flags, routinely in carriages or automobiles, to remain at a remove from street level and proximity to the male public. Some of these upper-class women were related to the well-known male leaders and came from influential families (e.g. Safiya Khanum) and were usually accompanied by servants, therefore maintaining class divisions. Their public engagement was through the removed space of a car or carriage in order to preserve a distance from the milieu of ordinary, and mostly male, Egyptians on the street. Over decades these photographs have been regularly reprinted and reiterated inaccurately; newspaper *The Madison Journal* published the photo with a fanciful headline labelling them 'harem women' (23 June 1919). Regardless, these images have played a crucial role in anchoring feminist activism through the visual as part of the nationalist narrative of this time in Egypt.[16] This photographic record of the public celebrations covering the release of the Wafd Party detainees has been wrongly associated with another infamous incident which happened a month earlier in March of that year. As part of widespread civil disobedience protests across Egypt hundreds of women nationalists were involved in a tense standoff with British forces outside Saad Zaghoul's house in central Cairo on 16 March 1919, resulting in the death of six women. However, this incident was not recorded on camera and the well-known images of female protesters in April at various public gatherings in Cairo and Alexandria triggered by these events have filled in the visual void in history of the March standoff led by women. In addition, these April photographs have been mistakenly captioned in the intervening years but nonetheless symbolize the aspirations of Egyptian feminism of 'ladies' demonstrations' (Baron 2005: 126). Moreover, these photographic images of female nationalists inserted the women into the iconic pantheon of the national imagination and went on to inspire subsequent generations of Egyptian feminists.

Despite British repression at this time, *al-Lata'if al-Musawwara* played a key role by publishing these seminal photographs to turn the veiled woman into a militant symbol of the emerging nation itself. However, these photographs of women on the streets are simultaneously indicative of other forces that sought to reinforce gender division and, in particular, class politics running through power relations in Egyptian society. Images of historical events can become malleable and, in this case, multiple ideologies used these photographs of protesting women which have been labelled as liberal feminist activists, Arab socialists and even Islamist protesters. As the 1920s wore on the participation of women in protests and street demonstrations became less of a novelty, and, arguably, the illustrated press helped normalize feminist politics to a degree in public space during this time of rapid change.

By the time Dar al-Hilal introduced *al-Musawwar* magazine to the illustrated press market some of the nationalist fervour had diminished as Egypt enjoyed a degree of self-determination as a British mandate. On 2 November 1928, the weekly edition of the magazine (no. 212) published a large image (Figure 3.2) on the cover of a traditional religious festival, *mulid*, in Tanta, halfway between Cairo and Alexandria in the Nile Delta. This week-long harvest event takes place annually in October at the end

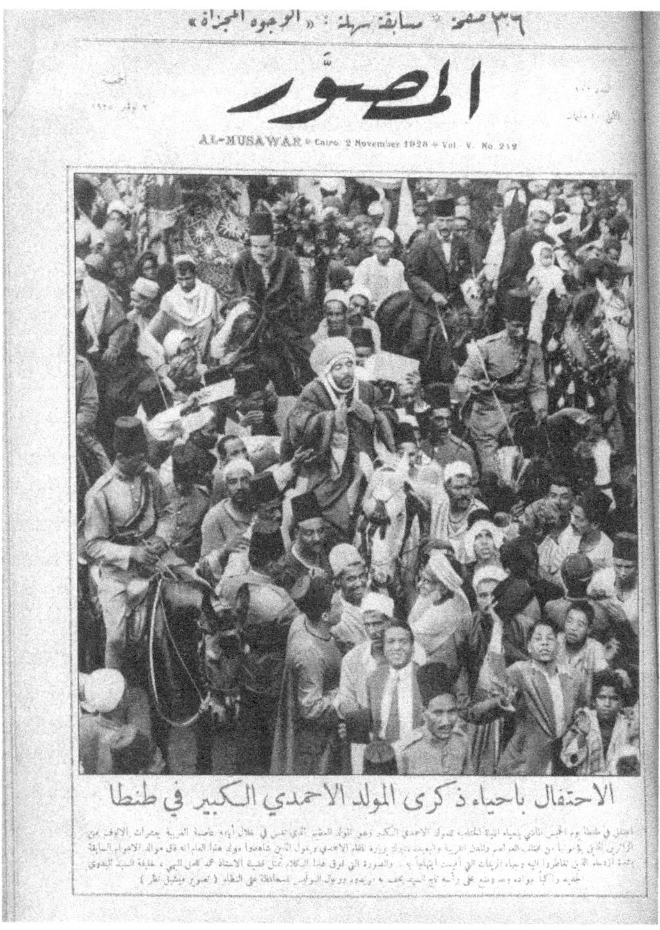

Figure 3.2 *Al-Musawwar*, magazine front cover, no. 212, 1928

of the cotton season and has been known to attract up to two million visitors. The *mulid* commemorates the life of one of the most venerated Sufis in Islam, al-Sayyid Ahmad al-Badawi, a thirteenth-century mystic who settled in Tanta and founded the Badawiyya order of Sufism.[17] Today the gathering involves around seventy different Sufi groups who erect tents outside the mausoleum to perform rituals, *dhikr*s, referring to the central Sufi ritual of praise that involves a ceremony at which music, body movements, song and chants induce a state of ecstatic trance. The photographic image of the *mulid* on the front page pivots between currents running through Egypt at this time, the forces of modernity and Islam's adaption into the contemporary world. *Al-Musawwar*'s camera lens looks down from on high at a large crowd of men milling around the *khalifa* (successor), Fadela Oustez Mohammed Kamel al-Bahey, riding a white horse and escorted by his entourage. This Sufi sheikh has his eyes closed but his head is raised towards the sky, as if in reverie, one hand rests on his chest, the other gestures towards the heavens. The Sufi sheikh is indeed an intermediary between the two worlds as a *wali* (saint or holy person) touched by a *ruh* (soul), and enters this holy place, full of *baraka* (divine grace or blessing). Moreover, he appears unaware of the buzz of street scenes around him or the camera and appears guided by an ethereal, invisible presence as he leads the *mawkab* (public procession) towards the mosque of al-Badawi. The event is founded on centuries-old cultural practices and traditions based on this Islamic group with legions of followers drawn to the mystical aspects of classical Sufism. Although al-Badawi is close to a national symbol of Egyptian Islam, tensions existed between two ends of the religious spectrum; on the one hand, the will to meet the contemporary world, and, on the other, the folk who yearn for union with God interwoven in this visceral form of religious belief. There are two forms of gaining religious knowledge: *'ilm kasbi* is acquired, aimed at worshipping God; the other is *batin*, a more internal access to God, closer to Sufi practices referring to the mystic *'ilm wahbi* or *'ilm ladunni* (divine achievement of knowledge) imparted through illumination. *Al-Musawwar*'s vision of modern Egypt is an ambiguous one as the front-cover image exposes these ideologies at play. The lens used to frame the male *mulid* subjects connects with the metropolitan gaze of the magazine's readership. Such dualities can be observed in debates in Islam at the time, as Catherine Mayeur-Jaouen states in her book on the Tanta *mulid*:

> From the 1880s, the rupture caused by Islamic modernism and its success as the dominant discourse in the twentieth century have led many commentators and the Egyptians themselves to a mistaken reading of religious tradition, seen as a tissue of backward superstitions. (Mayeur-Jaouen 2019: 2)

The illustrated press often privileged the metropolitan world over the impoverished countryside and rarely featured news or focused on life beyond cities. Although this image in *al-Musawwar* documents a scene in this famous *mulid*, it is encoded with an elevated perspective of the camera and, in turn, the concerns of modernity as the towering lens looks down to frame the subjects below, a cross-section of rural Egyptians, where a large crowd on a street surrounds the point of focus, the sheikh on his white horse. The police, two on horseback, two on foot, are close to the Sufi figure, easing his passage towards the mosque where he will set up his tent with his followers. Another three men on horseback appear to be part of the sheikh's cortege as they ride slightly behind him; one carries an infant and the men could be local patrons of the event or the sheikh himself. The majority of the male street crowd do not notice the camera looking down except for five of the gatherers. Most of the pilgrims are dressed modestly in galabiyas except for two men in the lower end of the frame who performatively return the camera gaze in flamboyant fashions. These two are dressed in fashionable suits and hold tarbushes in their hands looking upwards into the camera, aware of the photographic act and returning the magazine viewer's look. One gestures a salute towards the camera with his hat, cautiously smiling, the other companion grins a more nervous, unsure smile. Around them four others in the crowd have seen the camera but expressions are far less confident and more suspicious, uncertain and unsure of what the camera is doing. One young man, directly behind the two men in suits, looks aggressively up towards the photographer, while the other men are frozen in time, temporarily removed from the Sufi event and undecided how to react in this moment of self-awareness. Here the camera frame and the magazine page become intertwined in a traditional representation of Sufi Egypt in a world made up of visible and invisible. The camera lens makes visible the materials of the world, supposedly in an objective gaze, and those who see and notice the camera lens have just encountered the modern age as the bewitchment is broken. This encounter moment is fixed frozen in the photographic encounter and the event disseminated to faraway witnesses by the magazine distribution. But an invisible aspect is enclosed as the Sufi culture speaks to what is spiritual, metaphysical, imperceptible and exists only through its own absence. The modernity of illustrated magazine *al-Musawwar* and the tradition of the Tanta *mulid* collide to intersect two worlds at this time pulling in different directions in Egypt.

Other information on the front cover goes on to inform the reader about the number of pages in this edition and highlights a visual-based competition inside the magazine. Below the photograph a title and caption refer to the anniversary celebration but do not need to name al-Badawi in full because he is so revered in Egypt. The caption continues to offer a flavour of the event informing the readership about the large crowds and naming the Sufi sheikh arriving in the city as part of the news report. Indeed, one might expect to see more on the *mulid* inside the magazine to inform the reader further about this religious gathering; however, this thirty-six-page edition only included another single photograph from this annual event. There is just one additional reportage photograph from the *mulid* included at the bottom of page 5, underneath three images and a story on the inauguration of a new king in Abyssinia. The second Tanta *mulid* image shows Sufi followers inside a tent area sitting with their backs to the camera, eating complimentary meals as a line of local officials encircle them. The composition is less eye-catching than the front-cover image as the photograph seems pre-arranged, with some of the officials dressed in uniforms and suits posing in the direction of the camera. The scene is interrupted by one young boy, face turned towards the camera in a strained expression, but most of the pilgrims appear subdued and worn out, resting from the excess of religious reverie, and the police presence has ensured the order of neat lines during the camera exposure. The accompanying caption reports that the food was donated by the unpopular monarch, King Fuad, to feed attendees of the three-day *mulid* celebration and the image is credited to photographer Malik-Tanta. The rest of this *al-Musawwar* edition is typical for a magazine of its time and carries another forty-six photographic images that cover diverse topics; the King Fuad's visit to Siwa, police raids of hash farms and film actors, news, among other broad general interest topics. The magazine content is typical of the time as it emphasized the symbolic roles of the monarchy and state order through the active functions of the police and entertainment images which combine in a composite representation of ideological power. Therefore, this editorial content belies the primary concerns of the urbane bourgeois readership who have become hailed by modernity and disassociated from the mystic Sufi rituals of rural *fellahin* (farmers) in these traditional *mulid* gatherings.

Al-Ithnayn was arguably the most visually sophisticated of illustrated magazines produced in Egypt and advanced the level of visual literacy through formal design from earlier generations of the local press. The front cover from 9 January 1939 (Figure 3.3) is a non-Western cipher of visual culture and the photomontage consists of a collage made from the Hollywood blockbuster film *Cleopatra* as the image source. The composition comprises a side profile of Mussolini crafted on the face of the actor Henry Wilcoxon who played the role of Mark Antony in the film, as he looks intimately at the face of actor Claudette Colbert playing the infamous female ruler of ancient Egypt.[18] Published on the eve of war the image shows this Western rendition of Cleopatra who spurs the intimacy of Italian fascism, her head turned away to the side, as a text box in the lower edge of the page offers a fictional dialogue between these figures. The text is entitled 'Cleopatra and Anthony' and reads 'Mussolini: Come on let's agree together to restore the era of Cleopatra and Antony', and she replies, 'God opens, we are in 1939'. This phrase, *yeftaha Allah* (God opens), is a well-known spoken expression which refers to a Quranic verse, and in this context means doing something that is not worthy. Moreover, part of this rebuttal involved switching the name of Cleopatra to Masr (Egypt) in the front cover and the ocular content goes on to affirm this textual retort towards Italian fascism in favour of Egyptian nationalism. Meaning is further encoded visually by the female figure as she wears three stars in her crown, the symbol of the earlier Egyptian independence movement headed by the Wafd

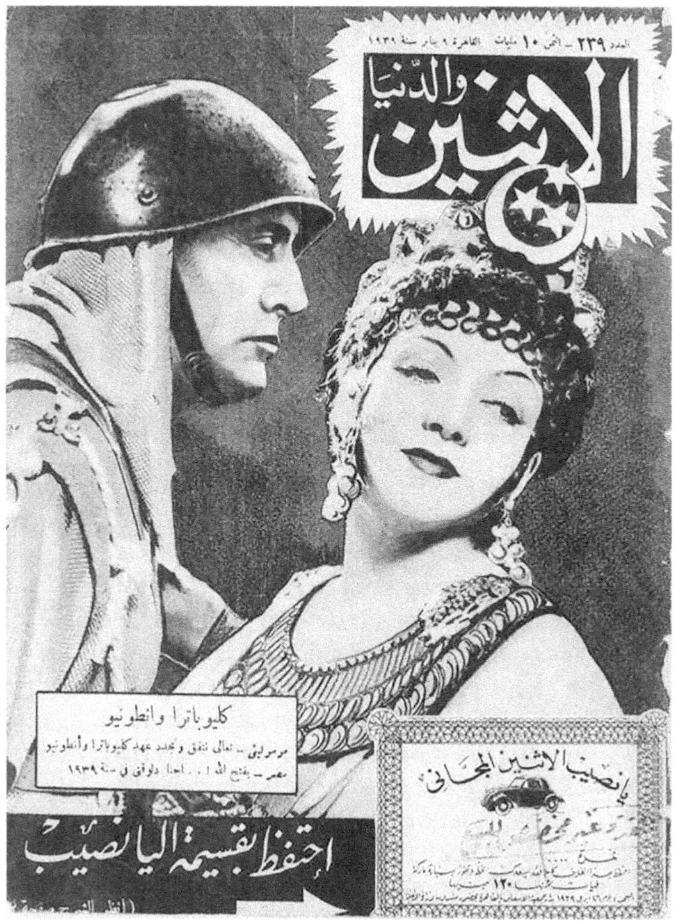

Figure 3.3 *Al-Ithnayn*, magazine front cover, 9 January 1939

Party. The remaining two text panels at the bottom of the page refer to a lotto prize competition, followed by the magazine title, edition and date at the top right of the page.

Al-Ithnayn's front-cover image breaks with earlier photographic practices in the local illustrated press through the use of photomontage; this juxtaposed image delinks the indexical truth of photo-reportage common in earlier magazines. Here the viewer decodes the symbolic language of the image and text to distinguish between more realist readings of the image versus the imagined nation. The photomontage itself has been rendered in a seamless fashion as the face of the Italian fascist leader is perfectly fused with the original film still image to look like a natural fit. This breaks with other radical formalist-led experiments in art movements in the West; for instance, the photomontages in Soviet aesthetics or Dadaist assemblages. Indeed, the image in *al-Ithnyan* may appear understated in comparison to other radical political montages of John Heartfield's left-wing periodical *Arbeiter-Illustrierte-Zeitung* (Workers' Illustrated Magazine), but in this case the specific visual language is not a radical artwork. Rather, it displays another sensibility towards the photographic that does not seek to disrupt the spectator's gaze in order to hail him or her and make them aware of ideological forces. At a quick glance one might not detect anything afoot in the *al-Ithnyan* image at all as it harmonizes design; Mussolini is not overtly out of place in appearance as his figure blends into and mimics the original film still. Even the modern military helmet he wears reiterates ancient Rome in tune with the fascist uniforms that were designed to resonate with past empires.

Regardless, this magazine image is daring in political terms as during the early twentieth century Italian imperial ambitions spread from Libya to other East African territories to the south of Egypt. Furthermore, foreign interests hinged on the strategic importance of the Suez Canal[19] and the economic crash in global markets at the start of the decade had resulted in a recession of cotton prices. Stability in Egypt pivoted on an equilibrium between British interests and local political forces to involve the monarch, King Farouk, the nationalist-led parliamentary party, Wafd, alongside the rising influence of the Muslim Brotherhood movement, among other lesser groupings. This uneasy situation led to the Anglo-Egyptian Treaty in 1936 which helped to accentuate British colonial ties in the country via the rule of the monarchy. This move set out to exclude political Islam from the future process while keeping Mussolini's expansionist policies in the region in check. The Muslim Brotherhood had started to gain support among the rural population by preaching to the *fellahin* and landlords alike the principles of a moral 'Islamic economy' (Hobsbawm 2010: 143) to further magnify urban rural tensions. Such political circumstances emboldened others and a proto-fascist group, Hizb Masr al-Fatah (Young Egypt Party), in 1933 emerged with the slogan 'Islam, Fatherland, and King' (Salem 1996: 660). Known as the Green Shirts, due to the uniforms worn at demonstrations, they gained ground in student circles by adopting a violent rhetoric against political elites. Eventually the group was responsible for an assassination attempt on the Wafdist Prime Minister Mostafa El-Nahas[20] as they espoused violence in military parades and used fascist salutes. Among their ranks were two future presidents of Egypt, Gamal Abdel Nassar and Anwar Sadat, who would be part of a military coup after the Second World War. Relations between the monarchist and extreme nationalist factions had always been factious as the young King Farouk regularly featured in the illustrated press at the time. In this light, fascism's marginal appeal in a country like

Egypt should be understood as a by-product or impact of the colonialist modernity.

Given the political mosaic of this volatile time the photomontage image in *al-Ithnayn* frames Egypt as spurning the advances of Mussolini and seeks to offer a unifying national image by hailing the readership to the specific iconic referent of the nation's ancient Pharaonic past. This photomontage sends out an unequivocal message to the public on the perils of flirting with Italian fascism, rebuked as essentially non-Egyptian, by appealing to a mainstream national sentiment and the political status quo over all other forces. Egypt consisted of nationalist groups and movements susceptible to fascism, namely, right-wing anti-colonial movements; moreover, the metropolitan mixing pots were vulnerable to the influence of Italy in the region. To counter this the photomontage calls on the nostalgia for Cleopatra to symbolize cultural purity in a potent message designed to align the readership with Wafd Party views. Despite the accord with the British forces the monarchy expressed, when called upon, anti-British views but radical young agitators were frustrated with the slow pace of reform through parliamentary politics. The obvious popularity of Cleopatra as a symbolic figurehead for local audiences was evident in the volume of theatre productions made with famous performers throughout the 1920s and 1930s. Popular nightclub singers, like Munira al-Mahdiyya, performed the queen's role of this heroine in Ezbekiyya, Cairo's vibrant nocturnal entertainment district. Later, in 1935, Aminah Rizq appeared in the cinemas to play Cleopatra in a retelling of the doomed romance for Arab audiences (Cormack 2022). The use of ancient visual symbols and colloquial spoken motifs is brought into the contemporary setting as Italian fascism is seen to be estranged from pure Egyptian national values, and out of place in the construction of its collective imagination. Such a strategy has been repeatedly deployed to appeal to the myth of nationalism in phases of revolutionary change and can be seen as an attempt to direct public attention towards the consensus of the Anglo-Egyptian Treaty, and, in turn, aligning Egypt with British interests in the overture to the Second World War.

Military state nationalism

The balance of political power in pre-independence Egypt rested on an uneasy alliance of local movements under the coercive influence of British interests who exploited the tensions between the Wafd Party and King Farouk's monarchist supporters. The Anglo-Egyptian Treaty had reinforced colonial rule as Britain strengthened its relationships with both dominant factions in the parliament. The agreement meant that the British High

Commissioner had the power to overrule Egyptian policies whenever they were considered detrimental to the interests of the colonialists to include, for instance, curtailing the Italian influence. Over the course of the 1930s civil unrest escalated as different factions vied for control on the streets, among them the Young Egypt Party's paramilitary Green Shirts, modelled on Mussolini's Black Shirts. Towards the end of the decade this movement had become an effective weapon in the anti-Wafd campaign under the service of the monarchy and extreme nationalism. Indeed, the Wafd Party resorted to establish its own Blue Shirts movement to, in turn, terrorize their opponents including elected deputies of monarchist parties. The full impact of these political tensions was mostly deferred during the 1940s but in the post-war period workers' strikes and student agitation reflected the popular resurgence of nationalist sentiment and anti-colonial determination, finally resulting in the revoking of the Anglo-Egyptian Treaty. In October 1951, under public pressure the Wafd-led government abrogated the agreement with the British as civil disobedience rose across Egypt.[21] In this violate period a faction of politicized military officers mobilized against the palace. On 23 July 1952 a group, with General Mohamed Naguib as their nominal leader, finalized their plans for a military coup and the 'Young Officers' moved against King Farouk who immediately abdicated. A few days later he left Egypt with his family on the same yacht his Turkish-speaking relative Khedive Ismail had escaped on over seventy years earlier. His departure heralded the end of the Ottoman dynasty in Egypt as the newly formed ruling body saw Abdel Gamal Nasser rise from among the ranks of the Revolutionary Command Council.

It was not until late 1954, after ongoing disputes with Naguib and an assassination attempt on his life, that Nasser ascended to the presidency of the Arab Republic of Egypt and became an iconic figurehead of anti-colonial struggle. A written constitution was approved in 1956 to formalize Nasser's position to lay the groundwork for the Egyptian army to rule over the country for decades; the only interruption being the brief interlude in 2012 when the Muslim Brotherhood's Mohamed Morsi was elected as president.[22] Some of the origins of this ruling military junta in Egypt emerge from within earlier fascist movements and as Sara Salem writes in *Anticolonial Afterlives in Egypt*:

> Nasserism as a political project was formed through the radical movements of the 1930s and 1940s, produced in and through the global politics of decolonization, and representative of major shifts in elite nation-building in Egypt and the broader postcolonial world. (Salem 2020: 2)

Nasser established an autocratic regime that set about creating a programme of nationalist-led takeovers of industry under the charge of developmental modernization. Egypt became a national liberation model which commanded significant influence over non-aligned countries and other decolonized nations across Africa and Asia through the influence of the station Sawt al-ʿArab (Voice of the Arabs) on Cairo Radio.[23] Nasser envisaged national development and national liberation as intertwined because neither could be achieved separately and he was emboldened by other international decolonizing movements. In this period Egypt challenged Western hierarchies in international systems and successfully played off the Cold War superpowers to serve its own national interests.[24] On the domestic front the Nasserist regime created a new country based on state-led capitalist development through industrialization. Initially this sparked a sense of pride of a nation awoken, on the move, busy and dynamic under a process of rapid modernization; at the time of the army takeover 72 per cent of Egyptians had no access to electricity. Part of this national programme involved the state control over Egypt's media industry through a balance of consent and coercion, as Golia writes:

> Newspaper employees owed their positions to the regime and qualifications and performance were not so necessary as loyalty. The state control of the press affected news-related photographs, but a controlling state shaped attitudes towards photography in general. Egypt's visual culture, both the fine and applied arts, was subject to direct and indirect forms of censorship, since those who crossed the tacit lines of sedition might lose their jobs or face arrest. The result was the declining quality of press photography and the scarcity of artistic photography throughout the 2nd half of the 20th century. (Golia 2009: 118)

This monolithic state bureaucracy of the Nasserist bloc became pervasive and invasive into the lives of citizens and economic businesses of every kind as military officers or other government appointees took over key positions. Government control established an archipelago of state censorship that was manifested in the administrative building, Mugamma, towering on the site of a British barracks on Tahrir Square. This imposing example of brutalist architecture became symbolic of the labyrinthine heart of the state and a space which every Egyptian citizen was required to visit.[25]

Photographs of Nasser were widely disseminated in public spaces, state institutions and media outlets as a complete vision of life under Nasserism emerged for a population united in production, consumption, aspirations and desires of citizens in the 'democratization of well-being' (Bier 2020). In addition to the ubiquitous framed portraits of Nasser found hanging on domestic and public buildings his image appeared on many daily objects, such as matchboxes, prayer carpets, medals, coins and stamps. For many Nasser embodied the conflicting desires of a postcolonial, self-determined nation with the hopes to win their rights deferred to this strong charismatic leader. Despite an assassination attempt in Alexandria, he was often seen with an ecstatic public in close proximity to ordinary citizens, thereby projecting the powerful image of power combined with humility; one which his many successors have tried to emulate.[26] Photographs of Nasser display his bulky physicality, his broad shoulders making him easily recognizable to crowds and often dominating other heads of state at political meetings. This contrasted with the image of the monarchy in the popular press who had been depicted as imperious individuals and somewhat detached from their public, operating in a lofty world, removed from the lived reality of Egyptians. In contrast, the Nasserist project used the photographic image as a tool of the nationalist state as its revolutionary leader reshaped the newly decolonized country. He cultivated his national identity through radio broadcasts utilizing his considerable oratory skills, but his photographic charisma also projected the image of a man of the people. In this sense he could be seen as the first genuine Egyptian leader since Pharaonic times, but soon he would become an autocratic ruler surrounded by a military system of dedicated supporters. This contradictory character at the heart of the military regime was evident through the use of coercion rather than consent under Nasserism; combining a new nexus trinity of military, state and economy as ideological pillars of Egyptian statehood.[27]

Nasserism's impact on Egypt was immediate through one of the most remarkable symbolic interventions, the construction of the Aswan High Dam over the Nile with work starting in 1960 and ending a decade later. The impressive national project combined diplomatic cunning, state power and engineering skills to leave a lasting effect on the country by transforming the lives of millions of Egyptians.[28] However, this change was not progressive for 'the Nile ecology and over 56,000 Nubians' (Fernea and Rouchdy 2010: 289) who were forced out in the years leading up to completion of the dam structure. The blocking of the Nile River created a vast reservoir, Lake Nasser, submerging the Nubian settlements and its ancient culture. Egyptian photographer Abdul Fattah Eid worked for Cairo-based *al-Ahram* newspaper and joined forces with the Social Research Centre in the American University in Cairo to document part of this forced resettlement of the Nubian people.[29] Eid's photographic collection was created in 1962 as part of this anthropological survey on the indigenous peoples who were moved from *naga'* (small villages) to a zone, Kom Ombo, north of Aswan. Eid's photographic archive consists of over 600 black-and-white images made on a 6 × 6 square format film camera to reveal the life and rituals of these peoples. The distinct photographs depicted rural life, ceremonies and monuments in the Old Nubia area and, in turn, this cultural transference to resettlements in the so-called New Nubia. The project photography is a collection of valuable documents that covers two phases of a culture in transition from an intimate standpoint to show religious shrines, wedding celebrations, farming labour, homes and *'aza* (funerals); much of which was soon to be submerged under Lake Nasser. This valuable collection of documents records the interruption of not only a traditional way of life but ecosystems centuries old, and the images are fuelled by the melancholia of loss. Many of the photographs are intersections between what was and what will become of this culture in the new government areas in the north of the dam. The images of resettled people show them adapting to, in some cases, large new public housing systems, and their attempts to uphold their customs in unfamiliar settings and cut off from the Nile River.

One particular photographic image from the collection (Figure 3.4) embodies this historical layering as the past and future meet in the resettlement zone of Ballana in Kom Ombo. The group portrait was taken inside a home

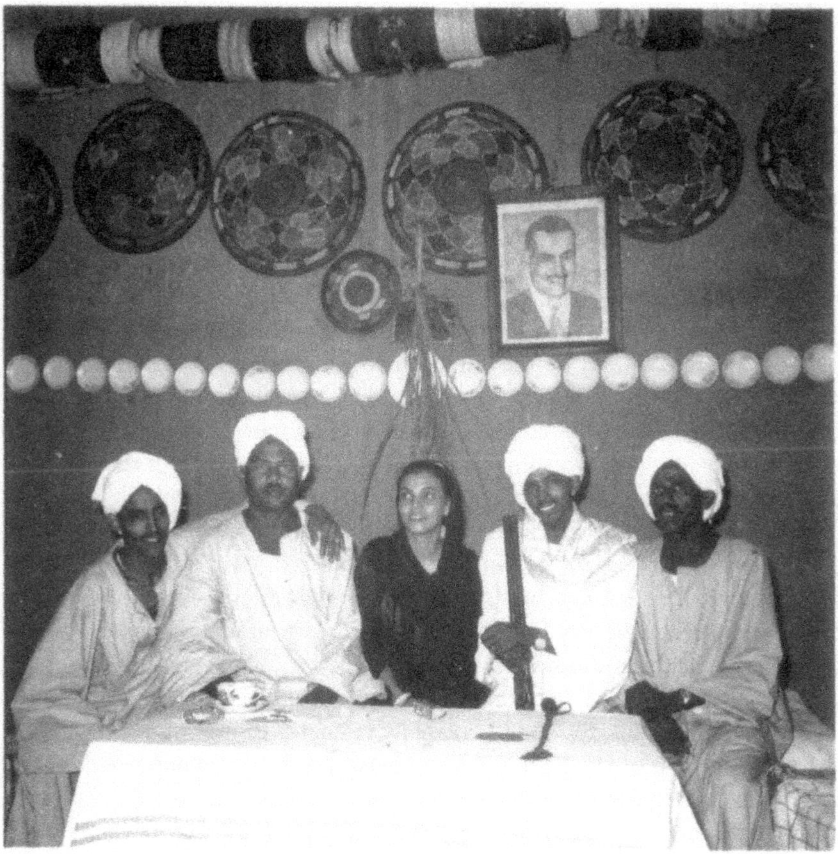

Figure 3.4 Nubian bridegroom with friends in Ballana, Kom Ombo, 1962

with flash-lamp as the staged scene depicts four Nubian men dressed in long-flowing, light-coloured galabiyas and a single woman dressed in black, placed in the middle of the four men. Above them on the wall hangs the ubiquitous portrait of a smiling Nasser along with traditional decorations of circular handicrafts in two horizontal rows, and at the front of the group lies a small table covered in a white cloth. The caption for the photograph states that Afaf El Deeb is part of the anthropological team. She joined a marriage celebration in the local home. The man on her right is the bridegroom who has come from Cairo for the wedding ritual; the bride has not been photographed. There are a number of symbolic meeting points in the image; the four men are of local Nubian descent but already one of them has migrated to Cairo, a consequence of the Aswan High Dam, as Egypt's industrialization process saw an estimated 50 per cent of Nubian men leaving village life for urban centres in the 1960s as part of large-scale internal migration. The woman at the centre of the photograph, El Deeb, was the wife of artist Adam Henein and they were well known in Egyptian cultural circles who lived between Cairo and Paris in a lifestyle in sharp contrast to the Nubian women in Ballana. In the photograph she is an honoured guest, seen loosely veiled, looking out of the frame at the moment of camera exposure in a somewhat distracted manner. She sits shoulder to shoulder, squashed up and in close proximity to the local Nubian men. This closeness of mixed gender sitters can be seen as transgressing certain behavioural codes because men and women should maintain distant, as borne out in the other photographs in the Eid collection of local life.[30]

Although El Deeb was Egyptian, she is at the same time perceived as an outsider in this context by the community and remains disconnected from this Nubian culture at a time of duress. The men pose in a self-conscious manner looking into the camera lens; the bridegroom smiles confidently leaning on a shotgun, while his companions are less assured in the situation to display a range of mixed expressions from sceptical, blank stares to tentative grins. The low table below them shows few signs of festivities, as one teacup and two saucers, an ashtray, a piece of card and an ornate fly squasher rest there. An earlier photograph in the series consists of the same men standing, almost blocking out the Nasser portrait and the table is busier with more teacups and other assorted items. Accordingly, it seems the image with El Deeb was taken afterwards and items of the table were removed; also an extra was man added to create a symmetry to the composition with her in the centre of the square frame. In addition, the group sat down to allow the focus to include the looming image of Nasser on the wall and, in this way, there are six people in the photograph as Nasser's large portrait takes up the same scale as the five sitters, reflecting the invasive role of the state in all aspects of social life. The photographer, Eid, was presumably director of the photo shoot, perhaps bringing in El Deeb to the composition and highlighting the role of Nasser in the centre of the frame. Such arrangements produce a scene that is perfectly ideologically aligned with nationalist unity propaganda to suggest the contentment of these resettled indigenous peoples despite the rupture of their culture in the interests of the state. This staged image projects Nasserism with the photographer as a mindful author of governmental values to propagate a vision of the cohesive nationalist community inclusive of women in the new Arab republic. The omnipresent image of Nasser seems awkwardly placed on the wall, as if even in a temporary addition to the domestic furnishings he is covering over, if not dominating, the traditional colourful woven decorations. Moreover, Nasser has intruded into the domestic space and broken with the ordered symmetry and overall sense of folk aesthetic of the homestead. Eid staged this image of Nasserism, with the portrait of the president an interloper into this rural life and indicative of how the military regime saw the citizen; in this case, through the imposition of the Aswan High Dam to disrupt Nubian culture in the displacement of tens of thousands in the name of the nation and economic progress. The image refers to the hegemonic power of Nasserist censorship, a coercive process to include internal workings of those responsible to construct a national image which intersects with anthropological truth to dominate the official narrative; a controlling tactic repeated over decades by Egypt's military rulers.

Over the course of the twentieth century Egypt absorbed photographic cultures and practices to set in motion a number of contrasting themes on the decoloniality of the image. Female protesters took to the streets in 1919 under the auspices of the nationalist struggle to initiate a debate on political visibility that, almost a century later, was a key part of the revolutionary politics in Tahrir Square. Through illustrated magazine pages a new sense of national modernity and social values were processed by a society moving towards its own sovereignty. The negligence of Egyptian statehood towards the visual archive began with the culture of Nasserism to become indicative of the military state's treatment of its citizens and how photography was used as a propaganda tool. The spiritual genealogies and religious beliefs alive in Sufi traditions speak to a singularity which links with the visual heritage as a creative energy that transcends the specific situation of a particular time and place. This range of distinctive intersecting ideological forces reminds us of the ways decolonial aesthetics in Egyptian visual cultures have been shaped in the transition from colonial to anti-colonial nationhood. The stifling atmosphere of decades of life under Mubarak was ruptured by the 2011 uprising in the sudden awakening of a new type of political activism and this seemed in tune with global debates on the role of the digital image at the time. The following chapter looks closely at this historic time in

Egypt's history and the subsequent discourse on how the image archive forms and preserves cultural memory. This is particularly poignant as the radical politics of this event have been erased from the public narrative under the repressive regime of the latest military leader, Abdel Fattah el-Sisi. In diverse ways the medium has shaped the ontology of the national image of Egypt and the evolution of the photographic became newly defined in the spirit of revolution in the 2011 uprising.

Notes

1   The Middle East Photographic Preservation Initiative is a partnership project between the Arab Image Foundation, Art Conservation Department at the University of Delaware, the Metropolitan Museum of Art, the Getty Conservation Institute and the Qatar Museums Authority. Bibliotheca Alexandrina initiated the Centre for Cultural and Natural Heritage project (CULTNAT) and houses a large archive collection of visual materials. However, the archive has been heavily criticized and is poorly organized despite the generous sponsorship from UNESCO. Another useful resource is the Akkasah Photography Archive, housed within the New York University campus in Abu Dhabi, UAE.

2   The concept of the 'contact zone with modernity', coined by Mary Louise Pratt in 1991, refers to the space where different cultures encounter and interact with modernity. It highlights the dynamic exchange and negotiation that occurs when diverse societies come into contact with modern systems, ideas and technologies. This contact zone is a site of both conflict and creativity, where power dynamics, cultural hybridity and identity formation are constantly at play. Pratt's notion emphasizes the complexity and fluidity of these encounters, challenging the notion of a one-way assimilation of modernity. It underscores the importance of recognizing and valuing the diverse perspectives and agency of individuals and communities in the process of globalization.

3   Part of the nationalist movement was reflected in the *al-Akhbar* (The News) daily, edited by Amin al-Rafi'i. It gained popularity for a while, but the Nationalist Party lost its leadership position in the struggle with other groups. The nationalist movement in Cairo was reinforced in 1921 when 'Abd al-Qadir Hamza published the journal *al-Ahali* throughout the war years.

4   The Wafd Party (Delegation Party) was a nationalist party in Egypt and was the most influential political party for a period from the end of World War I through the 1930s. During this time, it was instrumental in the development of the 1923 constitution, and supported moving Egypt from dynastic rule to a constitutional monarchy, where power would be wielded by a nationally elected parliament. The party was dissolved in 1952, after the Egyptian Revolution.

5   Women who appeared in these publications were excluded socially from the mainstream public. Their presence in the low-budget and low-circulation show-business magazines confirms the marginality dictated by their professions. For

instance, *al-'Arusa* (The Bride) was an illustrated magazine aimed at women and, for the first two years of the publication, all images of women printed were Western women, with few rare exceptions. *Al-'Arusa*'s policy was analogous to its male cousin, *al-Lata'if al-Musawwara*, which featured virtually no pictures of Egyptian women. However, by 1932 *al-'Arusa* had changed its name to *al-'Arusa wa-l-Funun al-Sinima'iyya* (The Bride and Cinematic Arts), and reoriented itself to cover Egyptian cinema actresses.

6 Unlike Dar al-Lata'if al-Musawwara and Dar al-Hilal, which both had their own agents in provincial cities as well as abroad, the show-business magazines were produced and distributed on a much smaller scale. *Al-Masrah*, for instance, was available solely at box offices of several Cairene theatres. Many others were heavily dependent on subscription and often did not live long. New titles were constantly emerging, which testifies to the popularity of urban entertainment, despite the chronic instability of the business.

7 Beth Baron has discussed the illustrated press inclusion of information and education on the subject and writes, 'Literary material included a pamphlet by Amin Hamdi of Benha on Amateur Photography (1922), a book by Abbas Effendi al-Harawi al-Khabir of Ain Shams on coloring photos (1924), and a sixteen-part series by Muhammad Effendi Zaghloul on photography in al-Nahda al-Nisa'iyya (1933–34)' (Baron 2005: 92).

8 Additional titles were *al-Mumaththil* (The Actor, 1926–1927), *al-Raqib* (The Observer, 1926–1927), *al-Mustaqbal* (The Future, 1927–1929), *al-Naqid* (The Critic, 1927–1928).

9 Under the slogan 'Know your body!' *al-Riyada al-Badaniyya* readers of both sexes are invited to know each other's bodies' secrets. Heteronormative articles such as 'Birth Control', 'Secret Habit' or 'Columbus and Syphilis' are aimed at male readers; others, such as 'Passionate Date' or 'My Emotionally Flaccid Husband', seem to beckon the female.

10 *Baladi* is a term for working-class women who were regularly represented as untrustworthy on crime pages of the *al-Ithnayn* magazine. In issue no. 242, on 30 January 1939 a loosely factual news report from Sayyida Zainab Square, Cairo, displayed a group of women selling vegetables with the illustrated story 'The Runaway Bride', which reported that a young woman pretended to be a villager lost in the city, asking men for protection through marriage. As soon as the groom brought her the obligatory dowry, she was gone with the money.

11 When photographs of women were used in the illustrated press, they were rarely Egyptian. One edition of *al-Musawwar* shows four images of women; Lady Carbury, an English pilot; Her Highness Badi'a, the Queen of Afghanistan; a latest fashion-from-Paris photograph; and the actress Lillian Gilmore as a tennis fan.

12 In the early twentieth century, a woman's face and name should not have been made public. Rather, it should derive from the identity of her father, husband or child. To this day, in working-class neighbourhoods a woman is not known (and certainly not called) by her name, but instead in relation to a male as, for instance, Umm Ahmad (mother of Ahmad).

13 Feminist Huda Sha'arawi would proactively remove such a face veil after attend-
    ing a suffragette congress in Rome in 1923, marking a stage in the history of
    Egyptian feminism. Women who came to greet her were shocked at first then
    broke into applause and some of them were inspired to remove their own veils.
    Within a decade many Egyptian women had followed suit, in particular those
    who wanted to be considered more modern orientated.

14 This image has been referred to inaccurately and misused in various publications,
    including the *Egypt Independent* newspaper in 2012, and this is indicative of
    the confusion concerning historical images of Egypt. Other times the image is
    claimed to depict Huda Sha'arawi, the Egyptian Feminist Union founder and
    nationalist icon.

15 Saad Zaghloul, leader of the Wafd Party, enjoyed massive support among the
    Egyptian people as Wafdist emissaries went into towns and villages to collect
    signatures in support of the movement's leaders. Seeing the popular support that
    the leaders enjoyed, and fearing social unrest, the British administration proceeded
    to arrest Zaghloul on 8 March 1919 and exiled him with two other movement
    leaders to Malta. In the course of widespread disturbances between 15 and 31
    March, at least 800 people were killed, numerous villages were burnt down,
    large landed properties plundered and railways destroyed by angered Egyptian
    mobs. For several weeks demonstrations and strikes broke out across Egypt led
    by students, civil servants, merchants, peasants, workers and religious leaders.
    This mass movement was characterized by the participation of both men and
    women, and by spanning the religious divide between Muslim and Christian
    Egyptians. The uprising in the Egyptian countryside was more violent, involving
    attacks on British military installations, civilian facilities and personnel.

16 The photographs from this time have been frequently reprinted. The special
    issue of *al-Musawwar* published on the anniversary of the 1919 revolution
    carried a cropped version, the middle slice with only three women. A differently
    cropped version of the photo appears in *al-Hilal*'s 1992 centennial anniversary
    album *Sijill al-Hilal al-Musawwar* (The Illustrated Record of al-Hilal). American
    newspaper *The Madison Journal* published the image in 1919 under the headline
    'Harem Women Make Public Speeches' (23 June 1919). For a detailed historical
    breakdown of this time, see Baron 2005.

17 There are over seventy officially recognized Sufi orders in Egypt, with some 15
    per cent of Egyptians either belonging to a Sufi brotherhood or adhering to Sufi
    practices. The Supreme Council of Sufi Orders, a government body founded
    in 1903, is responsible for regulating Sufi brotherhoods and is charged with
    ensuring that Sufi practices conform to Islamic norms and laws. For more, see
    Mayeur-Jaouen 2019.

18 *Cleopatra* is a classic Hollywood epic film directed by Cecil B. DeMille in 1934
    and distributed by Paramount Pictures. It is a fictional retelling of the story
    of Cleopatra VII of Egypt with actors Claudette Colbert as Cleopatra, Warren
    William as Julius Caesar and Henry Wilcoxon as Mark Antony. *Cleopatra*
    received five Academy Award nominations and was the first DeMille film to
    receive a nomination for Best Picture.

19 In 1940, it appeared that German successes in Poland, France and Norway would end the war. Italian dictator Benito Mussolini was concerned that Italy might lose its share of the spoils. On 10 June 1940, he declared war on Britain and France. He was sure that France and Britain would soon surrender and did not believe Italy would have to do much fighting. Mussolini wanted to occupy the French and British colonies in Africa and seize control of the Suez Canal from the British. In August 1940, he ordered attacks on British positions in East Africa and Egypt. Troops from the Italian colony of Ethiopia invaded British Somaliland and quickly overran its garrison made up of mostly locally conscripted soldiers.

20 Relations between the monarchy and nationalism had been always intoxicated by mutual distrust during the whole period under question. The fascist movement Young Egypt gained ground in universities by adopting a violent rhetoric against the old political elites as its Green Shirts displayed banners at military parades and gave fascist salutes in praise to the king. Among their numbers were future presidents of Egypt Gamal Abdel Nasser and Anwar Sadat, and the group had been admirers of Italian fascism. In 1937, they attempted to murder the Wafdist prime minister and the party then developed its own praetorian unit, Blue Shirts.

21 In January 1952, skirmishes in the Suez Canal Zone between disgruntled British officials and the locals resulted in the death of forty-six Egyptian policemen and on the following day, 26 January, violence erupted in Cairo and other cities. This eventually led to the nationalization of the Suez Canal in a popular uprising against colonial powers, spearheaded by future president Nasser.

22 Egypt has had only five rulers since independence: Nasser, Sadat, Mubarak, Morsi and el-Sisi, with the Muslim Brotherhood's Mohamed Morsi as the only non-military president. Nasser established this effective form of political control through discipline and the nationalization of Egyptian assets for the regime.

23 The new military regime recognized the value of radio and unlike the press, which the Nasserist government did not control until 1960, radio fell under the monopoly of the government. Nasser devoted considerable financial resources to the expansion of public broadcasting and the Voice of the Arabs first aired on 4 July 1953, one year after the Egyptian Revolution of 1952 as a half-hour radio programme on Cairo Radio. A year after its initial broadcast, the service's transmission time tripled and, by 1962, the service expanded to broadcasting fifteen hours a day and in the following decade to twenty-four-hour broadcasting. This functioned as Nasser's main vehicle in propagating his pan-Arabist views; it played a key role in promoting his image as an anti-colonial figurehead. The service promoted Arab unity and statements that highlighted Egypt's role as a decolonizing force in its rejection of Western imperialism. One example of solidarity was when Egypt endorsed India's declarations of Cold War neutrality in 1953, and went on to attract support from Nile Valley nations by broadcasting radio programmes in Amharic, Sudanese dialects and Swahili.

24 Such policies accelerated Anglo-American plans to outmanoeuvre Nasser, and when Western powers withdrew their funding for the Aswan High Dam in

July 1956, he nationalized the Suez Canal Company. Egypt then received swift support from Soviet Russia, China and India, but also from labour and liberation movements across Asia and Africa.

25 The distinct roles of private and public sectors were detailed in the Free Officers' National Charter 1962 as nationalization laws 117 and 118 were implemented to create a public sector and, by extension, make the state the central actor in production. By the end of the first five-year plan, the public sector represented 90 per cent of total investment, leading some to argue that state capitalism had successfully eliminated foreign control of Egypt's economy. However, the 1960s saw a deepening economic crisis as Egypt failed to develop a strong economic sector even before the impact of the 1967 War with Israel and the demise of the Nasserist project. For more, see the excellent study Salem 2020.

26 The Muslim Brotherhood, although initially allied with the military rebellion, eventually tried to assassinate Nasser, resulting in a massive crackdown. In this way, the Muslim Brotherhood was never compatible with Nasserism because it centred on the pillars of the military, the state and capitalism, leaving powerful legacies that would haunt Egypt's future. Therefore, although the 2011 uprising opposed the military system as embodied by Mubarak at the time, it also drew on the same nationalist sentiments formed by the 1952 revolution led by the Young Officers.

27 Magazine *Akhir Sa'a* published a report in 1958 on cross-dressing men in the regional city of Asyut as such gender fluidity was considered regressive by the self-defined Cairo cosmopolitans. The heteronormativity of the article does not clarify any further details on why these people posed for the camera, or how lives in rural communities may attest to a more progressive gender fluidity in a local context. The report is largely one-sided as the topic is presented as a backwards oddity to the mostly urban readership. However, such reports in the Egyptian illustrated press document historical drivers from non-Western sources outside of modernity.

28 The British began construction of the first dam across the Nile in 1898, which was known as the Low Dam, and Nasser moved to supplement this with a more ambitious project. Western powers supported the venture with a loan of $270 million; however, the relationship soured. Nasser signed an agreement with the USSR in June 1956, when the Soviets offered Nasser $1.12 billion at 2 per cent interest for the construction of the dam. The Soviets provided technicians and heavy machinery to work the enormous rock and clay dam designed by the Soviet Hydroproject Institute along with 25,000 Egyptian engineers and workers contributing to the construction. The High Dam (al-Sad al-'Ali) was completed on 21 July 1970 after ten years.

29 The Social Research Centre was part of the Nubian Ethnological Survey and consisted of a team of anthropologists and other social researchers that looked into the forced migration of the Nubian inhabitants of the Nile Valley south of Aswan to a resettlement area near Kom Ombo to the north. *Nubian Encounters: The Story of the Nubian Ethnological Survey 1961–1964*, edited by Nicholas S. Hopkins and Sohair R. Mehanna, covers this historic internal migration through

selected contributions from the archive along with more contemporary research on the legacy of this transformation of Nubian culture.

30　Indeed, one of the *mulid* photographs by Abdul Fattah Eid in the collection illustrates the defined roles for the locals as two women stand together underneath a large black sheet covering both of them from head to toe as a group of men dance around them. In this way, the women are present in a concealed fashion, faces and bodies hidden at a celebration.

4

Histories of the street

Digital image para-indexes

As Egyptian independence was won in 1952 the new Arab republic drew up a constitution to include law no. 156, which nationalized the press; by 1960 all major publishing houses were under government control, and all journalists had to join the Arab Socialist Union (ASU), part of the Nasserist national party. Egyptian independence movements deployed media technologies, prominently radio, to enhance state influence over the public thinking and accommodate the diverse readership with populist, socialist or even Islamist perspectives represented in the local media. Social trends and innovations in the media industry were closely aligned to state bodies in the transference of power from Nasser to Anwar Sadat (1918–1981) and, in turn, to Hosni Mubarak (1928–2020).[1] Nasserism's statehood was replaced by Sadat's open-door economic strategy, Infitah, as the media industry experienced a degree of relative freedom through Article no. 48 of the revised constitution which allowed private investment. However, state control of the media continued as Sadat placed loyal figures in key roles such as writer Anis Mansour (1928–2011), who became editor of illustrated magazine *Akhir Sa'a* and then, on 31 October 1976, was directed to found the political weekly *October*. This new weekly current affairs magazine set out to capitalize on Sadat's relative popularity after the October War with Israel three years earlier.

Sadat paved the way for the paranoid atmosphere of Mubarak's presidency as the visual culture was further directed by neoliberal economics under the tightening grip of press censorship as opposition publications, including the Muslim Brotherhood's *al-Da'wa* (1976–1981), were banned.[2] Although privately owned periodicals were permitted, all newspapers and magazines in Egypt are subject to supervision through the government's Supreme Press Council. As mentioned in Chapter 3, the first half of the twentieth century saw political factions use photography in illustrated magazines to frame the national family; in order to subvert the colonial gaze and form visual bonds through public albums of the emerging state. Post-independence photographic cultures became institutionalized under authoritarian rule as media freedoms were suppressed by censorship and coercion. The wide-ranging visual heritage of Egypt spans the breadth of the twentieth century to reflect local culture and media history that was prominent across the Arabic-speaking world. However, unlike Egyptian cinema, photography has not played the same key role in influencing visual culture, perhaps due in part to the military regime that was set up during Nasserism. This state system became a blueprint for invasive ocular control driven by suspicion and censorship of the visual up until the rupture of 2011 that positioned Egypt at the core of the debate on digital cultures.

The revolutionary activism on Egyptian streets in 2011 saw the digital image take on a key political role as arbiter of objective reality to counter the propaganda of state-regulated media as the Mubarak regime struggled to control public space. The veracity of the image made on various digital devices and circulated in networked communication systems was accepted as a statement of real events, often depicting police brutality; indeed, one of the catalysts of the 2011 uprising was the mutilated face of Khaled Said. In this context, the value of the low-resolution digital 'poor image' (Steyerl 2009) lay in its documentary capacity as a record of real-life events in an immediate way. Filmmaker John Grierson described documentary practice as 'the creative treatment of actuality' (Grierson 1933: 8) to define the apparent reality paradox at the heart of photographic-based image production. One of the myths of the medium asserts that a photographic image is an objective record of reality combined with the subjective expression of the maker; framed, composed and presented in a particular narrative context. In André Bazin's *What Is Cinema?* (2004) indexicality reclaims some of the semiotic theories of C. S. Pierce and goes on to purport that one of the most important key features of analogue photography is its direct impression of the real world, formed through light refraction and captured by the camera apparatus onto film emulsion. Susan Sontag suggested this key asset of authenticity is an inherent mimetic property of the medium: 'Images are indeed able to usurp reality because first of all a photograph is not only an image and interpretation of the real; it is also a trace, something directly stencilled off the real, like a footprint or a death mask' (Sontag 2001: 154).

Sontag discusses the reproductive nature of analogue photographic processes that exist through notions of stencils, masks or footprints that are themselves permanent registers of the object like a fingerprint, therein implying stability and fixture. Indeed, up until the advent of the digital image technology a powerful facet of photography and film theory revolved around indexicality, a material obsession with permanence, trace, memory and above all veracity. This suggests there exists a tactile link formed through an alchemy of light physics and chemical processes to form a picture of the perceived object in the world. Despite acknowledging the legacy of image manipulation in the history of analogue photography through various photomontage processes, censorship and other ruptures of image veracity, the photograph appears to have enjoyed an evidential status. Even the visual analysis of subjective camera framing or the use of darkroom techniques could not demean the realist claims onto the photograph as a bridge to some original chronological past that implies a moment of truth and unique point of origin.

Time and memory were much discussed by photographic theorists; Roland Barthes's *Camera Lucida* is a short influential book on the photographic process and memory, and his speculations on the indexical were perceived to be almost a naturally occurring phenomena associated with the medium. He writes, 'It is as if the Photograph always carries its referent with itself' (Barthes 1982: 80). Regardless of certain representative languages used in the production of a photograph, the image was often considered as standing in for something; not a complete copy of the real but certainly an authentic echo, as facsimile, stencil or trace were terms in regular use when discussing the analogue image. However, the digital realm challenged this ontological status of the photographic and reading the image in the digital age became far less assured. In the analogue formulation the indexical was considered as being material and fixed in character, formed by physical light in contact with the object to provide a certain empirical truth. In contrast, the digital media image is essentially viewed as an immaterial object, unstable and unreliable in a pictorial sense, while awash in its own computer processes. Light is refracted through a camera lens but in the digital realm photons are converted into computer data code. The non-indexical status of the digital image is a significant dispossession because it stands for the element of the image that visually communicates epistemic information to compel belief in the viewer. In the transition from analogue to digital image technologies many new media critics and visual studies scholars usher in the 'loss of the Index' (Paulsen 2013: 85) under the reign of the digital image. Anne-Marie Willis has described this phase, 'Digitization is a process which is cannibalizing and regurgitating photographic and other imagery, allowing the production of simulations of simulation' (Willis 1990: 199). New media figure Lev Manovich writing later in *The Language of New Media* has suggested this apparent post-photographic age signifies 'cinema is no longer an indexical media technology, but, rather, a subgenre of painting' (Manovich 2001: 294). The threat of digital non-indexicality encouraged W. J. T. Mitchell to warn in his seminal work *The Reconfigured Eye* that 'the emergence of digital imaging has irrevocably subverted these [indexical] certainties, forcing us to adopt a far more wary and vigilant interpretive stance' (Mitchell 1992: 225).

Such established critical theory narratives on the photographic image speculate about the indexical to lament its loss in relation to the digital age. These are compelling visual culture arguments but they have become less convincing theoretically as empirical evidence shows over the last years. The public use of online sharing platforms to circulate documentary images, the writing by contemporary media thinkers about the visual that affects us and the influential work of photojournalists show little sign of abandoning the index idea in many photographic debates.[3] The ocular continues to be invested in the truth value of the digital photograph today and the unreliable character or unstable nature of the digital medium comes from the data properties of the image, made up of computer code that can be endlessly reproduced in technological systems. However, when experienced online by viewers, if required to, the human eye is still drawn to the factual value of the image that points to a real thing, be it an ongoing unfolding event, and engages in a pictorial relationship and emotional response. Swapping the materiality of film emulsion of the analogue era for the apparent immateriality of data code in the digital age has not necessarily ignored the indexicality of the camera lens and the role of witnessing the photographic image allows. As history has proven the indices of photographic realism in the analogue time and its canon of critical theory were often unfounded and not as cogent as they might appear to have once been.

Indeed, not every realistic-looking image is necessarily formed by a camera lens at all as the advent of computer-generated image (CGI) software in photography and film production has become common practice and more aesthetically sophisticated. Photojournalist Jonas Bendiksen created a project about fake news which consisted of photographs of a provincial North Macedonian town called Veles which had generated clickbait accounts to influence the outcome of the 2016 US presidential election. Bendiksen's *Book of Veles* was initially received as a work of authentic documentary photography before it was exposed as a hoax comprising CGI images only without any indexical origin (Bendiksen 2021). Digital image technologies can engulf the visual experience through the use of augmented, virtual realities with the metaverse becoming more woven into the everyday social fabric of life. However, debates on indexicality have also been reclaimed and it is not yet abandoned in the digital age but reconsidered as a new 'para-indexicality' (Seung-hoon 2011: 183) where the index does not refer to a particular object, place or time. Others go on to suggest this is a type of quasi-index where the fixed-point certainties of Bazin's theory have been upended by a multiplicity of para-realism. Moreover, the image has always been more than a physical material entity because it exists vividly in the phenomenological realm; as W. J. T. Mitchell suggests, there are five distinct image categories in the ocular process, 'graphic, optical, perceptual, mental and verbal' (Mitchell 1986: 9). Therefore, the image has always enjoyed a speculative nature and rather than considering the concept of para-indexicality as unique to the digital age, there is a contingent fluidity and abstractness to reality. This multiplicity of being is beyond the frame itself, functioning as an immanent form and dispersed off-screen property. The post-analogue turn of the digital image can be understood as a rupture nodal point in a network, part of a quantum quilt, and no longer positioned on a linear timeline of the index as earlier Cartesian-led photographic theorists reiterated. Rather than witnessing the 'Death of the Index' (Paulsen 2013) the index re-emerges as a useful way to think about the status of the mediated, fragmented meta-digital image. Therein, the new digital index has not really been 'stencilled off the real' (Sontag 2001: 154) to maintain the linear concept of permeance; no matter how attractive the notion of an accurate record of something can be, the fixed point of origin appears outmoded. Thus, it reveals the limitations of analogue-led readings of the photograph based in semiotic theory and as theorist Kris Paulsen reminds us, 'the indices are, by nature, always open to interpretation and doubt' (Paulsen 2013: 89). In pure semiotic terms indices are more akin to symptoms that need to be decoded rather than truthful traces of past points in chronotropic time and space. The digital image can be a mimetic representation to situate events and may be meaningful while not having a sole indexical connection to reality. Rather, it is the appearance of realism that can be experienced to affect viewers emotionally, morally, psychologically and so on. The hypothetical debates on the indexical value can be misleading in this regard as the index has never had a tight grip on its own materiality and materiality alone does not imply veracity.

In the Arabic MENA region particular factors were impactful on the 2011 uprisings as the incompetence and corruption by governments meant that basic services were prone to outages and disruptions of electricity supply to affect, intentionally or not, communication networks. Such interruptions of the digital image transmission and connectivity have been described as an 'Arab Glitch' (Marks 2014: 257) or 'Arabic Glitch' (Sakr 2023), to imply that these forms of ruptures are inherent in the technology as all digital content is compressed, but it also an abstraction that is beyond the index and the wishes of the maker. Rather, the ontology of the digital image lies, to a degree, in the technology itself and what is experienced is a lower copy, a reiteration, that lacks the quality of the original version as loss occurs when the image is disseminated. What index survives is an abstracted approximation beyond the control of the author or the viewer and reminds us of the ideological conventions of such computer-based technologies (Marks 2014). Moreover, the fractured nature of the poor-quality image in 2011 across the region added to an aesthetic and symbolically embodied what the new generation of media activists were fighting against because, 'Many artists in the Arab world explore the aesthetics of low-resolution video as a metaphor for selective memory and forgetting' (Marks 2014: 260). The social engagement with digital images outweighs many other arguments, as through mobile phones, home computers and other devices non-professionals were empowered by an ocular activism of collective video editing, grassroots data circuits and shared information platforms. This created 'vernacular anarchives' of reality (Snowdon 2020: 81) as the region was transformed to be at the vanguard of technology innovation and digital debates through recording the lives from within an uprising (Sakr 2023). The paradoxical status of the digital image can be its photographic record with its own mimetic qualities, while, at the same time, having no single point of origin within the endlessly adaptable forms of digital formats. This appearance of realism is a perception experience only of the real world without necessarily substantiating it nor substituting the images of revolution. Anthony Downey posed the pertinent question, 'how does new media ... produce social formations and evolving ways of reimagining the often prescriptive and reductive rhetoric of political, historical and cultural debates?' (Downey 2014: 28).

Open Access Egypt

Lebanese artist Rabih Mroué in his lecture-performance *The Pixelated Revolution* (2012) commented on the use of low-quality mobile phones during the Syrian Revolution. He looks into the central role digital image devices have played in mobilizing people during the political events, and being shared through virtual communication platforms to, at times, become viral. Importantly he proposes these digital images were uploaded not only as individual expressive statements but as part of a collective 'common property' (Snowdon 2020: 42). In the Egyptian context three online image-based websites, 858: Archive of Resistance, 18 Days in Egypt, and Filming Revolution, were produced in order to document events in the production of a digital commons during the heightened atmosphere of 2011 via online spaces. During this key phase of social transformation and political upheaval the idea of revolution became the collective expression of solidarity rather than one of individuality and, in part, was connected by digital communication technologies. Despite the best efforts of many Arab regimes in the region to quell political dissent most experienced some level of unrest and digital media activism played a key role in the uprisings. The Syrian Archive collected digital content and video art collective Abou Naddara documented life during the war and these online spaces produced a memory of this conflict (Della Ratta 2018).[4] The digital networked image was a crucial actor in the sense of emancipation for citizens who found new forms of expression as their voices were heard, possibility even for the first time. Nevertheless, it would be misleading to not acknowledge other contributing factors of the rich political heritage of Arab and Egyptian leftist movements and Marxist agitators. Such groupings established an intellectual foundation in the region over decades, seen in the journals *Akhbar al-Adab* (Cultural News) and *al-Jadid* (The New), which laid foundations for dissent and discourse to contest the dominant ideology and test political alliances in Arab societies throughout the twentieth century (Haugbolle 2020). This radical historiography is evident among contemporary scholars, such as Adam Hanieh who has highlighted class struggles and internationalization in the region, as the secular activists in 2011 understood as a globalized and networked ceneteon the opportunity of the times. Egypt's Tahrir Square in Cairo became a media spectacle in the performance of revolution as image production and internet channels of distribution became political tools. Citizen activism used digital communication networks to address power relations, rediscover agency and mobilize the public in a time of historical flux.

In the Egyptian context Cairo-based video collective group Mosireen (Determined) were indicative of this age of media activism and were formed by the visceral culture of Egypt's street politics. They were a seminal part of the Tahrir Media Tent and initiated Tahrir Cinema where they projected video works made by the collective to public audiences followed by open-air discussions. This model was adapted by the Kazeboon (Liars) group who arranged similar documentary screenings and often held demonstrations afterwards, at times violent confrontations, in different neighbourhoods in Cairo.[5] The Mosireen collective went on to produce, collect and catalogue thousands of hours of video content over three years (2011–2014) which has become one of largest video documentations of revolutionary street politics available online in media history. The collective launched the Open Access site 858: Archive of Resistance, in 2018, to make available part of the visual material from this period. These archived videos can be viewed, downloaded, re-edited and, in turn, uploaded back to the archive due to the Open Access coding, in keeping with the egalitarian approach of Mosireen. The 858 project was supported by other collectives: Alternative Law Forum in Bangalore, CAMP in Mumbai and the Berlin-based group 0x2620,[6] and was modelled on the Public Access Digital Media Archive (pad.ma), built using open-source software. Other similar online projects exist; bak. ma is an online digital media archive of Turkish social movements which developed from the street politics of the Occupy Gezi movements in 2014. These contemporary digital media projects are an intersection of political activism, digital media practice and open-source computer technology which demonstrates a nonconformist way to document historical memory in times of conflict and the potential of archives to inscribe history with meaning. The 858: Archive of Resistance title refers to the total duration of the video footage in hours available on this online platform, made from over 1,500 raw video clips, and would amount to five weeks of real-time viewing if seen continuously clip by clip. This digital media platform encourages viewers to create an account to engage with the video content which has been logged and tagged by using date, location, topic and keywords to help orient the archive's content.

Another alternative archival model, Filming Revolution, is the multi-layered, meta-documentary website developed by filmmaker and academic Alisa Lebow, published by Stanford University Press in 2015. The interactive website uses a non-linear design to arrange the materials which consist of video content, images and various types of written contributions. The academic research project focused on the intersection between film culture and political activity formed during the 25 January uprising and its influence on independent Egyptian filmmakers. Lebow made two research field trips to Cairo to gather materials in December 2013 and June 2014, respectively, and since then the website has been intermittently updated with additional content. Part of the website consists of a series of thirty short video interviews with local filmmakers, artists, archivists and activist groups involved in grassroots media production. Through video interviews Lebow offered an opportunity for those involved to reflect on their particular experiences of 2011 and consider whether any lasting film innovation could be attributed to the impact of this revolutionary phase, either personally or collectively. The premise set out to explore how form and content can be consistent, the original approaches to the medium and whether such practices could be noted in a new generation of documentarian filmmakers. In addition to the video interviews, the website is further complimented by selected video footage of significant events from the time and text commentaries to provide richer context for the viewer. The interactive design of the website is non-linear in structure and offers no single, clear narrative route; rather, an array of constellations of relations are provided.[7] The graphic design of the website is divided by a vertical column on the right side of three tabs, projects, people and themes. A second column on the left side comprises pathway tabs of selections of the content curated by previous viewers of the website. Through this design feature, Filming Revolution has an added level of stratified interactivity; however, these routes are not so well defined and can seem convoluted. Lebow's conceptual framework is intentionally loose in design as the archival materials were generated over two fieldwork visits only to Cairo and the associative schema of the website design enables the users to interact with the materials selected for themselves. This graphic, intuitive archive approach is a clear visual response to her analysis of the fieldwork that 'loosely parallels the sentiments and strategies expressed within it [Filming Revolution], without attempting to master or constrain them' (Lebow 2016: 291). Reading Egyptian political narratives in this project allows for the dynamic juxtaposition between people, collectives and events, not unlike how such events on the ground may have been experienced. In this way, the Filming Revolution website has been carefully curated and organized to emphasize interactivity between various individuals, events and memories set within the wider situation. Such methods can embody the subjective nature of political struggles, as in the case of Egypt, where, as like history itself, an array of narratives have emerged in response to the 25 January uprising.

The digital storytelling project 18 Days in Egypt is also a more content-driven documentary-based website that invited the general public to participate by uploading short personal video narratives. The idea was developed by journalist Jigar Mehta and web developer Yasmin Elayat when the pair realized that Egypt was experiencing one of the first digital-era revolutions and media activism became a significant aspect to the street politics of the time. The website allowed subscribers to upload their own video works and create a stream of images, videos or text focusing on a particular topic of the revolution. The collaboration is more modest in aims and scope as the digital video stories cover the first two years only (2011–2013) and they have been arranged in a chronological design to list the series of short films available. The 18 Days in Egypt project received international funding from Tribeca New Media Fund, Sundance Film Festival and the Ford Foundation, among others, and the co-creators regularly participated in media workshops to promote it widely in the immediate years after the revolution. Despite the egalitarian merits of the approach its usefulness is somewhat limited for archival purposes as it did not successfully generate a large volume of noteworthy content or provide significant context to better appreciate the video documents. Also, the co-creators did not work from any ideological position and were, in comparison to Mosireen, more distant from and less influenced by the street politics of the time. However, the video project did provide a basic framework for unfiltered local voices to emerge, and serves as a vernacular record of this historic period for the public record; an alternative to highly controlled public platforms such as YouTube.

The political impact of the so-called Arab Spring in the Arabic MENA region was addressed at length by the mainstream media industry, both through regional and Western networks, and yet these events remain largely misrepresented. Vernacular digital image technologies were significant as communication tools in the freedom of expression for Egypt's marginalized communities to document and witness their own history; to forge connections between citizens and mobilize large crowds in public spaces. However, one of the key periods in the resistance against Mubarak's rule was when the regime shut down both the internet infrastructure and phone communication systems in an intentional 'Arab Glitch' (Marks 2014). It was precisely this inability to access news information that forced many out of their homes and onto the streets in search of information. Therefore, old types of social networks, coffee shops, mosques, churches, markets and street spaces replaced digital communication networks, and thus brought people closer together in unison, some for the first time. As Peter Snowdon comments of this time, 'Those who did stay home, undecided whether to join in the uprising or not, came to be known somewhat derisively as *hizb al-kanaba* [party on the couch]' (Snowdon 2020: 523).

Citizen activism was aided and amplified by this digital blackout strategy of the regime as real-world solidarities were formed in public spaces and the virtual and embodied became fused together in a new way. Both the 858: Archive of Resistance and Filming Revolution website preserve the memory of how technology influenced such social radical connections and historical narratives to contextualize the subjective nature of politics. In this formative time private lives and public spheres became more fluid and many media works brought forwards domestic intimacy previously unseen. One such noteworthy film, *Half a Revolution* (2011), produced by Karim El Hakim and Omar Shargawi, allowed the camera inside to show the interior home of archetypal activists of the time engaged in the violent struggle on the streets as they interact with and are impacted by the exterior world. El Hakim has described the film as a duty to the uprising and a rich personal experience; the film is one of many national and international films produced by the revolutionary spirit of the time to document this transformation.[8] Indeed, Egyptian life includes forms of spatial enclosures which are often interior domestic ones (courtyards, balconies, reception rooms) that also have a public-facing dimension. This social geography was a practical response to restrictions on exterior public spaces that were usually highly controlled by the state. Many documentaries of the 2011 uprising express this type of division to look at how Tahrir Square, plus other public spaces, for the first time became iconic of the nation. This transformative shift integrated public and private spaces with human rights demands and the political dimensions of the struggle, illustrating that the uprising involved a reimagining of domestic roles that came under the scrutiny of the state (El-Gundy 2016). 858: Archive of Resistance and Filming Revolution stand out as valuable research projects because they provide a platform for this revolutionary content to exist, at least online. In the aftermath of the uprising the Egyptian state has stepped up its repression of freedom of speech by targeting the semi-public spaces of NGOs, media collectives, art organizations, educational institutions and individual activists who engaged in a critical debate about the country. In 2015 Egyptian officials conducted a series of raids on well-known contemporary art and cultural spaces, among them Townhouse Gallery, Cultural Resource (Al-Mawred Al-Thaqafy), Contemporary Image Collective, Cimathèque and many other long-standing Cairene organizations. This harassment of creative expression included confiscating hard drives and documents, imposing fines, barring personnel from Egypt plus arresting key individuals for police interrogation. The Egyptian government has tried to stifle international grants to arts organizations, in particular NGOs, because they heavily relied on such support given the limited funding within the country. The aim of this oppressive state reaction was to not only supress political debate but to intimidate, estrange and exile the post-25 January generation formed in the creative atmosphere of revolutionary street politics. The government is suspicious of anything it cannot easily label and sets out to undermine what it does not understand. Over the intervening years censorship by the Egyptian state has gone on to describe alternative media outlets and art collectives as 'threats to the state' (Marks 2017: 3908). Such interference in cultural affairs created a sense of urgency for the Mosireen group to make the 858: Archive of Resistance project available and host the video data on servers outside of Egypt before further government crackdowns ransack this valuable video archive.

Image politics and media activism

The origins of the Mosireen project are situated in the image politics and media activism of a small community of fifteen core members that grew into a support network formed in the Tahrir Square's Media Tent during the eighteen days of the protest camp occupation (25 January to 11 February). Mosireen means 'determined ones' in Arabic and has a secondary connotation through an astute word play on 'Egyptian' (Masreen). In the momentous weeks leading up to the removal of Mubarak digital cameras became commonplace tools in documenting events on the streets as a means of resistance against the violence of the ruling regime. In this way, the Tahrir Media Tent initiative embodied the utopian spirit of the popular uprising and media activism, as the protesters would unselfishly pool their camera footage from the streets and videos were collectively produced and disseminated across available communication networks. This collective approach in production and dissemination of digital content also drew in mainstream international media producers looking for grassroots footage of key events as this activist media space expanded in scale and influence to play an indispensable role in the reproduction of the 2011 uprising. Part of this prominence included using the video records as potential historical evidence against the abuses of the regime in future trials. As Mosireen member Omar Hamilton commented in a video interview, 'The first mission was to collect and preserve of as much digital memory of the initial 18 Days as possible' (Hamilton 2017).

In the radical atmosphere of the time Mosireen were an important component of the media activism and their subversive vision took shape through principles of horizontal organization and collective authorship of productions. Such new political formations extended to refuse international funding or sponsorship; preferring self-governing autonomy and offering free training and support to anyone interested on a local level. The Mosireen attitude remained resolutely revolutionary in the aftermath of Mubarak's removal as they continued to document events on the ground and distribute videos of street protests, regime brutalities, workers' strikes and occupations during 2011. Some commentators reported Mosireen had become one of the most watched non-profit channels on YouTube at this time. To compliment the online distribution of video materials members on the streets downloaded content to flash drives, CDs and even Bluetooth connections as an attempt to get the work into as many diverse social spaces as possible, such as coffee shops, homes, workplaces, universities and importantly public screening events. The emphasis on social engagement and grassroots activism came about through public events like the open-air screening of video documents in central Cairo with an emphasis on post-screening group discussion and the reclaiming of public space for political debate. Many of these were impromptu events of crowdsourced video works and added to a sense of spontaneity and solidarity at odds with the hierarchical culture of most mainstream media organizations in the country. Indeed, the importance of street activism and political agency is paramount to their concerns. In a contribution to the book *The Arab Archive*, Mosireen state, 'I need to start with a disclaimer: what matters is having bodies on the street. I don't want to fall into the trap of giving images more power than they are due' (Westmoreland 2020: 36). Therefore, aesthetics were not the group's primary concern as the status of the digital image was negligible in a didactic sense when compared to the broader social purpose the video footage can facilitate. In the political struggle of the time digital images were part of a new-found collectivism between discussants gathered in solidarity. In this way, the image object was an interlocutor in forming new social relationships, knowledge and common cause, as a 'discursive document' (Devlin 2019: 3). Here the photographic image serves the purpose of a social agent which can be used and reused, thereby establishing space for critical discourse and even political being. The shareability of the digital acts as a bridge between people to bring about agency and resistance, thought and effect, to assume a role as an ocular-audio connector in an information flow circuit.

Despite Mosireen's didactical media approach, in times of historic change, video content can play a decisive social role to create different aesthetic forms which can seem to alter the evolution of photographic images. Often this is associated with the grand narratives of the twentieth century, such as the innovative film work that came about during the shock of the Bolshevik October Revolution and gave rise to the Constructivist-inspired redirection of cinema.[9] Soviet filmmaker Dziga Vertov once imagined a form of communist visual language in film that could inform and entertain while linking the workers of the world. In *Kino-Pravda* (Film Truth) he worked on a series of twenty-three experimental short films that intended to involve the audience and expose a deeper reality to the world through a visual rhythmical film language. In this light, the Filming Revolution project began with Lebow's research visit to Cairo in order to meet with independent Egyptian filmmakers and determine how their media productions had been shaped by this spirit of revolution. Writing about this question she went on to say, 'It is not revolutionary film that I sought in Egypt, but rather films that have been made in the lead-up to and wake of these transformative events, films which can be said to shape and be shaped by the context in which they were made' (Lebow 2016: 281).

Over the course of two research trips she gathered a local collection of video material through interview encounters that occurred in a period of political oppression. In the aftermath of the violent removal of the elected president Mohamed Morsi in 2013, Egypt was governed under emergency law and repressive measures with regular curfews imposed. Therefore, the interviews with the independent filmmakers were conducted during extreme conditions and exposed the stifling hiatus of the time set against recent memories of revolt. As this creative community became increasingly isolated and marginalized under military rule, Lebow began to envisage a non-linear, crystalline structure for the website project, as a deigned response to the atmosphere of the time. For her the research process exposed common themes and experiences, various filmic approaches of the participants that contributed to the interlinked, non-linear design of the virtual space. This structure allows for conversations to take place and ideas to interconnect in cyberspace because they could no longer happen in the physical world. The website architecture places the materials in a move away from the fixed chronological sense of events preferring an associative arrangement to reflect the filmmakers' diverse responses to the revolutionary experience of 2011. This interactive platform can be read in multiple pathways with no single route through history that facilitates a 'curated dialogue' of the historical (Lebow 2016: 285). Moreover, the research links are not overly determined; the network design can be navigated in various ways by the user and relationships visualized as content hover in cloud-like formations. This rhizome network of digital content is foregrounded in the conceptual design of the website itself to reflect the interconnected spirit of the 25 January uprising on the ground. However, this project is also a subjective vision of the researcher imposed onto the content and perhaps one unlikely to be formed in an organic fashion by the local filmmakers themselves. Despite best intentions and its undoubted research significance on alternative film production, the website also falls into another value system of curation, arguably an external gaze, in its treatment of the documentary content in order to see what it wants to see inside the troubled lens of Egypt in 2011.

In the aftermath of Mubarak's resignation global media interest peaked in Egyptian affairs but over time the mainstream media lost interest in the struggle. Events on the ground became more discordant and the narrative of the revolution complicated along ideological lines. However, groups of media activists continued to upload video works to contest the claims of the interim military government, the Supreme Council of Armed Forces. Mosireen's media activism recalibrated as the Tahrir Media Tent's materials grew by several terabytes to become somewhat unruly and what media scholar Peter Snowdon has defined as 'a video corpus produced by Arab revolutionaries as they filmed their revolutions as the vernacular anarchive' (Snowdon 2020: 81).[10] Within a fluid period of history digital images continued to be distributed and repurposed by such groups. The footage often revealed the all too evident brutality of the military; in one particularly horrific incident a peaceful demonstration was attacked outside the Nile TV station at Maspero in central Cairo. In this violence twenty-four protesters died and hundreds were seriously injured. Mosireen responded with their first collectively authored and edited film work entitled *The Maspero Massacre*, and uploaded it to their YouTube channel. The short nine-minute documentary includes interviews with witnesses and horrific crowdsourced clips of army personnel carriers crushing the demonstrators, shooting and beating a crowd of the mainly Coptic Christian protesters. The affecting video manifests Mosireen's form of media activism and coordinated efforts to counteract the military regime's use of local TV stations to spread the false claim that the army had been violently attacked by the crowd with three soldiers killed. This accusation was disproven, in part, by the group's media activism, and the army's statement had to be retracted in favour of the activists' version of events (Human Rights Watch 2011). The 858: Archive of Resistance consists of seventeen videos of raw footage relating to the Maspero incident alone, gathered by the project members and their network of supporters. The video footage follows a timeline to include the army attack, witness interviews and accounts, press conferences, hospital scenes, funerals and subsequent street protests. This digital content offers a complete and invaluable documentary video record of what happened at Maspero as a human rights violation and documents the visceral reaction on the ground. This media activism was part of a public response and one of the most politically strident acts by Mosireen to collectively illustrate the principles of militant media activism.

Such video documentation clearly exposes the human rights abuses carried out by the regime to be indicative of why such indexical records are worthwhile, as this type of video footage could, for instance, support legal investigations at some point in the future. Regardless, this does seem unlikely in the short term as the political context is extremely hostile to human rights agendas and media activism. The current hiatus deems sharing, collecting and organizing of media content as subversive and hostile to the state. In the intervening years political struggle has left the streets of Egypt and Mosireen will not inspire or compel protesters to demonstrate despite the worsening political and economic situation. The camera, once a potent political tool, has been become apolitical and is used most often to record the prosaic everyday life in social media platforms. The 25 January uprising has become airbrushed from public memory through the propagation of official state narratives and Mosireen's purpose seems all but invisible in the public sphere. One stark example of this rewriting of history was the Ramadan soap opera *al-Ikhtiyar 3* (The Choice 3) where the melodrama series chronicles the 2013 military takeover which was engineered by the country's then defence minister and current president el-Sisi.[11] However, the potential of the 858 video records is latently retained for the public and to some degree in the online environment to one day challenge the sense of ingrained injustice; a right removed from public space. As filmmaker Snowdon speculates in his book on digital image politics, 'Do these images reveal the people to us and demonstrate their power? Or do they function as another kind of mask behind which the reality of people and their true forms of their power can disappear?' (Snowdon 2020: 704). Few in the public sphere dare to unmask the image presented by the military regime narrative found in popular soap operas, media punditry or social media spaces. The political repercussions of the 858 project remain unclear as new contributions and social engagement have been limited since its launch in 2018. In part this could be due to the website existing out of time, on the wrong side of history, for the lived reality of most citizens as an atmosphere of public disillusionment pervades post-25 January Egypt. Independent media projects, like 858, are representative of the dialectical relationship between the para-indexicality of the digital image and the evidential role it can provide in the witnessing of history, even in uncertain, troubled times.

Mosireen members persevered for years after 2011 to create the 858: Archive of Resistance website with only extracts from the vast collection of the video footage available on this digital platform. The reasons for hosting only a portion of the video footage are multifaceted and involve the scale of data generated by the collective project and the management of such video materials on servers. To archive this type of visual content is extremely time-consuming and requires expensive and advanced digital management resources. Taking into consideration this project was made up of volunteers certain operational challenges and technical restraints arose. Furthermore, the revolutionary nature of the content has rendered the video footage more controversial over the intervening years as the individuals who produced it and the people who were recorded might have changed alliances or be put in danger by renewed public exposure. Another potential risk is the creative commons licence itself and the open-source Pandora software that gives access to the footage and could be used by malevolent forces to compromise the integrity of the project. Open Access sharing enables downloading and re-editing of the raw footage that could be easily construed for counter-revolutionary narratives at odds with the ideological ambitions of the Mosireen project. Part of the laborious process for the group was to determine what footage could put activists or others at risk given the current hostility towards revolutionary politics. In a video interview included in Filming Revolution,[12] Mosireen member Sherif Gaber seemed to dismiss some of the ethical concerns faced by the collective in selecting video works for online publication: 'The state in Egypt does not seem to need hard evidence in order to detain or imprison those it deems dangerous, and thus it might not make much sense to worry about providing them with such evidence' (Gaber 2015).

By this, some of the collective appear to take a more pragmatic approach to ethics but also raise a valid point on the arbitrary nature of police harassment and the video footage archive itself may not be of concern to the security state surveillance. Mark Westmoreland comments that the responsibility lies with the subjects in the video footage to request Mosireen to remove content because they are not able to include such safeguards: 'to place the burden on others to contact them [Mosireen] with requests for removal' (Westmoreland 2020: 26). Given the magnitude of the video footage generated and gathered for the archive, the reduction to 1,664 video clips of 858 hours was a viable quantity to be catalogued but not if it had to be ethically evaluated. Indeed, many video-based archives can be daunting on many levels and the 858 collection works because it is worth remembering that Mosireen became the custodians of a vast amount of video content during the stark reversal in revolutionary fortunes. As Maspero and other events have proven, the apparatuses of the Mubarak regime continued to oppress after 2011 and as the momentous events faded from popular memory the wider public deviated. In the current hiatus the activist movements failed to navigate the new political terrain, and the Mosireen collective attempted the data management of this extensive archive material in a time of crisis as the revolution was phased out. The 858 project itself came about in a natural fashion rising up from the grassroots spirit of collective resistance in Tahrir Square and embodied a certain archival anarchy of the fluid political culture on the streets, as they strove to 'preserve the disorderliness' (Gaber 2015). Their nonconformist approach towards the video archive was perhaps unorthodox to some and certainly did not simply involve posting footage online to the website. Rather, Mosireen's method strove to return the images to a virtual collective commons to embody the street atmosphere of Tahrir Square and other autonomous areas of Egypt. The 858 media project upholds this subversive discursive agency established through the ad hoc screenings and discussions during 2011.

The group perceive their activism indirectly, their involvement in the revolt was 'not as journalists' (Mosireen 2018), and they see the video collection as more than an objective resource documenting the human rights abuses. For them the archive is a retelling narrative on what happened, a collective street history of Egypt and one more culturally specific to this time. The 858 media platform is augmented by low-key footage of 'images that don't yell' (Mosireen 2018) to consist of everyday scenes of Egyptian life unfolding through this time of struggle. One particular clip highlighted by the group (Figure 4.1) consists of male strikers in the Ceramica Cleopatra factory, sitting on sofas playing dominoes in the port city of Suez.[13] In this video clip the camera displays a convivial scene that is tender; the lens peers from the edge of the room, the workers do not notice the camera at first, then expressions become self-consciousness, glances exchanged, words muttered, chuckles and laughs. But in comparison to other more spectacular videos in the 858 archive, little happens; the camera moves a little closer to the workers, then another man is seen filming the same workers on his phone but seems unsure why, looking towards the Mosireen camera operator for affirmation. Some of the strikers in the group leave; others join but the game continues to unfold in real time uninterrupted. This unedited video clip of ordinariness is not overburdened by its own revolutionary potential but does still await and anticipate its moment of archival discovery by the viewer.

Mosireen go on to suggest the collection could be extended to include non-documentary footage from fiction films as part of the 858 vision of collective memory. But when viewing the video content now the question arises, who are the images intended for? How do they function over a decade on and even recalibrate power relations? The 858 project seems like an incomplete resource for a future generation of Egyptian activists to rediscover, mediated by time, and one that might again resonate forcefully. The state's attempt to erode the revolutionary memory and its vicious oppression of any dissenting voices has tended to create the impression of

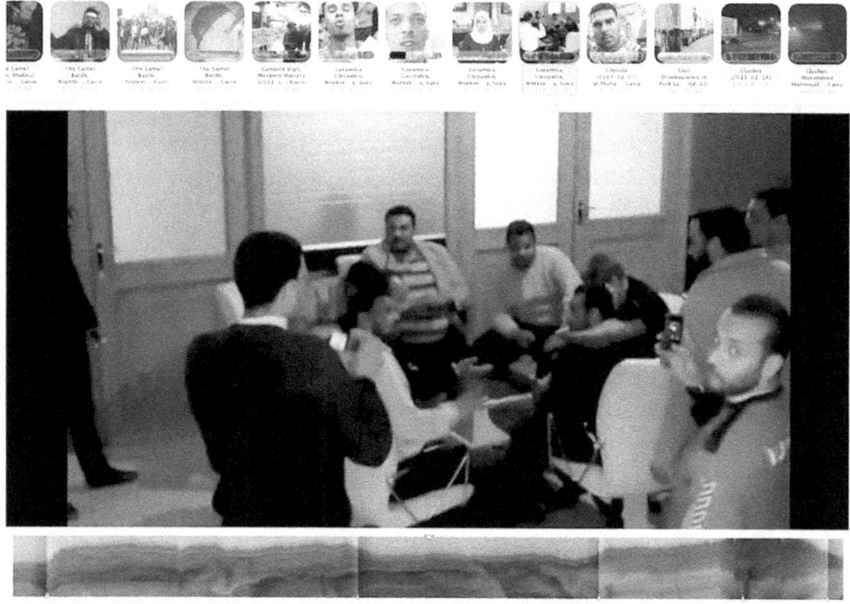

Figure 4.1 Mosireen archive video of group of striking workers playing dominoes, Ceramica Cleopatra factory, Suez, Egypt, 12 March 2012

the uniform imagination of counter-revolution politics that no longer sees any alternative radical vision. Therefore, this Mosireen collective lives up to its revolutionary didactic purpose because it acts as an indignant witness of events to oppose the official state narrative and cultural hegemony. Moreover, as these video documents prove, history is more nuanced than may appear at first and in specific ways there is a visual language of representation that expands beyond the purely political and folds into the subjective. The archive is latent, a time capsule, a veiled treasure of knowledge, that awaits the encounter with the viewer to offer an authentic narrative of this time, as the 858 statement suggests, 'It [858 archive] is one collection of memories, one set of tools we can all use to fight the narratives of the counter-revolution, to pry loose the state's grip on history, to keep building new histories for the future' (Mosireen 2018: 28).

Recollecting revolution and the visual subject

Egypt, like much of the Arabic MENA region, was swept up in the optimism of 2011 as the digital image played a key role in the representational politics and revolution narratives acquired a new-found urgency. Internet technologies and digital media production seemed to nurture a capacity for social change in the difficult labour of emancipatory politics. The celebratory discourses on media technologies as tools were somewhat overblown despite the valuable role of disproving the propaganda from counter-revolutionary state forces. It is important to acknowledge the part digital cameras played on the streets to witness events on ground level and feed into the communication networks that enabled the dissemination of revolutionary content to local and global audiences. However, issues remain in relation to the methods of codification of pictorial content that are harder to position within the algorithms of communication technologies; despite improvements in AI systems on platforms such as YouTube, many are ill-suited to preserve factual documentation of historical memory. Social media networks have only basic search functions in relation to image content and these functions are based on the textual recognition of words tagged onto and embedded with the visual object. YouTube videos must include textual markers and background information with a title, description and associated hashtags to ensure the visibility of the image content for search engines. In this way, the digital image is read in code and uses algorithms to make it translatable for online environments. Computer-assisted analysis can process vast quantities of visual content online and image identification has improved, in particular, in the area of facial recognition technologies connected to surveillance systems and con-troversial 'pre-emptive' crime methods.[14] This algorithmic gaze scoops up everyday images from internet traffic to improve its own AI recognition ability and often determines who is watched and what is seen online. However, at the same time, even more advanced image recognition technology is not best equipped to appreciate the complex pictorial qualities the human eye perceives and computer-assisted programmes fail to register the symbolic importance of a person's face, an event or even a gesture in the inscription of history. The Mosireen collective and the video projects 858: Archive of Resistance and the Filming Revolution are valuable because of their political underpinning and structural approach to technology that created solidarities as a whole and not just a black hole in digital content.

Despite the best efforts of media activists and other protest groups the ownership of the 2011 digital imagery may not reside in Egyptian hands at all and much of the content has been retained by Silicon Valley's tech-capitalists. Global technology companies have policy guidelines and impose rules over what content is made available to future generations. Governments also interfere; for instance, media channel Al Jazeera is prohibited in Egypt and social media platforms compliantly block content from the Qatari network on the behest of the Egyptian state. Historical narratives are being rewritten or even forgotten; for example, YouTube deleted thirty-three million videos deemed 'terrorist propaganda' (Warner 2019: 106). One of the most extreme examples of video archive loss has occurred in the Syrian conflict where hundreds of YouTube channels documenting the war were eliminated including the Shaam Network, a popular opposition group (El Deeb 2017). The Syrian Archive project co-founder Hadi al-Khatib has described the situation thus, 'We are writing our memories not in our own book but in a third party's book. We don't have control of it' (al-Khatib 2017). This Syrian group have lobbied YouTube to reinstate the removed channels but video content from only twenty local channels has been restored with 150,000 videos blocked by company protocols.

In Egypt, the time of revolution is long over as the military regime tightens its grip on the country. Both the Mosireen collective and its 858: Archive of Resistance and Filming Revolution websites are, in fact, available inside Egypt. However, online surveillance technology has become part of the state's censorship of critical voices with an estimated 34,000 websites blocked to the public (Freedom House 2019). This includes independent media groups and NGOs, such as Mada Masr, BBC Arabic, Human Rights Watch, and infrequently social media platforms themselves depending on what content has been uploaded by users. The open availability of the 858 website appears exceptional given the political climate, in particular, because of the close connections between many members of Mosireen and the independent media groups; for instance, Mada Masr, who have endured regular raids, arrests and its news website has been permanently blocked. Therefore, it seems as if there is a distinction between the state harassment of contemporary media dissenters and the memory of the 25 January uprising which the state has chosen to reappropriate rather than completely erase from the public sphere.

Accordingly, this grand narrative has been co-opted into the official history of the nation but as another mythologized national event, among others in a national timeline ending with the military *coup d'état* saving Egypt from Muslim Brotherhood rule in the 2013. In this way, 2011 has become air-brushed and depoliticized into the historical blur of sentimental nationalist narratives. The combined effects of state censorship and 'communitive capitalism' (Dean 2014: 1) have strengthened the rule of the authoritarian regime to crush the political imagination. Despite the user-friendly allure of social media spaces and the technological lustre of this twenty-first-century form of 'Capitalist Realism' (Fisher 2009: 2) the digital commons failed to materialize in Egypt, in part due to state harassment and surveillance. Anxiety over the COVID-19 pandemic could usher in a new age of unconditional surveillance, a disastrous boost unimagined a few years ago, since the pandemic has been defined as a 'dress rehearsal for the next crisis' (Latour 2021: 2). Media activists in places like Egypt and Syria did embrace social media platforms to easily share content and host videos as part of a political struggle against corrupt regimes. However, by now this potential archival space is mostly lost and ill-suited to be the creative commons once imagined because the technological infrastructure is commercially designed and ideologically privatized. Media theorist Jodi Dean goes on to apply class struggle to digital content:

> Mainstream media babble about Facebook and Twitter revolutions was right, but for the wrong reasons. It was right to draw our attention to networked media, to suggest a link between the protests and ubiquitous communication networks. But it was wrong to think that protests are occurring because people can easily coordinate with social media, that they are primarily struggles for democracy, or that they are indications of a push for freedom on the part of networked individual. (Dean 2014: 1)

Online archive projects and spaces hosting documentation of the Arabic MENA region include the witnessing of violent events that corroborates the indexical value within the digital image. The visual rush of 2011 brought the body with the body politic together when visual acts were performed, as Lina Khatib has written about Egypt, 'political agents are acutely aware of the resonance of the image projected by this performance' (Khatib 2012: 165). Much photographic theory saw the image moment in space as a binary one that discounted other elements of who is within the camera frame. Photographic critic Justin Carville outlines this part of representation in visual studies, as he writes, 'In the dualistic emphasis of photographer and viewer, the subject of the photographic image remains passive and invisible' (Carville 2010: 346). Mosireen emphasize how the digital image is part of a fluid process of generating meaning in mental and physical ways to question the implied hierarchy of archival structures and, as Downey comments, 'Artistic practice opens up a horizon of future possibility within which civic imagination can flourish' (Downey 2014: 44). Therefore, the 858 archive is not a space to log documents but one where the mediated video footage can bring forth new solidarities and build networked social connections.

Social relationships around the image object can be seen as a feedback loop between photographer, the photographic subject and viewer. This take on representational politics has been discussed in *The Civil Contract of Photography*, by critical theorist Ariella Azoulay, who examines the photographic act involved in looking and consuming images from the Israeli-Palestinian conflict. According to her the photographer with the camera, the photographed subject and the spectator of the image object are involved in a closed-circuit loop that is an ethical pact of vision. She goes on to outline an equality of the represented subject in the image at the moment they are photographed and looked at by the viewer of the image in 'an attempt to anchor spectatorship in a civic duty toward the photographed persons who haven't stopped being' (Azoulay 2012: 16). In her organization of this ethical gaze she moves on from using emotion-led terms like 'empathy' or 'compassion' and prefers to reconceptualize this as a law-based binding contract between photographer, subject and viewer in civil space (Azoulay 2012). In her book she examines the representation of Palestinian subjects in contemporary photojournalism to discuss the politics of seeing that implicates the key, but often ignored, human rights of the represented subject. Under the suspension of time in the photographic act all social hierarchies are removed so photographs can temporally emancipate those involved in the civil contract process to become new citizens in photography. Through this process a new community is formed around equality, as she writes:

> Anyone who addresses others through photographs or takes the position of a photograph's addressee, even if she is a stateless person who has lost her 'right to have rights,' as in Arendt's formulation, is nevertheless a citizen – a member in the citizenry of photography. The civil space of photography is open to her, as well. That space is configured by what I call the civil contract of photography. (Azoulay 2012: 81)

The video works produced by the Mosireen group came about in a process of collective making as an alternative to the privatized working methods of the mainstream media industry. The video footage contents came from the pool of group members and supporters with additional help from their wider network active on the streets. All videos on the 858 website can be searched for in multiple ways and, for instance, the 'sort by shooter' tags have been used to credit the filmmaker of the raw clip when the information was available or appropriate. Other videos have come from external supporters or other media groups who are listed in the video data and this levelling out of hierarchies has been later extended into the architectural design of the website itself. The video footage of street politics and violent clashes can mingle with everyday images of men playing dominoes, among other low-key quotidian scenes. The video fragments on the 858 website invite the online viewer to engage in an act of reconstruction as the raw footage can be downloaded, re-edited and new versions added to the 858 website or other online video platforms. This open-source computer process positions the viewer as editor-maker with a potential of re-authoring video clips that can include the original role of the photographer, the subject or other immanent encounters as digital images circulate. The collective's intention may appear somewhat convoluted if archives are seen as neutral repositories, but Mosireen are aware of other factors beyond what is immediately visible within the image frame. The videos can testify as candid documents or unedited clips aware of their own means of production. In addition, the archive invites the viewer to engage with the visual material to produce digital works in order to add to an ongoing archaeology of struggle. This nonconformist anarchive questions the values of digital images as a common property associated with speed, accessibility, sharing that expresses a condition of dematerialization (Snowdon 2020). This perspective on the image's exchange value reclaims what artist Hito Steyerl describes in her influential essay 'In Defense of the Poor Image' as the 'political punch and creates a new aura around it' (Steyerl 2009). The aura here in not related to the index of the real or concerned with the permanent truth status of the original image; rather, the digital image is a transitory copy of disruptive movements and glitches. In this way, the palimpsest of 2011 politics is a process in which particular people enact events in a transformation of the visual act performed on the global public stage (Khatib 2012).

Perhaps an impediment of the 858 website relates to the edification of details in the project as the contextual information is unevenly handled, notably in terms of the represented subjects in some of the video content. Mosireen never extensively resolved the ethical debates within their collective media productions and there is, in some cases, paradoxically a prefixed distance in the vision between maker, camera and subject. The collective had a right to record the intolerable injustices of this time and the membership was motivated by noble principles to create a democratic society while the archival project sets out to retain and preserve the raw memory of this historic phase in Egypt, as a political struggle met with a turn in digital image cultures. Sometimes the act of photography can be a desperate one and immediate in turbulent periods of revolt but those videoed are persons trapped within the set frame of characters in the performance of revolution and have been deprived of privacy. In the 858 video archive, images of the dead and injured invade the viewer's imagination, bodies are disturbingly crushed by military vehicles on the streets, cadavers laid out in morgues, mothers cry uncontrollably. As stated by Gaber, the 858 website published this video collection without consent of those subjects within the frames and would only remove content if asked to by those involved. This can be read as part of a wider symptom of ethical glitches in media culture; white victims of violence are often granted a dignity not necessarily conceded to others. For instance, the thirty-two fatalities who died in the bomb attacks in Brussels in 2016 were never represented as bloodied victims of terrorist rampages because their privacy was respected by media channels. In this case a tacit social contract modifies media content: the victims are named but seen respectfully, family photos are solemnly used to replace mutilated bodies in news reports and symbolic marches conceal the true horror of disfigured bodies torn apart by violence. Contrast this with much of the representation in the Arabic MENA region where media screens can display maimed casualties of bombings, as documentary filmmaker Mohammad Ali Atassi stated in reference to the Syrian War, 'How can we persuade a mother or a sister or a wife, or a son, that someone has the right to publish the image of their tortured son or his corpse? How do we allow ourselves to do this, in the name of what is right, according to which human principle, heavenly legitimacy, legislation, logic, or art?' (quoted in de Angelis 2020: 78).

The majority of the video content on the 858 website comes from a turbulent three-year period in Egyptian politics (2011–2014) and consists of non-professional footage, filmed by amateurs and enthused by a radical spirit of grassroots media activism. The visceral street politics of the time has been preserved in the 858 website and shaped by a visual narrative of the image index and underpinned by the ideology of revolution. A unique spatial pluralism pervades the historic content available online and the Mosireen collective, like most of the other local activist collectives, pursued a new form of progressive citizenship, as nationalism mixed with demands for social justice and egalitarian change in Egypt. The 858 project is a subjective trace that seeks to place the digital image at the axis of value meaning. The video clips become edifying instruments in an open political debate on equality as the unbearable oppression of physical and psychological environments has accrued over the years in Egypt. The video content will continue to be present, if only during the time it is being viewed, to preserve the past and sustain the hope for a different future. This form of watching borrows from Azoulay's hypothesis that looking at a photographic image reinstates engagement with the visual subject as an active process. As Steyerl writes elsewhere, 'Visual representation matters, indeed, but not exactly in unison with other forms of representation. There is a serious imbalance between both. On the other hand, there is a huge number of images without referents; other the other, many people with representation' (Steyerl 2012: 32).

The 858: Archive of Resistance project can be contextualized within a histography of experimental film activism and nonconformist anarchival practices (Snowdon 2020). This independent non-aligned subversion of digital image politics often involves the low-resolution aesthetic, a poor image, and sets out to reorder social hierarchies and decolonize media cultures. Although the digital networked image is a perfect contemporary exponent of this low-resolution formalism, there also exists a history with earlier precedents in analogue histories of the medium. Part of this tradition includes the Global South aesthetics in the radical manifesto 'For an Imperfect Cinema', by Cuban director Juan García Espinosa. It is unconcerned with most Western film history in favour of a cinema of the people and casts aside preoccupations with quality as 'the imperfect cinema is no longer interested in quality or technique' because 'Art will not disappear into nothingness; it will disappear into everything' (Espinosa 1979: 27). In his revolutionary framework for cinema Espinosa argues for a filmic language that can overcome class division and dissolve the distinction between producer and consumer, audience and author; foreshadowing the writings on aesthetics by French philosopher Jacques Rancière where he proposes art can dissolve into the everyday realm. Espinosa's decolonizing of film history has earlier precedents in Vertov's *Man with a Movie Camera* (1929), with its experimental approach where a sensorial transformation of the environment takes place to make strange a political vision in the quotidian. This Kino-Eye is a dissolution of the existing world at a time of radical transformation a decade on from the 1917 October Revolution in the newly formed communist state. Vertov set out to not only reflect the widespread cultural changes taking place, but to alter the very nature of the public audience themselves through this radical viewing experience. In his theoretical writings he expressed the notion of film being able to construct visual bonds among the workers, with a vision to transform the greater social, political and economic structures. Through a new language of cinema the workers would develop class consciousness as members of a society within the revolutionary politics of communism. This new-found awareness is beyond the lived experiences of the individual workers in daily life as he describes it as 'organizing the worker's vision' (Michelson 1984: 4). This is more than a subgenre of film theory or experimental media practices but a radical political fusion of art and life on a vast scale. This can be seen as a decolonial delinking from Western cultural traditions to establish independent and self-determined ways of knowing (Holert 2015).

Marxist frameworks of visual bonds are developed through didactic filmmaking and can be read in some of Azoulay's ethical theories on the web of relations between the producer, object and spectator. Herein, the viewing experience of an image reinstates political engagement and forms a loop between maker, subject and audience based on an equality of gazes. Mosireen's text Revolution Triptych addresses the video collection, and comments, 'The images are not ours; the images are the revolutions … How dare we profit from the mangled bodies, the cries of death of mothers who lost their children?' (Mosireen 2014: 48). Such militant conceptualizations of image production are political because the visual artefact becomes a mediator of community-based solidarity; not simply an indexical record of events. The 858: Archive of Resistance project and, to a somewhat lesser degree, Filming the Revolution were indications of a fuller expression of representational politics and cultural specificity emerging from the 25 January period in Egypt. Mosireen were a media group that moved beyond linear documentation to mediate the video footage and archival content that awaits the eye and hand of the viewer to release the spirits of those who witnessed the intolerable poetics of struggle. Recuperating from the political punch of the photographic image can possibly create disruptive movements of thought and effect for future public audiences. Such subversive digital image archives initiate another remarkable chapter in the genealogy of alternative media collectives and information technology subcultures. The networked videos in these two significant Egyptian-based projects have become part of a histography of resistance and digital image activism that involves a heritage of pamphlets, cine-trains, underground video collectives, conceptual art practices, imperfect cinema and maverick media workers. Furthermore, these projects reclaim the historical ideas associated with communication loops and circuits in the solidarity bonds of what may be immanent until acted on; the videos exist simply to keep the human imagination open. The Mosireen collective is a notable part of the twenty-first-century digital commons because of their approach to media production with a genealogy in its local history beyond the video content alone. As they remind us, 'Let us not over-celebrate archives. Archiving revolt is a critical act, but it is a secondary one' (Mosireen_Soursar 2020: 36). The significance of this grassroots media collective lies in their communal practices of production and positioning of the image as an arbiter of meaning in order to shape a new egalitarian future for Egypt's citizens.

These two digital archival projects embody what is visible at the intersection of cultural engagement, political activism, popular protest and social participation in the Arab MENA region (Downey 2014). Foremost in this process was the contested debate on gender-based violence and the representation of women within the revolutionary spirit of 2011 activist circles who grappled to maintain solidarity, while state forces exploited these tensions through the controversial policing of female protesters. All too common regressive political, social or cultural forces were at play that undermined the equality politics of 2011 and image representation was part of the discourse. The murder of Khaled Said in 2010 by the Egyptian police was the epitome of the development of the image as a resistance tool (Khatib 2012); however, state brutality of women was not so uncomplicated for the public and became discordant rather than unifying. Two incidents during late 2011 demonstrate this difference starkly in image politics and show how divisive this topic was for the fledging activist movements, pointing towards the widespread misogyny in society where *nasawiyya* (feminism) is mocked as an insult (El-Rifae 2022; Khorshid 2021).

A digital photograph circulated of a female protester being beaten by police as her brassiere was exposed and in this viral image, she became known as Sitt al-Banat (best of girls) in Egypt or the Blue Bra Girl in the West. A short time earlier feminist Aliaa al-Mahdy had provoked controversy when she posted a nude self-portrait on her blog that became a loaded image for the broad-ranging collation of opposition movements and caused moral outcry in the public sphere. Both of these image events provoked diverse reactions in the public context to expose the complexity of image politics in regard to female representation and depictions of gender-based violence. Chapter 5 will examine how female gender representation has been visually censored and how the area of political visibility has been mediated through portraiture and online local trends that intersect with global media cultures. Despite the radical social ruptures and revolutionary zeal of the 2011 era, the horizon of possibility where 'civic imagination can flourish' (Downey 2014: 44) has floundered and heteronormativity is upheld in Egypt as a foundational pillar of contemporary society. The next chapter looks at how photographic images have navigated female identity and personal expression within the challenging if not hostile environment that impacts on the lives of women regardless of social standing. In order to address this it is necessary to examine the history around the colonial encounter with the local visual traditions of Egypt and situate this contemporary issue in a cultural context which has its origin in the moral codes of Islam through the division of gender roles. Orientalism formed an erotic visual lexicon that met with the religious beliefs and heteronormative roles in the Arabic MENA region at the time and formed the basis for the debates on feminist modernity through the camera lens.

Notes

1 For more on Egyptian media history, see Armbrust 1996.
2 *Al-Da'wa* was an Arabic-language monthly political magazine published in two periods, 1951–1953 and 1976–1981. It was one of the media outlets connected to the Muslim Brotherhood and was banned in 1953 and again in 1981.
3 Images of conflict continue to affect viewers despite the prevalence of fake imagery online. The World Press Photo competition continues to promote humanist photojournalism as certain images can resonate deeply with the general public. A case in point is the 2015 photograph of Alan Kurdi, the two-year-old Syrian boy whose drowned body was photographed on a beach in Turkey and circulated online to millions of viewers.
4 The Syrian War has seen the establishment of various media projects and the Syrian Archive sets out to collect, verify and preserve a digital memory of the conflict. The database contains verified documentation content in order to facilitate investigations of human rights violations. Abou Naddara is a Syrian video art collective best known for its documentation of life during the war. The collective's members are self-taught and anonymous, but the group has exhibited video works in important art spaces and cultural intuitions internationally.
5 The Kazeboon group started as a response to a violent attack at a protest on 17 December 2011 in Tahrir Square. A young woman was beaten and

dragged along the ground by Egyptian army soldiers, exposing her torso and bra. A picture, known as Sitt al-Banat, appeared on the front page of *Tahrir* newspaper, accompanied by the word 'liars'. The image was widely shared to become an important visual symbol of abuse of power by the Egyptian military and galvanized the organizers of the Kazeboon campaign to screen videos, hold discussions and street protests. Through screening events the group intended to reach an audience beyond the established activist culture in Tahrir Square, and the group challenged the government and state-run media narrative to reach ordinary Egyptians in the country. The most ambitious Kazeboon project consisted of the creation of an online interactive map that prompted people to identify military figures from the Mubarak regime attempting to occupy civilian jobs in the newly forming administrative apparatus.

6 Pad.ma's manifesto, '10 Theses on the Archive', urges users to start assembling an archive from content at hand, before it is lost or privatized. The manifesto is a radical declaration of autonomy through the culture of creative commons philosophy. Platforms like YouTube (owned by Google), Facebook, and Academia.edu confiscate the content uploaded to them for their own commercial exploitation. Members of CAMP and 0x2620 developed the free and open-source media archiving platform used by Mosireen (pan.do/ra), which allows users to manage large, decentralized video databases and collaboratively annotate the videos and create other metadata.

7 The Filming Revolution website attempts to match the open-ended, rhizomatic emergent structure of the 2011 uprising by translating it into a homologous platform (non-linear, non-hierarchical, spatially and temporally open-ended). In a sense, this parallels the sentiments and strategies expressed within it, without attempting to master or constrain them. Filming Revolution functions as creative project and resource simultaneously, open to interpretation and inviting users to engage with the ideas of the filmmakers and activists.

8 This documentary film, *Half a Revolution*, has been screened at more than forty international film festivals, including Sundance Film Festival in 2012 and Dubai International Film Festival in 2011, and was awarded Best Documentary Film at the Al Jazeera Documentary Film Festival and the Audience Award at the Karama Human Rights Film Festival in Jordan. Among the other notable documentary and fiction films based on the 2011 uprising were *Crop* (2013), by Johanna Domke and Marouan Omara; *Al-Fagoumy* (2011), by Essam El-Shamae; *After the Battle* (2012), by Yousry Nasrallah; *Moug* (2012), by Ahmed Nour; *al-Midan* (2013), by Jehane Noujaim; *Arij: Scent of Revolution* (2014), by Viola Shafik; *In the Last Days of the* City (2016), by Tamer El Said; and *Au Caire de la révolution* (2014), by Samir Abdallah.

9 Like the photomontages and designs of Constructivism, early Soviet cinema concentrated on creating an agitating effect by montage and making strange. The filmmakers Dziga Vertov and Sergei Eisenstein, as well as the documentarist Esfir Shub, regarded their fast-cut, montage style of filmmaking as a film Constructivism.

10 'Anarchive' refers to distinctive digital media practices and vernacular videos hosted online from more traditional understandings of the archive. The term has

been used to define low-resolution digital imagery that has been selected and hosted online, in less systematic assemblages normally associated with archival management.

11 *Al-Ikhtiyar 3* (The Choice 3) has been slammed for falsifying historical facts and whitewashing the government with its depiction of the July 2013 military coup that overthrew Egypt's first democratically elected president, Mohamed Morsi. The series chronicles the hours leading up to the military takeover, which was engineered by the country's then defence minister and current president, Abdel Fattah el-Sisi. The coup in 2013 ended Egypt's brief experiment with democracy following 2011. The show's second season, which was broadcast in 2021, sparked outrage for its depiction of the Raba'a massacre, the worst mass killing of civilian protesters in modern Egyptian history with around 1,000 deaths.

12 See the Filming Revolution website for the interview with Mosireen member Sherif Gaber: https://filmingrevolution.supdigital.org/clip/79/the_mosireen_collective (accessed 26 September 2023).

13 See the 858 website for the complete video clip: http://858.ma/ANP/editor/F (accessed 22 September 2023).

14 NBC News reported in 2019 how IBM supplied such image technology to the New York Police Department that can categorize people according to ethnic features, with obvious concerns raised that many ethnic communities were already 'over-policed and over-surveilled' (Solon 2019).

5

Censorship gazes on female portraiture

Misogyny, imagination and court concubines

The acceptable limits of visual representation are played out in the depiction of the human form, and gender relations are, arguably, one of the most contested cultural sensibilities in the Arabic MENA region. This chapter looks at this issue of the visual censorship of female representation through three intersecting contemporary photographic works within the Egyptian public sphere. This imposition on what is permissible in the photographic image came to the fore with the colonial camera encounter and contrasted with Western art history. Much of this European heritage included the visual tropes of Orientalism which dwelled on the forbidden harem scene and principally the domain of the odalisque figure. Jean-Auguste-Dominique Ingres's iconic painting *La Grande Odalisque* (1814) is emblematic of this cultural imperialism, which was fixated with this motif of the sensual harem woman and overlooked ocular representation of the real-life court concubines. In the cultural operation of colonialism, photographers built on this art foundation to generate collections of erotic odalisque images, often sold as postcards, to exploit this imaginary vision of the Orient for Western audiences. Well-known photographic studios in Egypt, such as German and Swiss partners Lehnert and Landrock,[1] produced large volumes of photographic works which at times included pornographic misogynist images, in different staged scenes, by using models to feed the European marketplace. There exists a stark contrast between the representation of women in the white male gaze of colonial photography and the court gaze of Ottoman and Persian portraiture during the nineteenth century. Although both situations expose a dark misogynist imagination in the framing of the human subjects who are exploited by a patriarchal camera viewpoint, there do exist some notable differences between these two forms of image production.

Within Orientalist visions the odalisque is a powerful visual symbol of the objectified female subject whose ambivalent nature floats through Western art and into much of the history of photography. These sensuous, sexualized representations were exclusively made by male imaginations and designed to appeal to the male gaze of the imperial traveller or adventurer passing through this exotic landscape. This external audience drew upon the Western imagination of the Arabic MENA region to conjure up the potent motif of the enclosed harem space. This concealed space appeared to offer the lure of boundless pleasure the camera seeks to explore, a lasciviousness of desire under the gaze of the European eye. In *The Colonial Harem* (1986), Algerian poet Malek Alloula analysed popular French photographic postcards of local women made in the early twentieth century. These staged photographs depicted the imagined scenes inside the hidden harem space to feature semi-naked women. These postcards did not depict Algerian women in any authentic cultural sense, but rather appealed to the colonial imagination of the occupiers, the French male projection onto the Orientalized female, who is seen posing in luxurious environments, suspended in time, listless and always available to the viewer's eye.

The exotic iconography of the harem is a crucial motif, one that arouses the viewer's desire to cross this forbidden threshold and was, in Western visual art, part of the European colonial imagination. In this context, the well-known figure of the odalisque became a key representational motif beyond the Arabic-speaking world. However, 'odalisque' is a term with origins in the Ottoman harem, where these women commonly worked as servants to the real concubines and did not work as sex slaves themselves.[2] Moreover, in the Ottoman court setting, odalisque women were never directly represented or seen and were usually hidden from the public eye. The Ottoman Empire's earliest use of photography dates back to 1842 and in Iran two years later, where both royal courts made their own, non-Western types of photographic portraits of harem concubines among other subjects for personal, not public consumption. The distinctive photographic images were produced under strict conditions to accommodate the Islamic values of the ruling sultan and crucially diverge from the European odalisque representational form. Under the instruction of the late Ottoman and Persian rulers Islamic dress codes for females were stringently adhered to in the photographic portraits, made by local photographers and shot in the hidden confines of the harem for the eyes of the privileged few only. The photographic portraits of the harem workers produced in this time do not conform to well-known Orientalist notions of the harem's physiognomic conventions popular in the Western colonial context. As Turkish historian Saadet Özen has stated:

> With their thick eyebrows, wearing tutus inspired from the ballerinas that the Shah saw in Europe, and not least because of their serious, direct gaze to the viewer, these women challenged our immediate visual codes of the harem aesthetically, bodily and behaviourally. (Özen 2017: 53)

Persian ruler Nasir al-Din Shah (1831–1896)[3] was an enthusiastic photographer himself and produced collections of portraits of his inner harem of concubines and other courtiers. His interest in the medium began at the age of eleven and he employed the Russian photographer Antoin Sevruguin as the official court photographer;[4] however, the shah restricted the visual representation of his estimated hundred wives and concubines. The photographic images produced by the shah include individual portraits and group shots of his concubines that at times featured himself in the camera composition. This personal archive is one of the most extensive of its kind and it has been widely examined, as the archive offers an invaluable insight into the intimate world of life inside these quarters of an Islamic palace. However, Nasir al-Din Shah's images contrast in arresting ways with the European odalisque vision, devoid of modes of lasciviousness and seductive inertia found in Orientalist depictions. In the shah's vision the viewer is unable to inscribe such overt sensuality to what can appear to be rather dead-pan and desexualized scenes. Intriguingly, in addition to his court duties, Sevruguin did produce erotic portraiture with female models for the Western market. He included the erotic model in these staged photographs in his own photographic studio away from prying court eyes. Sevruguin's odalisque images included suggestive text captions to further recharge the male Orientalist gaze, as the image's sexual appeal imagined a place of endless and timeless desire.

In broad terms, the local Iranian version of the harem as depicted by the shah saw women represented far more modestly and chasten, underpinned by an imagined vision of a paradise populated with houris.[5] These real-life concubines appear more androgynous to the viewer's eye and speak to distinctive, non-Western erotic properties. This vision is a counterpoint to the colonial erotic version and contrasts with the European imagination with discernible physical differences evident in body shape, facial expression, hair and, in particular, in the absence of nudity. Moreover, in such portraiture a distance is set between the viewer and the subject, as the gaze of the camera lens is veiled, in a way adding to the sensuousness of the figure in this local context. Here the viewer may be invited, in a voyeuristic fashion, to unveil the female model themselves and much is left to the imagination to generate sexual frisson. This invitation to desire-imagination defines the representation of these real-life concubines and contrasts with the sexual objectification of the female form in colonial representations. A key cultural notion at play here is *namus*, meaning 'dignified respectability' in Arabic, which contrasts with the more uninhibited, languid passivity of the male gaze characterized in visual depictions of women in Western art history. In more contemporary times the abject explicitness of Western art has been read, by some conservative Muslims, to signify moral corruption or even a culture in decline which contrasts to the piety and piousness of Islamic values. However, scholars argue that this religiosity is patriarchal and embedded in the misogyny of the cultural structures to omit and suppress female representation. Ali Behdad discusses this issue: 'There is no space for mothers, sisters, and daughters, whose absence is a visible sign of their marginal role in a court that was marked by gendered segregation of space and strict control over the visibility of women' (Behdad 2016: 148).

The use of photography in nineteenth-century Ottoman and Persian courts usually followed strict Islamic statutes and represented the harem concubines as fully clothed; however, in some cases portraits did show unveiled royal consorts or even curiously transgressive gender portraits of women dressed as men. The abusive nature of the harem system in these royal courts saw women as slaves of the ruling dynasty. Inside the harem hierarchy the odalisque was considered of lower status and akin to a chambermaid worker who might become a houri concubine if deemed worthy enough by the ruling sultan. Regardless, a fundamental misreading of this royal court social hierarchy exists within the colonial imagination, since the odalisque was depicted inaccurately and as the local photography of real-life concubines reveals, it differed greatly from Western depictions. A significant divergence is evident on the issue of nudity alone and objectification of the body that extends to include the physiognomy of the sitters themselves. These radically divergent visions of the erotic image, between the colonial odalisque and the local concubine, can exemplify debates on misreading in the contemporary image today in regard to representational politics.

In the Arabic MENA setting female representation is one of the most controversial image types and, arguably, the remaking of the performative self is key to present-day debates on gender identities. Some traditional Islamic codes are inflected through the social fabric to regulate what is considered appropriate behaviour, be it haram (illicit) or halal (permissible). The contentious nature of self-representation in the photographic image, especially on social media platforms, points towards the complex matrix of cultural censorship and power relations in society and, in this regard, how Islamic beliefs can construe the role of the image. One notorious incident in June 2021 involved the Misdemeanours Economic Court taking action against a young female Instagram influencer, Renad Emad, who was sentenced to three years in prison for 'violating society values and principles' (Gamal El-Din 2021). She attracted attention for posting short music videos of herself singing along to popular songs on TikTok, a platform known for its amateur short videos. This incident is part of a widespread crackdown on online freedoms of self-expression that particularly target women, as over eight were arrested on similar chargers between April and July 2020 alone through a series of court actions.[6] This prosaic social media content was deemed by the court to be 'inciting debauchery'

(Ghoneim 2020) in the youth and everyday internet content can be considered profane under conservative moral ciphers. The patriarchal nature of state law seeks to arbitrate what is permissible and enforce a vision of acceptable halal female behaviour in a division between public and private spaces. Human rights lawyer and head of the Cairo Centre for Development and Law Entisar Elsaeed commented on the state's treatment of these female online influencers, 'Our conservative society is struggling with technological changes which have created completely different environments and mindsets' (Farouk 2020).

This chapter goes on to address three contrasting photographic image-based works in which the depiction of the female body has been contentious within the Egyptian public sphere. The digital photograph of then twenty-year-old feminist activist Aliaa al-Mahdy took much of Egypt by storm in the aftermath of the 2011 uprising when she posted her naked self-portrait on her personal blogsite, A Rebel's Diary. The image went viral in hours garnering global media attention and overshadowed the cases of other Egyptian feminist activists, such as Samira Ibrahim, who challenged the enforcement of 'virginity tests' on female protesters. Al-Mahdy's divisive image posting failed to rally support both from the Egyptian public and the majority of Arab feminists, revealing the harsh reality that few were prepared to unreservedly endorse her gamble of fusing her own body with the body politic. In the aftermath of the scandal, she was forced into exile to eventually find solidarity among the ranks of Femen, the European direct action-based protest movement whose Islamophobic approach presumes 'Muslim women need saving' (Abu-Lughod 2015).

In the Arabic MENA region some lifestyle websites are aimed at female audiences and uphold heteronormative values. The Egyptian-based https://adlat.net sets out to uphold such traditional beliefs through a message board blog format that offers users tips and advice on a range of subjects aligned to conservative social values. The title, adlat, relates to an old-fashioned name for a working-class woman and part of the website categories comprise posts offering advice on gender roles and personal relationships along with contemporary fashion trends within an Islamic context. In this section a community of volunteer bloggers post information about clothing items of particular interest in the fashion threads and the blogger will find an online commercial photograph to illustrate this fashion recommendation or clothing item under review. The source images are often scavenged from free stock photography agencies on the internet; however, before the contributor will upload the photograph she will, first, censor the image by using digital software, frequently Photoshop, before reposting to the adlat.net forum. This alteration to the digital image is carried out to maintain prudence and piousness in regard to female representation.

Cairo has a number of specialist English-language bookstores that include Western art history publications as part of the in-shop display. This small selection of books can include popular photography anthologies encompassing a wide range of image types which commonly consists of nude art categories as part of the contents. This canon of Western photographic history presents a dilemma in the Egyptian public context and a process of state censorship has entailed hand-painting each photographic image, in each book edition, to obscure the full erotic effect of the human body. The collection of censored photographs from these books can be read as indicative of visual culture sensibilities under the state policing public space. These well-known photographic books are produced by international art publishers and cover the chronological pantheon of, mostly, male photographic maestros.

In these three different visual cases female representation in public has been contested, altered and each one questions the ideological underpinning of visual censorship to dictate what can and cannot be seen. These diverse image works are a type of archaeology of photographic censorship and the images switch between digital, art history, vernacular and editorial contexts. There exists a cultural vigilance and sensitivity around the female form in reference to the photographic image, and censoring can overlook iconoclastic intervention and aesthetic transformation of the image object. The original photograph has undergone a process of censorship to be mediated as an object of desire, be it a commercial fashion photograph or an example of Western art, and is situated in certain artistic traditions of photomontage and image surfacism. Another ontology of the photograph is evident in these recuperated images as an aura hovers over the surface tension created between the censorship act and the value code of the original. The emerging hybrid photographic image provides a conceptual basis for rethinking visual culture and modernity encounters as part of globalization within the networked and computational world. In the case of al-Mahdy's self-portrait, she set out to produce a direct-action feminist proclamation, which collapses into Orientalist traditions of the odalisque; to subsequently, and somewhat tragically, misconnect with its intended public audience in Egypt.

Enacting the selfie #nudephotorevolutionary

The selfie-portrait of twenty-year-old Aliaa al-Mahdy went viral when she posted a photograph to her personal blog.[7] The image caused a frenzy of activity in October 2011, with over 1.5 million hits on the website in a week (Mourad 2013). It sparked praise and derision in equal measures; the alumni of the School of Sharia in Cairo's al-Azhar University called for capital punishment. The timing of the photograph is crucial in understanding this adverse reaction, as Egypt was facing the first parliamentary elections after Mubarak's removal in a cloud of uncertainty that exposed the political vulnerability at the core of the 2011 uprising. In this precarious atmosphere al-Mahdy's digital self-portrait ignited tensions in a society trying to establish boundaries in the turbulence of political dissent and social change. Discontent and frustration built up, with the lack of significant political and social progress to unmask the paradoxical dilemma at the heart of revolutionary fervour, as street clashes erupted at regular intervals between different factions of the protesters and the state security forces. The sexual harassment of women and gender-based violence had become major social problems at public gatherings with perpetrators remaining unprosecuted and security forces more than compliant in failing to protect female citizens. Moreover, the authorities actively engaged in the infamous 'virginity tests',[8] the de facto state-sanctioned rape of female protesters used to politically supress women and intimidate them from taking up roles in public space. In late December 2011, a Cairo court ruled in favour of a young protester, Samira Ibrahim, who won her case against the military for abusing her human rights and 'finding virginity tests to be illegal' (Kraidy 2017: 174).

A-Mahdy's controversial digital self-portrait image, entitled *Nude Art* (Figure 5.1), depicts her naked, staring blankly into the camera, in ways reminiscent of other nude female figures in Western art history; Sandro Botticelli's *Birth of Venus* shares something of the pose adopted by al-Mahdy. Taken on this basis the image itself would barely be seen as controversial in a broader visual culture context. However, al-Mahdy appears aware of the erotic capital of her composition as she meets the viewer's gaze directly and seems intent on provocation through the compositional approach. In Egypt there appears to be little direct censorship of sexual imagery online and, like most of the contemporary world, globalization has brought with it the pervasive pornography industry which remains, despite censorship of political content, unrestricted to the general public. Therefore, far more explicit material is available online in Egypt and al-Mahdy's photograph is a composed selfie, an amateur self-portrait which has been imagined with an awareness of the Western nude portraiture. This performed nature of the image is evident because the photograph includes a number of motifs to reveal some artistic aspirations by the author. Al-Mahdy stands alone in a wooden-panelled room and wears black stockings, red-tinted ballet shoes and a matching red-coloured flower in her hair. Apart from the red-tinted objects the rest of the photograph has been changed into black and white and the adjustments were made in post-production software to again reflect some artistic embellishments of behalf of the maker. She categorizes the photograph under an art section on her blogsite and the image circulated on social media platforms with the hashtag #nudephotorevolutionary. Her

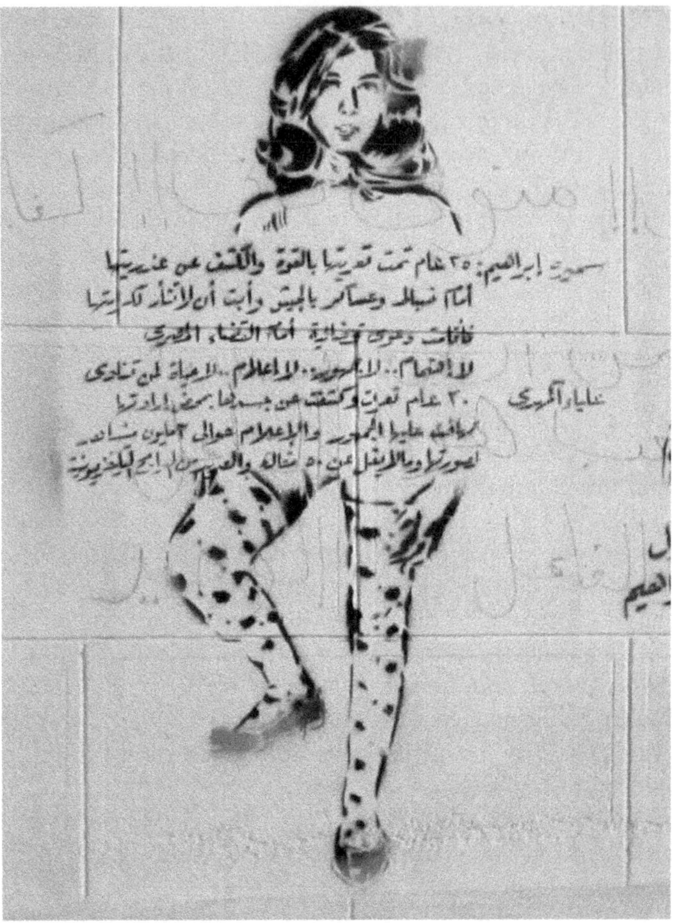

Figure 5.1 Graffiti stencil in Cairo attempts to recognize Aliaa al-Mahdy as a feminist icon of the 2011 protest movements. However, her image became more contentious in the media storm as support dwindled.

black stockings, red shoes and flower are somewhat affected, arguably by the stockings and colorization, but in the end these embellishments compromise her feminist activism in the local context. The overall aesthetic impact of the image is somewhat vernacular rather than fine art as intended by al-Mahdy, and as Marwan M. Kraidy comments, the image's effect is rather 'reminiscent of a *Playboy* centrefold, the photo's sexual aura absorbs its political symbolism' (Kraidy 2017: 167). Moreover, al-Mahdy's pose and facial expression contribute to the sexual potency of her photograph over the political, as she stands with her leg raised and her foot rests on a stool in order to expose her genitalia to the camera lens and the gaze of the viewer. As Kraidy points out the image appears influenced by a soft porn aesthetic of well-known magazines or even amateur erotic photography reinforced by the *mise en scène* of the monochrome wood-panelled room. Indeed, the image approach is a subjective construct mediated by the male gaze that might overshadow female sexual expression. She looks out, head turned down submissively, to the viewer to hail attention as her expression is one of bashful confidence, perhaps slightly unsure of her own sexual capital but still assured there is something to be exchanged with the viewer. Moreover, the monotone hues of the image have transformed her naked body from the naturalism of colour towards an objectified gaze. Al-Mahdy was, according to her own comments, in control of the image as the sole author, model, digital producer, promoter and publicist. The self-portrait image-making itself was not the transgressive act; however, it was by virtue of making it public through the dissemination on her blog, at an unstable time in revolutionary politics in Egypt, that the image became divisive.

Therefore, the controversy around the image was not caused in the pictorial surface alone, as the significance of the image lies in the challenge to social codes hard to digest for the majority of both women and men in Egypt. The fluid ideology of the protest movements met with the traditional mindset of Islamic groups who were involved in street politics too and had finally embraced the opportunity presented by the removal of Mubarak. Al-Mahdy's image entered this revolutionary fray to polarize opposition activists even on the left of the spectrum who felt betrayed by her overt gesture because it seemed to mimic external Western values. Al-Mahdy's photographic act was not culturally codified within the definition of revolutionary politics of Tahrir Square and some extreme voices threatened violence against her; in December 2011 an innocent young woman who resembled al-Mahdy was badly beaten in Cairo. One of the few to support al-Mahdy's image politics was the outspoken feminist Mona Eltahawy, who wrote in an article for the *Guardian* that this was an attack on social and state misogyny, 'She is the Molotov cocktail thrown at the Mubaraks in out heads, the dictators of our mind' (Eltahawy 2011). However, other detractors came from the local liberal and secular sides who criticized her for making the revolution personal at a politically sensitive time in the run up to first parliamentary elections. Even feminist voices were estranged from her explosive action because, for them, she put the social revolution before the political one. Eventually, al-Mahdy went underground in Cairo fearing for her public safety as, conversely, her image became briefly a feminist icon and was audaciously stencilled onto the walls of the Ministry of Interior near Tahrir Square, alongside other female revolutionary protest figures, such as Samira Ibrahim, from this time.[9] Yet this alignment within graffiti street space was short-lived and even the prominent April 6 Youth Movement[10] eagerly distanced themselves from her as the controversy grew when they stated she was not a member of the organization, as had been rumoured. Tarek al-Kholi, one of the leaders of the April 6 Youth Movement, was asked about al-Mahdy by the news channel Al Arabiya and he said, 'the movement does not have any members who engage in such behaviour' (Stack and Kirkpatrick 2011).

The vast majority of unequivocal and tangible public support came from external audiences who saw the #nudephotorevolutionary photographic act and its negative public reception within Egypt as an infringement of hard-fought women's rights. As al-Mahdy's image circulated online in an appropriated storm, arguably in part driven by voyeurism, for some, this dissemination projected her image into a pantheon of feminist icons. But matters worsened for her when a solidarity photo stunt by Israeli women was published that only served to feed her detractors in the region (Rawi 2011). Another example of international solidarity came from a UK-based feminist campaigner, Maryam Namazie, who launched a support calendar, entitled *Nude Photo Revolutionaries Calendar*, consisting of twelve individual self-portraits by women in homage to al-Mahdy. This was launched on International Women's Day in 2012. The online publication included quotes by al-Mahdy alongside her image, which was combined with black-and-white self-portrait responses from other women in Europe and the US as each portrait included general slogans. Other solidarity photographs followed as al-Mahdy continued to solicit support and publish online through her blog by requesting others to send her nude portraits with even men contributing selfies in this open expression of body politics. Despite such gestures of international solidarity and sense of enthusiasm for such feminist-inspired online campaigns, the composition of these photographs differed significantly from al-Mahdy's original self-portrait. The homage photographs and visual memes were more modest in pose, avoiding the sexual charge of the original, and set out to mediate the nudity issue to resemble more prudent forms of naturist representation or even advertising culture. For instance, the image made in Tel Aviv consisted of a large group of forty women where they carefully covered up their bodies behind a banner reading 'Homage to Aliaa ElMadhi. Sisters in Israel' and 'Love without Limits' written in Arabic and Hebrew (Rawi 2011). Other photographic responses included restaging the image composition by cropping the head of the sitter in order to keep the identity of the subject anonymous to the public while many others simply transferred the original photograph into non-photographic media such as drawing or painting formats.

Over the course of 2012 al-Mahdy's profile resurfaced intermittently as she used her blog, A Rebel's Diary, to petition for more photographs in support of her form of body politics. She was eventually drawn into the direct-action protest group Femen,[11] and strategically protested naked outside the Egyptian Embassy in Stockholm in December 2012 to draw attention to the influence of Sharia law in the Egyptian constitution; the Muslim Brotherhood's Mohamad Morsi had become president in elections. By now al-Mahdy was in long-term exile in Sweden and her staged Femen event was a well-produced media stunt in contrast to her homemade domestic photograph over a year earlier. The resulting YouTube videos and photographs gained little traction or influence inside Egypt and failed to ignite public reaction like her previous photographic pose had in 2011. Certain clues about the reception and impact of the original self-portrait can be discerned from aspects of the image itself and importantly the timing of its public dissemination on social media. Regardless of the merits of her political ambitions by this attack on state misogyny and hypocrisy of the activists, the effectiveness of this feminist critique on the patriarchal nature of Egyptian society remains in doubt as her image was a highly provocative act, if not too explosive, for a religious-based society to process.[12] Al-Mahdy purports, with justification, that the image was controversial because of the prevailing norms of the state regime and society in Egypt and she has gone on to declare the need for gender issues to be on any reform agenda. In an interview with Vice Media, she said, 'I'm not ashamed of my body. And I expressed that with every item I was wearing' (Asad 2013).

Through her full-frontal nude selfie this atheist blogger was catapulted into infamy and unlike other female activists on the streets, was not abused by state forces to take such radical action. In contrast, the case of Samira Ibrahim or the violence against the Sitt al-Banat (Blue Bra Girl)[13] highlights the extreme levels of police brutality experienced by women activists. However, the dignified responses by Ibrahim, Salwa el-Husseini and others were in contrast to al-Mahdy's doomed photographic act. Many commentators believed she was mistaken because posting the image was 'offensive in being both aggressive and objectionable' (Kraidy 2017: 174). The image al-Mahdy produced is significant as it did pierce the revolution myth of 2011 by puncturing the bubble of gender equality and exposed the widespread misogyny within activist movements. The criticism levelled at al-Mahdy accused her of putting personal freedom over wider political goals, but this weak argument ignores the need for progressive social change on gender issues alongside political reforms. Tunisian Mohamed Bouazizi, fed up with regression and humiliation, immolated himself in a personal sacrifice, an act of desperation that became the catalyst for the Arab uprisings, and he was never attacked for the personal nature of this action. The adverse public reaction to al-Mahdy's image unveils a harsh reality of misogynistic tendencies, sexual harassment and gender-based violence that was, even in Tahrir Square, all too common, and this remains a depressing constituent of Egyptian society. Unlike other photographs documenting the violent treatment of women protesters at the hands of the security forces that solicited public outrage, al-Mahdy's image transgresses straightforward victimhood. In the contested protest space of the street, women endured sexual harassment and, at times, gang rape by groups of men in uncontrolled sexual frenzies, at times lasting hours, while the police have carried out highly questionable 'virginity tests' (Amnesty International 2012) on female activists arrested during protests.[14] These violent abuses of female bodies are a dark mirror that few contemporary political figures choose to address head on in an atmosphere of denial. Implicit social values and codes shape gender relations and create a cultural distinction between private and public behaviour. Al-Mahdy has attempted to position herself in a generation of blogger activists who communicate equally to both local and global audiences through the internet. Perhaps she hoped to strengthen progressive social values inside the country during the power vacuum in the transition from the Mubarak police state to democratic elections that heralded Muslim Brotherhood rule. This goes some way to explaining why, despite al-Mahdy's campaigning, the image provoked such a negative reaction with few in Egypt ready to defend her in the public sphere. In the aftermath of the image's publicity there was a discernible lack of consensus from other Egyptian feminists as none followed her to use the body as a tool of freedom of expression in the political setting. Al-Mahdy's self-portrait may have left her personally empowered but estranged from a society polarized over gender issues in a post-revolution quagmire. Al-Mahdy has continued her type of campaigning internationally and remains part of Femen but at the price of little recognition from Arab feminism; one exception is Eltahawy who continues to support her. Writing in the online journal Jadaliyya in January 2013 Sara Mourad articulates succinctly the issue of al-Mahdy's feminist status in the Arabic MENA region:

> Equally important is an evaluation of transgressive gender politics in light of a religiously-inflected social conservatism that is tightening its grip on a post-Arab Spring official public discourse. The purpose is not to discredit Aliaa or belittle her. Clearly, she has the right to use her body as she pleases. However, a naked body is not just – and not always – a signifier of political transgression, cultural resistance, and sexual liberation. (Mourad 2013)

The removal of autocratic leaders from the body politic in Egypt in the end yielded no substantial social progression on gender issues and did little to address misogyny in society. The toppled leaders and their cronies lost, temporarily, control during this time but in the upheaval a hostile gender environment persisted under societal indifference or denial. The presidential election of Mohamed Morsi in June 2012 indicated public support for the Muslim Brotherhood's conservative brand of politics among the electorate in Egypt that made the traffic of images highly sensitive in the public sphere. Against an increasingly paranoic backdrop al-Mahdy's deep-rooted political motivations were questioned by other activists, among them leftist blogger Khodar Salameh, who even accused her of 'a crime against the Egyptian revolution' (Kraidy 2017: 161) because she called for a sexual revolution when the political one was still incomplete. However, this position attempts to cover up the cracks in the opposition movements as personal expression must be part of a successful revolution that triggers cultural and social change to topple misogyny (Eltahawy 2011). Her self-portrait image may have been a visual cliché in the West, or even a photographic one-liner in photographic art history, but in Egypt it was a visual signature that was not to be corroborated by the wider society. Her heartfelt feminist motivation and sincerity resulted in estrangement and exile to exclude her from any potential political discourse in Egypt; her campaign contributed little meaningful change to the causes she sought to address. The viral nature and global reach of the internet has configured her controversial self-portrait outside of Egypt, and regrettably in another rather Islamophobic discourse fuelled by her Femen protests. Al-Madhy's image has been largely written out from the national narrative on visual materials dating from the 25 January revolutionary time with little support from both secular feminist sides, while the image remains a curious marker of political miscalculation.

Representation in digital photomontage

The notoriety of al-Mahdy's brand of protest feminism clashed within Egypt and has to be seen in the broader context of a society aligned along conservative religious values. Censorship exists in the organs of the state because many perceive it as a necessary role and are coerced into believing in censorship on an individual and collective level. Therefore, it prevails as a form of tacit knowledge, implicit and implied through the fabric of the social relations, and appears to be rooted in diverse but imagined national community. The female style images hosted on the adlat.net website originate from global fashion industries found in Western image culture and, in a more regional context, in the Turkish design industry. Differing styles in the fashion industry are the source for the digital images circulated on adlat's message board website as posts offer heteronormative advice on the performance of gender roles in traditional topics: cooking, heterosexual relationships, housework, childcare, lifestyle choices, cosmetics and in particular fashion advice tips. The website culture predates the era of global social media platforms, such as the ever-popular Facebook in Egypt, and operates like an online version of an old-fashioned women's magazine with subscribers and internet membership from across the Arabic-speaking region. Working in themed networks on message boards the postings are supervised by teams of online avatars with maternal pseudonym names. The website homepage contains a short statement announcing the kind of content to be found inside, including information on 'housework', 'couple relationships' and 'hair, skin and everything that matters to increase your beauty, and your wedding night appearance' (Adlat 2023). Other topics include pregnancy advice, family relationships and how to care for your child.

The architecture of the website is basic to allow each contributor to upload images and post commentaries that are supervised by a community of administrators. Many of these online personalities, Om Tatu, Om Alaa, Om Seif, Shimaa, have sizeable numbers of followers and discuss wide-ranging issues, offering advice to online members as surrogate mother figures or even agony aunts. However, the category 'Elegance and Beauty' is of particular interest for this chapter due to its treatment of the photographic and comprises posts addressing contemporary conservative female fashion trends. Often the adlat blogger will post a review of a clothing item of interest and they will seek out an online image to best illustrate the fashion recommendation. The source images are scavenged from the internet, often from stock photography banks, and sometimes in more Islamic-styled outlets in the region with models wearing headscarves, which are popular in the local marketplace. Before the contributor uploads the photograph, they will first censor it in digital software and only then post it to the adlat.net web community forum. Each contributor is striving to invent their own distinct signature style of censorship by using the digital software to manipulate the image in order to complement the type of clothing and, in turn, gather more online followers. After altering the image, the contributor will put her signature on the image as if she is the author of an appropriated artistic image. Furthermore, the signature is meant to identify the distinct fashion styles of the contributor as author of the tip for the web community, while the followers, in turn, will vote on different merit awards for a valued post. The merit badges are wide ranging to include 'best Photoshop manipulation' (Shalabi 2023) or even 'ideal mother'.[15] Therefore, these Islamic influencers can appear to speak for and to a traditional perspective of working-class women in Egypt, if not across the Arabic MENA region.

The adlat website attracts volumes of posts in the 'Elegance, Fashion and Clothing' section alone, comprising a vast array of strangely altered fashion images, sourced on the internet from various fashion companies and modelled by women unaware of what will happen to their look when manipulated by these Egyptian iconoclasts (Figure 5.2). In this process conservative Islamic

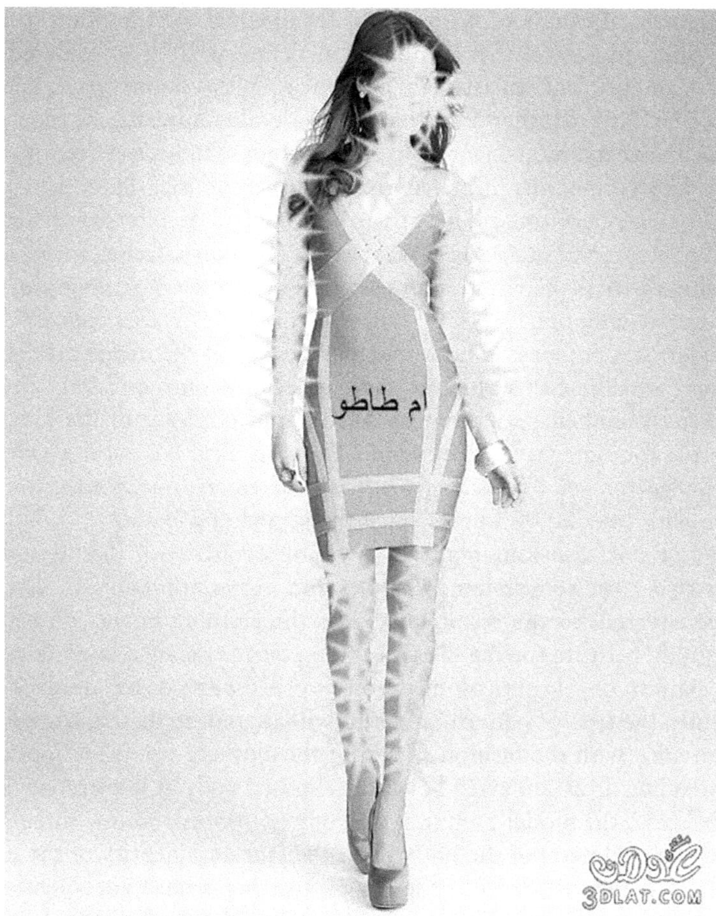

Figure 5.2 Visual censorship of fashion photographs on adlat.net. Volunteers have different styles in the photoshopping of the female models.

aesthetics are visualized by these local Egyptian women who express themselves and their vision, while being hailed by global fashion industries. Such digital photomontages are cultural expressions that seek to restrict the full sexualized charge of the body, concealed behind a censored public space in order to not cause offence to the public and reassert the modesty to the fashion model. Given the patriarchal nature of the social context and certain limitations of gender roles in Egypt, it is mostly working-class women who use these message boards to express what relates to their lives, while upholding heteronormative values of mainstream society. Often the discussions on the message boards offer advice and support on themes considered feminine in this specific local situation. Within these female-only communities, specialist figures offer advice on the self-image to define what is considered both attractive and prudent, an aesthetic judgement. In this online space, personas such as Om Tatu (Mother Tatu) have considerable influence as they define this local aesthetic judgement inflected through a subjective lens to shape identity and community in a heteronormative context. There is a coded visual language here and a logic at work as Photoshop filters transform the original photographic images in specific ways. This public-facing, social-shaped censorship restricts the visual representation of women in strange ways that can seem to lampoon or even satire avant-garde movements or ironic postmodern art practices. The vernacular quality of the image productions made by the volunteer censors provides a window onto a visual culture of non-Western aesthetics, disconnected from and unaware of the history of artistic photomontage. Leading iconoclast Om Tatu has won a Diamond Merit badge for her Photoshop work, as she receives accolades from her fanbase with over 20,000 posts since she joined in 2013..

The aesthetic decisions made in covering details with digital software follows two basic censorship principles and visual approaches. First, skin must be covered, so the result looks like the clothing hovers on top of a female body because the digital tool often paints a strange layer to replace skin, a pattern or vibrant colour on the exposed parts of the model's body. Frequently, the type of pattern or colour will attempt to match, complement or harmonize with the fashion design of the clothing itself; the fabric of a white wedding dress can extend over the exposed body as if a strange disease spreads across the model's white skin (Figure 5.3). Second, the intention to conceal exposed parts of the body hides the face and identity of the model; apparently recommended in order to protect her from malevolent online stalkers or internet trolls. This approach is more strictly applied when using photographs that include regional models, mostly from Turkey's fashion industry. These two guiding principles of image manipulation pass through local values and aesthetic codes to represent the female model in a more modest light of primary concern. The types of visual experimentation and creative gestures include ebullient digital filters like starbursts, metallic liquid paints, spray paints or even superimposing multiple heads. In some images, the volunteer censor has altered the details so much the photograph turns into a strange sci-fi-like image, as if to offer a portal or wormhole into another universe and altered image world. The imposed social judgement on female representation comes about from within a strictly gendered community and operates within the pervasive nature of globalized image culture. This conservative matriarchy constructs its own appearance of femininity through relationships, reaffirming heteronormative social roles and gender inequalities in contemporary Egypt. The popularity of the adlat platform

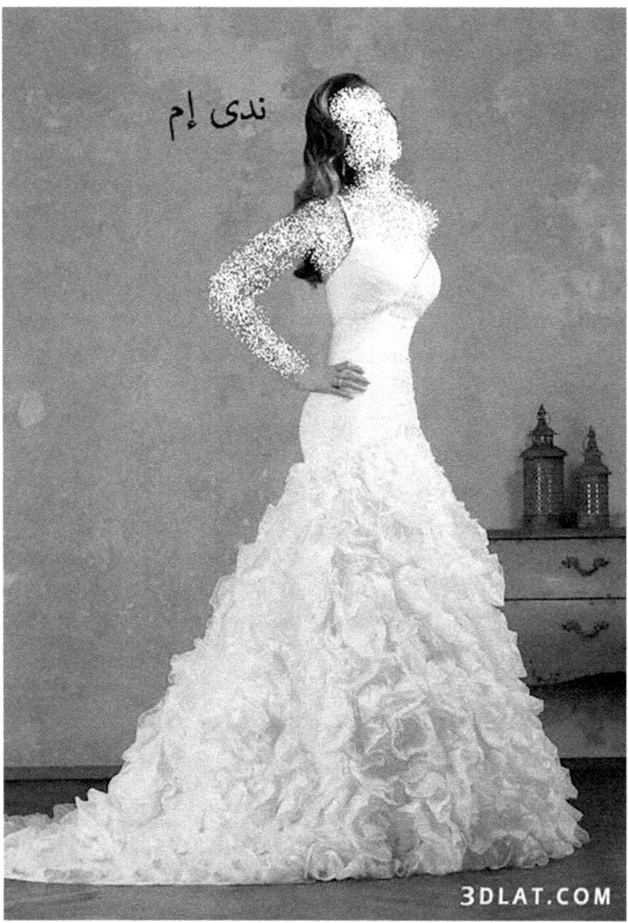

Figure 5.3 A different style of visual censorship used with this wedding dress. Most of the models are Western and photographs are taken from stock photography or commercial websites.

reveals the disequilibrium and dilemma where women are hailed, firstly, by the desires of global fashion imagery and, secondly, by piousness in a more modest version of beauty. Two opposing forces meet in the digital photograph and compete to shape the future of female representation as they navigate between the image as freedom versus the censorship in Arabic MENA cultures.

The online adlat image maintains the visual balance of censorship that distorts photographic indexicality, and privileges the image surface to shape the cultural performance of heteronormative everyday life. As contemporary visual culture influences global society in a multitude of differences while we drift towards the 'slow cancellation of the future' (Fisher 2009: 189), the adlat website is an antiquated use of technology to promote outdated gender roles that still have a foothold in the cultural imagination of Egypt. As Sherine Hafez writes, 'Because bodies are media of transmitted knowledge, they archive information, convey meaning, and perform memory, thereby becoming catalysts of social transformation' (Hafez 2019: 39). These photomontages mediate conservatism and the image to act as reactionary reminders of censorship, a blunt retort and ill-informed attempt to counter the encounter with global photographic cultures. In the tabulations of Egypt these photomontage works could be understood as almost a type of Islamic rather than vernacular modernism (Pinney and Peterson 2003) that expresses a photo practice in reverse, occurring in response to global trends but trapped within an aesthetic time lag so great that censorship is seen as creative. These instrumental photomontages seek to reconcile religious beliefs and accommodate local cultural sensibilities rather than disrupt the viewer and open minds. Moreover, this amateur digital image work has other shortcomings because it lacks a deeper critical framework to develop within, as such iconoclastic experiments set out to suppress explicit forms of expression in stark contrast to the feminist charge of al-Mahdy's 2011 nude self-portrait. Adlat's anonymous form of self-expressive acts ultimately constitutes the bowdlerization of the photographic image in the service of regressive misogyny and counter-revolutionary politics in the regime of the visual.

Visual censorship and dominant narratives

Imported books in Egypt are scrutinized by government agencies for their appropriateness for sale and various photographic images have been censored from the history of art in anthology publications available in local bookstores. In the years after the 25 January uprising, between 2012 and 2014, a range of publications have been doctored, including well-known photographic publications such as *The Photo Book: A History, Volume 1* (Badger and Parr 2004) and *Photographers A–Z* (Koetzle 2011).[16] After passing through the Egyptian state-run organization al-Riqaba 'ala al-Musannafat al-Fanniyya (Censorship of Creative Arts), a veiled filter stands between the viewer and the original photographs. The image content of these publications constitutes the representational regime in the history of art, mapping out part of the visual culture embedded in European aesthetic traditions. These large and ostentatious photography books are anthology productions that offer a set pantheon of artistic maestros and movements that appeal to wide-ranging audiences. These canonical collections also reveal certain covert misogynist tendencies commonplace in the culture of popular photography and this visual economy uses the human body as a site of ideological struggle.

The original photographs in the book collections found in Cairo consist of different photographic practices and aesthetic experiments of principally Western photo artists of the twentieth century. Predominately male and made with analogue photographic technologies, the images were produced by some of the most renowned photographers in an unrepresentative history of the medium.[17] Many of them reproduce a male gaze that projects the ideas and values of the time in which they explore the self-reflexive lens often focused on the passive female muse. This art history collection includes the unpalatable visual work by the controversial American photographer Terry Richardson and the kitsch portraitist David LaChapelle, among many others, who operate under the label of artistic freedom. In some ways the practice of such canonical figures in the history of photography seeks to transmit abject sensitives to shock or even disturb the overly normative vision in the bourgeoisie viewer. In other photography works in these collections, a less provocative approach can be seen; for instance, in the classical erotic oeuvres of impressionist Erwin Blumenfeld, whose work objectifies the female form in a shadowy vision of translucent bodies and covers models with veils to emphasize the model's breasts. Other more innovative images are included too which share modernist turns of freedom, like Marianne Breslauer's *Autoportrait*. Here, both female model and the photographer are one, but she still poses naked for the viewer in a mirror, looking into the camera viewfinder in the act of creation and adopting a self-referential manner as if parodying the male gaze of her counterparts. These varied photographic practices speak to Western-coded values and cultural sensibilities in the arts to privilege visual experimentation that was aesthetically developed to reinforce the sense of artistic autonomy, and often uses the naked female form as an important referent.

In contrast the Egyptian al-Riqaba censorship office staff labour to restrict the erotic capital of the visual and doctor the original photographic surfaces by hand, to alter each page in each book edition, painting over the original photographs to transform the book collections. Photomontage and avant-gardism have been an integral, disruptive part of the photographic history and such image intervention normally disturbs the indexical referent and forms a new meaning. However, the Egyptian state censorship applies its own logic not to evolve but supress any new visual meaning of such collections from Western-based photographic history.[18] At the same time, this Egyptian censorship indicates something is deeply amiss, both in the image politics of the original photographs in the publications and in the local response to their spirit of artistic autonomy. The Egyptian censorship workers are, like the adlat volunteer censors, anonymous interlopers in the process who judge the representational object, the referent of the naked model, made by the photographer and seen by the viewer. This covering of the photograph in these books has happened mostly through strange ink-like shapes applied to mask certain body parts or occasionally even over the whole photograph. Various censorship hands and multiple workers appear to have reworked the different images in the original books, covering the page surfaces with different colours in curious, unannounced and uninvited ways. In other images, more subtle, delicate tracing or dotting handiwork of ink is found, or, in contrast, roughly applied to paint on an imaginary dress, undergarments or bikini. At other times such handiwork may give way to thick black blocks, or just arbitrary blobs, to cover the female naked body. Both genders are sometimes in fact covered to conceal the potential of any forbidden erotic details to escape, while in other photographic images the original is deemed too excessive to be seen at all. In such cases, large strips of industrial black tape cover the full image frame and, curiously, such tape rests over the reproduction much like the blades of a closed analogue camera shutter. Moreover, this black tape can actually be peeled back carefully to reveal the hidden, original photograph buried underneath.

The intriguing variety of hand-drawn gestures was used to mask the photographic images that may even indicate the level of fatigue at any given time, as on occasion the process looks hurriedly carried out, perhaps in order to complete the daily quota of handcrafted reticence. Equally, one can decipher different censors having different signature styles in their practice or even a distinctive authorship. In others, the severity of the visual disciplining applied relates to the perceived transgression or provocation of the photographer in the image-making, in a similar fashion to how al-Mahdy provoked such a harsh reaction. Heavy-handed acts conceal not just the alleged offending parts of the anatomy but the whole image by burying the photograph under black adhesive tape, forsaking the photograph to be locked under a dark oil-like surface, thereby consigned to a black hole of representation. Additionally, other photographs are treated with more respectful, light touches of watercolour brushstrokes to maintain the equilibrium between what is seen and unseen with delicate, responsive colouring, masking or creative ink blobs applied on each individual image. This lighter-handed censorship is still an intrusion but is done with an almost embarrassed undertone or whisper; as if not overtly wanting to disturb the gaze or diminish the impact of the original. Sometimes, in the case of colour photographs, matching inks were used, occasionally blending into the image composition to the point of opaqueness and camouflage, as if not overtly wanting to interrupt the viewer's voyeuristic relationship to the photograph.[19]

Despite this diversity and degree of censorship involved in the mark-making these new photographic surfaces reveal an ideological logic to prevent, block or limit the ways of seeing. This type of censorship process is a laborious one, a painstaking task to conceal large volumes of images individually by hand-painting each edition of the book anthologies, as each edition often contains hundreds of photographs ahead of public sale. This interruption subverts the photographer's original intentions and what can be anticipated by the viewer. And yet, through this distinctive censorship process, a visual strangeness is heightened to produce an uncanny resemblance to avant-garde or even postmodern art practices. The Egyptian censorship process may appear to resemble experimental, aesthetic innovations in the Western canon of photography through photomontage or collage practices but this association is only skin deep because the censorship acts are directed towards the public sphere only, unaware of the theoretical framework of art movements or photographic cultures. Indeed, even parody or irony cannot be credited to the censorship agents who have proven determined to repress freedom of expression across the society. Since the inauguration of President el-Sisi in 2014, the regime has stepped up repression of the visual by closing down art venues, banning books and imprisoning photographers. The Egyptian state places itself as an arbiter between cultural productions and the public, between art works and the viewer; by the logic of censorship it can determine, in a patriarchal fashion, what is sayable, seeable and doable. The censorship bureaucrats have formed photomontage images of conservative values that are an archive of visual censorship to reveal certain aesthetic sensibilities of this process. The Western photographers created the original images found in these photographic history collections and many of them claim to speak to an autonomy of the arts and freedom of expression albeit with a tinge of twentieth-century misogyny. Beyond this vision are the Egyptian visual censors whose pens, tapes, inks and brushes await to insert a veil over the Western photographic image in the name of censorship. On the pages of these books is another encounter between the Egyptian state and Western modernity which has been seen in various historical contexts since photography became part of visual culture.

Iconoclasm of the body image

The apparent collision of visual cultures in the reproduction and dissemination of photographic images relating to gender in Egypt opens up many intriguing misrecognitions. The historical aftermath of European colonial exploitation through the dominance of the Orientalist gaze continues to underwrite much of the use and reception of the contemporary image in global culture. In the case of Egypt, a series of gazes are exchanged; the creative ambition of the photographer, the visible and invisible forces of visual censorship and photographic literacy in regard to the image in the public sphere. The logic-void of censorship clashes with self-expression, contemporary photographic cultures and artistic motivations that alter the moral status of the image beyond straightforward aesthetic concerns. In this way, the photographic image in Egypt has become a purveyor of political and social meaning for local dissemination as it mediates modernity in this specific context.

Despite the regressive influence of censorship in many regards, be it the photographic works found in the Cairo bookstores or in the international fashion models on the adlat website, there are Egyptian minds and hands operating as light-touch iconoclasts of symbolic transformation. Their (in)adeptness, perhaps, belies an attempt to be self-determined from the values of Western modernity in cultural terms. For instance, in both the censorship treatment of the history of photography books in Cairo and the adlat community, a sense of garbled artistry can be seen that goes on to produce new image forms and meanings that emerge strangely. These new photomontages appear to be invested with a radical recuperation and the cultural force of reiteration. The visual censorship process is an act to inadvertently create a new meaning that does not advocate a world without images, in fact quite the opposite. Bruno Latour puts forward the idea of 'iconoclash' (Spicer 2017) to introduce this portmanteau to consider the motivation and logic underpinning iconoclasm. He suggests that no matter how harsh the iconoclastic act is on the image, its effect will create an irreconcilable tension between the destruction and proliferation of images, with distinct codes and values attendant. As Latour states:

> Thus, we can define an iconoclash as what happens when there is uncertainty about the exact role of the hand at work in the production of a mediator. Is it a hand with a hammer ready to expose, to denounce, to debunk, to show up, to disappoint, to disenchant, to dispel one's illusions, to let the air out? (Latour 2002: 8)

Within the context of the three image projects discussed in this chapter (al-Mahdy's self-portrait, the adlat website and photography books), the role of iconoclasm is evident as the viewer's ability to see the images has been hindered. These visual case studies intersect in intriguing ways because it was the lack of censorship in al-Mahdy's case and its unimpeded circulation that provoked the harsh reaction; almost justifying the twisted logic visual censorship in Egypt's public environ. One well-known image from the above-mentioned censored book series serves to embody Latour's iconoclash argument in the work of Japanese photographer Nobuyoshi Araki. His book project *Dirty Pretty Things* (2007) is part of the publication *Photographers A–Z* (Koetzle 2011), where the artist's page consists of a diptych image showing the same female model reclining in the same pose, looking into the camera in both frames. In Araki's original version she poses, rather predictably, topless on the right side, and in the other frame the same model is wearing a black vest garment, in a diptych-like portrait. However, in the book edition sold in Cairo the censors painted on, with a degree of care and accuracy, an almost identical black vest shape to modestly cover the model's bare torso in this mirrored composition. The result in this censored version shows little difference between both photographs and the unknowing viewer could be confused by these interlinked photographs as scant change can be noted at first glance, doubling into an ocular puzzle. Araki's misogyny is blocked here as the paired images defer the gaze and the abusive frame is postponed from his creepy male vision. Araki's infamous photography of *kinbaku-bi* (rope bondage) and other sexually explicit images of women raise questions about the power dynamics in the process between the photographer and the subject in this genre of photographic history. Controversy arose when one of his long-term models, Kaori, accused him of stalking, sexual harassment and exploitation over a period of fifteen years as she was inspired to speak out by the #MeToo movement.

The deeper motivation behind censorship of gender in the photographic image has been curiously dealt with in the Egyptian context through three photographic case studies under review in this chapter. The online advice community of *adlat*, al-Mahdy's controversial nude art in 2011 and the governmental censorship of photographic history can, in broad terms, exist as objects of interest, curious artefacts that are delinked from Western visual culture. Through these different censorship acts and reactions the photographic emerges from a need to mediate the global visual culture encounter and censorship is aware of the image's potential to reproduce perception, thought and act. The impact on the original photograph sets out to reinforce the control and discipline of what is permissible in a specificity of a given place and time. In the image politics of Egypt, the female body remains contested, guarded and harassed in public space and viewed under the apparent natural logic of concealment. Rather than diffuse the original photograph of its set intention, these visual impediments and surface obstacles to the ocular experience use ink, paint and digital software tools to imbue the viewer's imagination with a strange resonance. By veiling the visual these censored photomontage images are laden with attendant meanings to the local audience, to connect the representation of the physical world with the mental image process, the conscious and unconscious. Within Egypt, cultural sensibility exists in visible and tacit forms to become understood through subtle social codes of control to conservatively shape the values of the visual in public sphere. However, this is not a denial of erotic expression as the media space is adorned with sexual energy, most evident in the cultural signifier of the belly dance archetype.

The policing of the female body in the photographic creates a haunting presence as anonymous actors, unseen players exert control to impede the viewer's experience and direct them to what one cannot see; the sensual aura around the image. Indeed, the true nature of censorship is based on the psychology of frustration, deferral, delay, to refract the gaze as this denial is invested with its own erotic capital of desire. Despite the dominant role of the photographic image in vernacular life, mostly through social media platforms, photography as a form of open personal expression or a thinking tool remains marginalized politically with little agency since the fervour of 2011. Islamic-based sensibilities have toiled to reconcile local traditional beliefs with the polysemic power of the photographic medium with its mimetic capacity in the representation of the female body. Historically, Islam has tended to dominate social and cultural affairs by its central role in everyday life and through its operation within the Egyptian state apparatus, despite the influence of the Coptic minority and other indigenous voices with diverse heritages. Notwithstanding some notable exceptions, an example being Van Leo's studio images of actress Nadia Abdel Wahab who posed naked in 1959, the open depiction of the naked female body is read as somehow at odds with the indigenous visual culture; as al-Mahdy has shown, accused of falling into Western-styled modernity, apocryphal to bona fide Egyptian values. As cultural commentator Ismail Fayed has written on human rights in the online Mada Masr newspaper when addressing the suicide of LGBTQI+ activist Sarah Hegazy, 'Feminism, the LGBT+ rights movements, and "universal rights" in general were all seen as imperialist tools to undermine the "morally pristine" universe of the authentic subject' (Fayed 2020). Many of Hegazy's supporters believe the Egyptian state harassment of such communities as negatively affecting Hegazy's mental health and contributing to her suicide.[20]

The altered photographic ontology of three interlinked image works under consideration in this chapter have encountered heteronormativity and conservative ideologies working with state control systems and media channels to influence public attitudes in Egyptian society. Such networks form an archipelago of censorship to control the general debate in public space by seeking to divide along moral lines the communal values of freedom and self-expression to even intrude into the realm of private desires. Contemporary photography in the Arabic MENA region has to navigate between the legacy of Orientalist representations and heteronormative structures of patriarchal power embedded in an authoritarian visual regime and propagated within the broader society. Only beyond these restraints can photography truly flourish and visual culture be enriched not only to speak for gender rights but also as part of a wider agency to develop local methods of egalitarian representation. The Western fixation with the hijab headscarf too often perceives it as a motif of female oppression and, in turn, to indicate religious piety or even fundamentalism. This reductive argument is seen in the Neo-Orientalist fad of 'Chador Art' (Bekhrad 2014: 55) in contemporary Western culture as it continues to fetishize and embolden the misreading of female representation in Muslim cultures.[21] Censorship has been used to arbitrate modernity for the public as it permeates within the private layers of Egyptian society where the image plays a key role in social debate on what is permissible. Arguably what is needed is a radical if not unimpeded critical discourse on visual culture issues to include the operations of the photographic and by this to moderate the effects of global image circulation. The mimetic qualities of the photographic medium, its indexical capacity and innate malleability in the digital realm make it a powerful candidate or symbol to underpin the debate on gender relations among the diverse cultures of Egypt. The motivation behind censorship can inform us of subjective expression because it also addresses creativity and notions of personal freedom. Given the glare of surveillance capitalism, hidden spaces and concealed corners can perhaps be a sanctuary to nurture new formations and decolonize from the dominant Western gaze in the history of photography; a lens which values of explicitness and self-exposure in a burden of representation in cultural politics.

Al-Mahdy's unreserved self-portrait is timely in this context because it was a photographic moment which crossed over cultural boundaries as her artistic motivation encountered the harshness of Egypt's social reality. When fantasy fuses with the physical world the consequences can be perilous because fantasy is an imaginative framework only or a type of projected screen to mediate our subjective existence. The violent reaction to her image in public space and online cultures, even during the revolutionary zeal of 2011, was not a rejection of images alone or her proclaimed brand of feminist politics per se. Moreover, her transgression was not in the right to compose this self-image in private, but the misjudgement to publish it online in public space as the image became too easily perceived as beyond the lived experience or concerns of most people in Egypt. Furthermore, the explicit nature of her homemade photograph became entangled with the hauntology of the odalisque symbol of Western-led iconography and differed from local notions of sexual seduction with its concealment of flirtation. It was her miscalculation to visualize this gap through her composition, pose and act that fell short of Arab feminist support and the revolutionary solidarity she strove to personify. Censorship of female images is seen by the regime as a public service, a necessary task to uphold the social fabric of the diverse nation. As al-Mahdy was to tragically discover visual representation has been trapped within the mythic vision of Egyptian nationalism, an imagined community and national family at the expense of other cultural narratives and marginalized identities.

These three different photographic case studies delineate how the female body is policed and suggests a broader cultural anxiety in the depths of the collective psyche. In the protests of 2011, Egypt, like Tunisia, saw street images of bare-chested male body protesters, receiving bullets and injuries in a sacrifice of selfhood as part of the political struggle where the body was political. Yet, al-Mahdy's body politics has not been celebrated because it pierced the nationalist myth narrative and the hypocrisy of gender politics; rather her photographic act embarrassed many local viewers, and it has seen as a national betrayal that triggered an abject sense of disgust in society. Censorship does not respect borders and disturbs individual identity, political systems and Egyptian social order and cultural values. Cultural theorist Marwan Kraidy insightfully comments on this disturbance of the collective psyche in his *Naked Blogger of Cairo*, 'Behind the insistence that all sexual matters must remain private lurked a fear of the abject, which characterizes our horror when we confront the threat of a collapse of the boundary between the self and the other' (Kraidy 2017: 55).

No criticism of body politics was directed towards the self-immolators Mohamed Bouazizi in Tunisia or Abdou Abdel-Monaim Kamal, a fifty-year-old restaurant owner and father of four from Ismailia who set himself on fire outside the parliament in Cairo a week before the 25 January uprising started. Rather, both figures were key to the revolutionary politics during 2011 and the radical, rebellious male bodies are accepted as symbolic martyrs in the public sphere, a space where women have limited access to political agency. In the discussion around women's corporeality many feminist scholars claim the same levels of emancipation and freedom of expression is not extended to female activists in regards to their own bodies during the 2011 protests (Bayat 2017; Hafez 2019; Korany and El-Mahdi 2012). Over the course of Egypt's cultural history in the twentieth century local woman skirted and provoked the social convention, especially through entertainment industries and at times in anti-colonial struggle, but their activism went largely unrecognized in a process of 'organised forgetting' (Hafez 2019: 184).

Though al-Mahdy never claimed to represent any section of Egyptian women and insisted she acted out problematically her own notion of individuality, her photographic performance was fused with the symbolism of Egypt in a female form, emerging in art and cultural spheres in nationalist movements of the early twentieth century.[22] King Faruq was overthrown in the popular rebellion led by the military in 1952 as political Islam grew as a social force, noticeably after Egypt's defeat by Israel in the 1967 War. Over the course of the twentieth century a new morality with a tinge of

Islamic piety permeated within the country as piousness became an increasing part of Egyptian modernity that constrained feminist expression among other indigenous traditions in rural areas. Al-Mahdy's volatile image opened up an abject abyss for many where unity and collectivist nationalism were weakened and, as Kraidy points out, this formed a deeply troubling association in the political flux of the time. In a sense, al-Mahdy's exposed body became redolent of another time of national embarrassment when Anwar Sadat's capitulation to Western hegemony in the peace treaty with Israel and his open-door economic strategies contributed to his assignation by Islamic extremists in 1981. Kraidy suggests that al-Mahdy was allegorical of Sadat as she represents an Egypt that is fully exposed, 'unprotected, denuded, an Egypt that has totally surrendered to western values, an Egypt that has moved too far from its putative authenticity' (Kraidy 2017: 182). The estranged photographic gesture of al-Mahdy is a stark counterpoint to the state as arbitrator of morality in the control of women's bodies; this takes on a visual role through the policing of book pages in photographic publications or by the violence of female protesters. As Hafez writes, 'women's bodies are enshrined in nationalist ideology as iconic subjects of the state's protection, [which] inversely legitimate the state as a governing [and disciplinarily] power' (Hafez 2019: 133). Extreme measures are enough to internalize discipline and cultural codes that are manifest in female communities' self-censoring visual depiction in the public sphere, as the adlat website of volunteer demonstrates graphically. Al-Mahdy may have mistaken premeditated undressing as part of a gender revolution in Egypt but her act did expose the limits of visual representation and, in turn, the interconnectivity of misogynist control systems focused on controlling the female body.

Chapter 6 looks at innovative photography in Egypt because this form of artwork responds to the subjectivity of gender representation and has been shaped by visual censorship over decades. Moreover, this form of creative photography remains outside of Egypt's mainstream media sphere and governmental control to enjoy a degree of autonomy in personal expression and thinking beyond the direct image object itself. This generation of photographic artists has emerged in the aftermath of the 2011 uprising and continues to produce and exhibit work within Egypt that examines cultural representation, identity and photographic cultures. Such work can be seen as indicative of an indigenous reimagining of the photograph in Egypt based on decolonial aesthetics that mediates between Western and local cultural traditions. The move to include art photography projects in this final chapter is a pertinent one because it enables a reflection on themes, historical phases, theories addressed in earlier chapters of the book. This involves decoloniality's specificity and singularity in relation to visual culture and these present-day photographic artists are shaped by colonial hauntology and how image politics can alter the perception of everyday life in Egypt. Such wide-ranging forces have influenced the work of Nadia Mounier and Ibrahim Ahmed who have chosen, in contrast to other peer artists, to set up a creative life in the challenging local setting as they embody the aims of decolonial aesthetics.

Notes

1 Swiss Rudolph Lehnert (1878–1948) and German Ernst Heinrich Landrock (1878–1966) formed a photographic business and produced a large archive of photography in the early twentieth century. They established a photographic business in Tunis around 1910 and after the First World War in Cairo. They listed themselves as postcard publishers rather than photographers, presumably so they could concentrate on the romanticized images of the region. Their output consisted of postcards, larger souvenir photographs for albums and reproductions in books. In 1930, Lehnert returned to Tunis, opening a studio independently. In 1985, over forty years after both men had retired, much of their collection of negatives were given to the Musée de l'Élysée in Lausanne, as well as the government taking over the Cairo studio to turn it into a bookshop. In addition, their work is available through auction houses and the bookshop in Cairo sells a selection of the archive as black-and-white prints from their work produced in Egypt. However, a less well-known part of the photographic output also included pornographic work of female and male subjects to satisfy the European market.

2 The odalisque (Turkish: *odalık*, room person) was a chambermaid or a female attendant in a Turkish *seraglio* or harem, in particular to assist the court ladies in the household of the sultan. Later this figure became eroticized by European travellers and depicted in romanticized paintings.

3 Nasir al-Din Shah (1831–1896) was well known for his interest in visual arts, in particular painting and photography. He was a talented painter and amateur photographer. Several of his pen and ink drawings survive and his extensive archive of photography documenting palace life is a unique visual record of the time. He established one of the first photography studios in Golestan Palace in 1863, and appointed one of his favourite court attendants, Aqa Riza Iqbal al-Saltana, to learn the techniques of photography. By the 1870s, the shah had at least three official photographers who accompanied him on his travels both inside and outside the capital. On his three trips to Europe (1873, 1878, 1890), the Persian ruler made entries in his diaries about his visits to well-known photographic studios. Part of the archive and photography made during this time is available in the Harvard University Library Archives.

4 Born into a Russian family of Armenian and Georgian origin, Antoin Sevruguin grew up in the region. Antoin took up photography to support his family and his brothers Kolia and Emanuel helped him set up a studio in Tehran. Because

he spoke Persian as well as other languages, he could communicate across the social strata and the shah employed him when he took up a special interest in photography.

5 Houris are beings in Islam, described in English translations as 'full-breasted companions of equal age', 'modest gaze' virgins of paradise.

6 Another case involved a high-profile Egyptian belly dancer, Sama El Masry, who was sentenced to three years in prison and fined 300,000 Egyptian pounds ($18,500) for 'inciting debauchery and immorality' as part of a crackdown on social media postings. She was arrested during an investigation into videos and photos on social media that the public prosecution described as sexually suggestive. The dancer, aged forty-two, denied the accusations, saying the content was stolen and shared from her phone without her consent.

7 Aliaa al-Mahdy is a prolific blogger, as her personal blog, A Rebel's Diary, dates from 2011 to 2021 with intermittent uploads of content.

8 Marwan M. Kraidy has written at length about the use and historical context of such violations of female bodies in Egypt and other Arabic MENA countries. In Egypt the violations were usually part of pre-marriage rituals performed by older women on a bride-to-be and were not discussed in public. However, in 2011, the military brutalized women in the infamous 'virginity tests', made famous by Samira Ibrahim's court case taken against the state. In late December 2011, a Cairo court ruled against the military, finding such human rights violations illegal and dismissed the authorities' claims that they served to protect soldiers from rape charges.

9 A graffiti mural consisted of a stencil of Samira Ibrahim and al-Mahdy's self-portrait; however, her modesty was intact as a long text covered her body. The text stated, 'Samira Ibrahim, twenty-five years old, nakedness and a virginity test in front of officers and soldiers were forced upon her, and she rejected that her story not be told, so she lodged a judicial complaint with the Egyptian judiciary. No interest … no notoriety … no media … no one answers. Aliaa al-Mahdy, twenty years old: she went naked and unveiled her body entirely of her own will, the public and the media rushed toward her, nearly three million people saw her picture, and there were no less than 50 articles and numerous television programs' (Kraidy 2017: 175).

10 The April 6 Youth Movement were at the vanguard of the 2011 uprising and are known for their leftist, socially progressive politics.

11 Femen is a self-proclaimed activist movement whose naked protests are highly controversial. The group regularly targeted Islamic organizations and culture in provocative and insensitive ways that can be seen as Islamophobic in character. One campaign saw Femen militants waging 'Topless Jihad' protests in Berlin, Brussels, Kiev and Milan. See https://femen.org/about-us/ (accessed 26 September 2023).

12 Surviving examples of explicit portraits of Arab women are rare but the Arab Image Foundation collection includes images of Egyptian actress Nadia Abdel Wahab, who asked local photographer Van Leo to capture her in eighteen different poses as she removed each article of her clothing. In the final

photographs, taken in 1959, she stands defiantly clad only in her underwear and high heels.

13 Sitt al-Banat, known as the Blue Bra Girl in English, was a young protester who was beaten by police on the streets and the images were captured by a local photojournalist Ahmed Gaber. Later the woman in the photograph was revealed to be political activist Ghada Kamal and she appeared on local television to talk about her experience.

14 Samira Ibrahim was highly controversial for taking legal action against doctors who carried out the so-called virginity tests on female protesters in Egypt during 2011.

15 The merit awards consist of many categories that reflect the dynamic range of the website. Some of the most contested merit badges include Special Themes, Best Member of the Year, Supervision, Order of Chef, Ideal Mother, Distinguished Writer, Photoshop, Special Administration and Support of Justice.

16 The archive of photographs was taken from a total of three publications: *Photographers A–Z* (Koetzle 2011), *100 Contemporary Artists* (Holzwarth 2009) and *The Photo Book: A History, Volume 1* (Badger and Parr 2004). Most images in the archive come from the first source, a Taschen compendium of mostly twentieth-century works arranged in biographical order. All of these books were available in limited numbers in branches of Diwan, a bookstore found across Cairo.

17 Many of the photographic artists in the books are well known, including Nobuyoshi Araki, David Bailey, David LaChapelle, Helmut Newton, Robert Mapplethorpe, Cindy Sherman, Irving Penn, Bert Stern, Larry Sultan, Mario Testino, Wolfgang Tillmans, Andy Warhol, Bruce Weber, Weegee and Garry Winogrand.

18 For instance, Michel Frizot's extensive compendium *The New History of Photography* contains only a handful of images from non-Western photographers and this excludes Arab practitioners despite their historical role in influencing the medium. Female Palestinian photographer Karimeh Abbud (1893–1940) is an example of a photographic artist from the region and other eminent photographers missing from the selection include Van Leo, a Cairo-based Armenian photographer who worked mainly as a studio portrait photographer. In recent years, the Arab Image Foundation in Beirut has saved the legacy of photography in the region and rewritten the historical narrative in this regard.

19 A selection of these book images is available in Close 2017.

20 In September 2017, Sarah Hegazy attended the anticipated concert in Cairo where the Lebanese band Mashrou' Leila, whose lead singer is openly gay, performed. She was photographed when she raised a rainbow flag as this act led to controversy and her eventual arrest. For more, see: www.al-monitor.com/originals/2020/06/egypt-sarah-hegazy-death-gay-rights-crackdown.html#ixzz7AIkkyN21 (accessed 26 September 2023).

21 Joobin Bekhrad has used the term when discussing Iranian female photographic artists such as Shirin Neshat and her *Women of Allah* series to state that this representation is 'somewhat Orientalist [in] nature, some have argued—featuring

women in chadors, veils, hijabs, and the like, with "exotic" supplements such as calligraphy' (Bekhrad 2014: 55). Ali Behdad states that there is an unevenness to the photography work produced in the Arabic MENA region, mostly dependent on the West, and persists today in the contemporary trend for 'chador art' (Behdad 2016: 167).

22 Nationalist movements in the late nineteenth and early twentieth centuries appeared to mimic Western arts; for instance, Delacroix's *Liberty Leading the People* (1830), including the use of the female form for political allegory. Mahmoud Mukhtar's sculpture Nahdat Misr (Egypt's Awakening) from 1920 consists of a female figure with her right arm resting on the head of a sphinx. The sculpture combines the sphinx with a peasant woman baring her body to invoke Egypt's past grandeur and modern liberation.

6

Contemporary lenses within Egypt

Seen and unseen storytelling

This chapter looks beyond previous visual case studies, which included popularist, vernacular and political image cultures, to focus on more intimate personal forms of visual narratives emerging from contemporary art photography practices. The dubious nature of the Egyptian state's interference into visual matters has altered, if not impeded for decades, the development of a sustainable homegrown art photography scene. Despite notable exceptions in the arts ecosystem many organizations and individual photo artists labour under harsh conditions to face state censorship, few professional opportunities and, in broad terms, the dominance of cisnormativity in cultural affairs that impacts on creative expression. Therefore, contemporary photographic art has developed in a rather uneven fashion and, to date, has not had quite the same presence in the region as, for instance, Lebanese visual art counterparts like Walid Raad or Akram Zaatari among other key cultural actors. Beyond the visual rush in the exceptional time of 2011, communities of photo artists have operated in more modest, low-key fashions without attracting the critical attention from global photo arts organizations, unlike their counterparts in Beirut's Arab Image Foundation.[1] However, despite this lack of critical framework within Egypt for young practitioners many photographic artists have still managed to create work of significance by finding nuanced forms of personal expression that instil a subjective, non-whole truth, be it through the poetic, abstract or allegorical approaches to visual culture. Such uses of photography have developed a distinctive form of subjective realism that fuses the imaginary or symbolic with the everyday to arguably connect photography with deep-rooted local sensibilities. This specific cultural force has become more commonly inferred in Arabic literature to be sometimes described in literature as 'magical dualism' (Ghazoul 1994), meaning a meta level exists in creative expression. This is type of literature uses indirect approaches of subjective experience in regard to personal narratives regularly underpinned by political and social constraints. Literature scholar Ferial Ghazoul has used the label to discuss the oeuvre of Egyptian poet Mohamed Afifi Matar, in order to suggest there is a divided self of inner and outer states, public and private environs where a vibrant creativity is alive and 'one finds on the one hand symbolist force and on the other a solid link to Egypt and to Arab and Islamic culture' (Ghazoul 1994: 13). This means what art is seen in public can seem restrained or abstracted and in Ghazoul's viewpoint connects with a tradition core that unifies the artist to the wider society. This contrasts with the modernist artist as exile in Western cultures where the artist is often estranged from broader forces.

The photographic artists in this chapter consist of a generation who have been impacted by such local traditions alongside the transformational potential of the 2011 uprising. In this way, their practices embody the separation of self in a complex discourse on belonging, representation, identity and decolonial aesthetics. The photography projects explored include the work of two unique contemporary image-makers indicative of this fragmented condition, Ibrahim Ahmed and Nadia Mounier. These artists are part of a generation who reimagine the local from within the society through the medium of photography and they use the image object as a way to mediate colonial pasts, forces of globalization, cultural capitalism and the heter-onormativity of mainstream society. In part they achieve this by working with decolonial aesthetic qualities of the locality alongside their own individual subjective gazes because the singular can transcend the specific. This enables a generation to emerge who have much to say about the state of the nation, challenge patriarchal power of the state apparatuses because the personal does become political; reminding one of the imagination's capacity to vibrate society in unseen, unfamiliar ways, in order to bring about new awareness. These visual artists present a current wave of Egyptian photographers who are looking both outwards and inwards; capturing life among the sprawling cities and turning the social world into the source of visions by exploring shifting identities and the traces of the colonial past. The photographic projects included in this chapter have been formed by their individual experience of creative life within Egypt and they turn the camera on themselves in a self-portraiture that constitutes an art process drawn from the local sensibility and is visible inside the country. Although many of this generation have taken up career opportunities abroad the two artists in this chapter have not become part of the cultural diaspora and the imprint of their practice continues to be in Egypt because it is a necessary part of their creative life. Others have advanced their art photography by working globally with institutions, particularly in Europe, North America and the Gulf, through exhibitions, commissions and publications to develop career opportunities outside of Egypt. However, in these cases the Egyptian artist becomes contextualized as Middle Eastern, losing something specific as their work is viewed in global centres while they participate in cultural production for the international art world industry.[2]

The photographic artworks in this chapter, in effect, are not embedded in the global channels of the cultural hierarchy and connect to what is significant for them within a more indigenous context. This delinking is an important part of their artistic strategies because, despite all the intrusions, restrictions and limits imposed on creative expression in Egypt, the meaning of visual art is mediated by the viewer. In this sense, the audience affects the reception of the artwork and a discourse opens from this encounter between photographer, image and viewer. The above-mentioned literary concept of 'magical dualism' (Ghazoul 1994) has been influenced by the preceding literary genre of 'magical realism' (Roh 1995) in order to articulate what can be thought of as a fractured lens or an imaginary signifier on local types of visual art works which are shown within the national setting. A recent feature in the journal *Photo Researcher* reconsidered Egypt's photographic heritage anew and an editorial discussed this turn in photography of and about the country:

> It [Egyptian photography] appears to be a fruitful investigation and a good time to look at this fascination, which we consider to be an ongoing, continuous one. Not only photographers turn to the cities and the landscapes, to deserted towns and proliferating new housing projects, as well as to the people and to the well-known and stereotypical sights. Today, scholars and artists with international backgrounds turn to the endless numbers of photographs of Egypt which are still being found in archives worldwide or create their own, outstanding, new imagery. (Stühlinger 2017: 2)

Each artist's body of work here echoes back to connect with earlier visual cases and chapter content by intersecting with concepts, themes and image theories discussed. This can be seen as a way to rethink cultural values that contrast with more dominant visual culture narratives and consider the singular qualities of Egypt's photographic heritage. Contemporary visual culture has been shaped by this recent generation over the last decade or so, and in contrast to other global contexts, the majority of non-commercial work produced is almost exclusively focused on human-centred topics. These more artistic strategies in photography can be seen in two contrasting ways as, firstly, to experiment with portraiture as a way to situate the self in relation to wider forces or, secondly, to address social issues head on through documentary practices,[3] in spite of grave personal risks for photographers working in social themes in Egypt. In light of this, topographical or architectural photography, among others, are not commonly represented and landscapes seem to be less attractive as a genre of visual expression or subject theme for many local Egyptian practitioners. Outside of some notable contemporary photographic artists,[4] few artists have direct their gaze towards the desert landscapes or reproduced industrial typologies with their cameras. This informs us on the local visual traditions through the use of the medium as topographics in Egypt remains dominated by the nineteenth-century colonial context, despite some notable contemporary exceptions. In contrast to the impact of the 'new topographics'[5] movement in the Western history of photography, Egyptian counterparts demonstrate scant interest in non-anthropomorphic subjects or topics for the medium. The dominance of visual representation in documentary and portraiture genres over others in the medium acknowledges the impact of Egypt's own history by drawing on its artistic heritage and vernacular culture, in order to reimagine the gaze rather than simply emulate other external ways of seeing. The urban lived environs and vast open indigenous landscapes are perceived differently to Western art photography traditions and the cultural imagination in Egypt is reconfigured around a particular visual ontology made through the camera lens. Furthermore, unlike their counterparts in the Western context, photographers work with a different notion of public space with its political limitations, economic controls and ideological coercion that are part of everyday life in contemporary Egypt.

The character of the photographic art and broader visual culture made, shown and seen within Egypt has been created under the proposition that personal expression intersects with the political to some extent. However, such a proposition can be suspicious to the state because ideas are subversive and meaning is complicated by the response of the public viewer in different contexts. The Egyptian state favours the contingency of the European *l'art pour l'art* approach because it persuades local artists to produce work that is not overtly if at all critical of the authoritarian regime. Therefore, the discourse on the true role or value of art, between a committed didactic meaning or more autonomous aesthetic position, is manifested beyond the theoretical context to be existential. The question of artistic strategies and decolonial aesthetic boundaries has been widely debated and there exists a sensitivity around the political role of art and whether there is or can be such a role for art to be part of political praxis. G. Frederick Hunter states, 'In a situation of social oppression and conflict, autonomy in art is not merely impermissible, it is impossible' (Hunter 1985: 41) because the repressive framework impacts on the self. Much of this debate in relation to the photographic image was explored by earlier theorists; Walter Benjamin presented the issue as both a political and aesthetic one in his 1937 essay, *The Author as Producer*. Alongside other critical Marxist perspectives on the left, namely Bertolt Brecht, these figures enunciated a common-held position that aesthetic autonomy is a mystified form of creativity, an art aura, at the expense of the ideological structural components of cultural production. Moreover, Benjamin applauded the demise of this aura in the photographic image in his influential *Work of Art in the Age of Mechanical Reproduction*.[6] Other criticisms suggest that a committed political artwork is, in fact, open to becoming consumed by the status quo that it sets out to attack or even the photographic image can aestheticize suffering instead of being a catalyst for foundational change in a society. However, in the context of contemporary photographic art in Egypt neither position can be essentially valid because the self intersects with the political through censorship. Furthermore, no matter how autonomous the creative process sets out to be contemporary art is contentious in the society where it is often perceived as morally dubious. As Jessica Winegar writes in *Creative Reckonings*, 'Most artists wanted to be true to themselves and their cultural background while pursuing a career in a field that was widely recognised to be a foreign import. They also wanted to be useful members of a society in which technology and science were valued over art' (Winegar 2006: 49). Aesthetic theories of Theodor Adorno are based in Kantian moral arguments to contrast autonomous art with committed artworks, in keeping with other renowned thinkers in the Western canon. As such this may not be fully applicable and pertain to the local context of Egypt where societal values, cultural traditions and coercive censorship are navigated on a daily basis by local art photographers. Adorno's critique of committed artworks argues that by aligning itself with social or political causes, an artwork can lose its ontological determination which is, for Adorno, a duty to the singularity of artistic creation. As he noted in his final book, *Aesthetic Theory*, first published posthumously in 1970, 'If art tried directly to register an objection to the gapless web, it would become completely entangled' (Adorno 2013: 133). But the ontology of the photographic image can be seen through the phenomenological lens as the experience of the perceiving self that intersects with the web of social forces. A viewer sees pictorially a photograph differently because of neural factors[7] and as it is made up of referents that can have different kinds of intent, correlated to different kinds of objects. As Robert Sokolowski simply points out, 'taking something as a picture is different from taking something as a simple object' (Sokolowski 2000: 12). Despite the digital destabilization of the image and the uncertainty surrounding the analogue photograph, technological transformation or advancements are not the same as progress in photographic literacy and visual cultures. In a sense, the contemporary photographic image is a simulacra, an appearance of an object, without necessarily possessing its substance or full properties; as Jean Baudrillard suggested it is a process in 'the successive phases of the image'[8] (Baudrillard 1994: 6). However, despite the estranged realities of postmodernity, social relations and connections are created by the image process and its dissemination requires time and patience from the viewer to restore depth to ontological categories.

The empirical relationship between the art producer and audience is encountered through the artwork event which contains coded messages for a viewer with the potential for an awareness to come about of cultural structures and ideologies at large. In the Egyptian context, the same artwork may appear to be wholly driven by an autonomous creative impulse with no clear specific political ends. Therefore, a duality in the art object can be difficult to recognize at first as meaning is conveyed through sometimes enigmatic signifiers to a non-local audience and the artwork awaits the subjectivity of the viewer to complete the communication loop. As the photography case studies in earlier chapters have shown (Figures 4.1 and 5.1) the visual can have a disruptive effect on a bourgeois audience. Moreover, debate on the aura around photographic images can also serve political ends, notably seen in nationalist renewal or even fascism during volatile periods in twentieth-century history in the opposition to British rule (Figure 3.1). It is this type of one-dimensionality of the photographic image as deployed in Egypt that poses the greatest threat to any readings of the medium, a domain in which capitalism has been nourished at the expense of emancipation. The most convincing subversive property of autonomous art can be its marginality, that is, its detachment or decentring from the ideological in mainstream entertainment. The status of photographic art is found in the synergy between the specificity of place and the subjectivity of artistic creation as singular entity. Political concerns and artistic autonomy can converge in substance and form and are not differentiated spheres of discourse in Egypt due to the intrusive nature of the state and other key actors. Awareness of military authoritarianism rarely occurs through didactics alone and autonomous photo art practices may seem non-political at first glance, but on a second look what emerges to the audience is shaped by an internal perspective that brushes up against censorship in this cultural context.

There exists a certain duality in photographic art practices as the being of the human subject in the camera frame, through poses, gestures and expressions, acts out more than the self and permeates the social fabric in a new politics of looking (Ranciére 2011). This echoes in earlier experiments with modernity in Egyptian visual history through perspectivalism and chronotopes, and it is central to the cultural mediation of the medium. The local photographic idiom is beyond one indexical origin that fixes the body in a set time and place; rather, the body subject is allegorical on the visual surface of the image. In somewhat similar terms, Christopher Pinney discusses the interchangeability of cultural properties in the case of Indian photography when he states, 'photography is concerned with the body as a surface that is completely mutable and mobile, capable of being situated in any time and space' (Pinney 2003: 211). The field of spatio-temporal uncertainty is indifferent to the schism between the subject and object, image and the world, and prefers to embrace other scopic regimes that break with the rational, the Cartesian perspective in the representational zone. Thinking of the photographic image as a composite layering is a mindset, a fluidity delinked from the fixed indexical stance of Western art history. This responds to the encounters with modernity through photography that have been part of the hauntology of Egypt's colonial past to ascertain its own cultural autonomy in decolonial futures.

The artistic strategies and bodies of work made by the two photographic artists Nadia Mounier and Ibrahim Ahmed are developed in this chapter because they have gone a long way to mediate the burden of the past and cultural legacies in the regimes of vision. These photographic artists have formed imaginary realms to dissolve reality and transform what the image describes because they flourish within the vernacular cadences of life in Egypt. Both artists are part of a broader generation who constitute a deep look into the reality of the everyday in order to transcend its specificity in singular reconciliation. Literary critic Luis Leal had made observations on magical realism to suggest that it 'discovers what is mysterious in things, in life, in human acts' (Leal 1995: 121). The photographic work of these cultural producers, Mounier and Ahmed, is distinctive by their decolonial aesthetic treatment of the photographic image and artistic processes anchored inwards in a gaze that addresses the specificity of the local over the general. In different ways both have made the conscious decision to remain in Egypt despite the regular impediments of their creative expression and career development. They position their visual art in the local cultural context for a predominantly local audience to remain committed to a distinctive artistic vision, and by this they delink from the dominance of the Western canon of photographic history.

Staging the self in portraiture

Nadia Mounier (b. 1988) is a photographic artist and curator who graduated from the public university in Helwan, Cairo, in 2010, and completed a postgraduate programme in visual studies at MASS, Alexandria, an independent arts space in Egypt. Mounier opened her first solo exhibition, *I Will Defend Myself* (2017), in the Contemporary Image Collective, and has been included in prestigious group exhibitions both in Egypt and abroad. She has been awarded prominent residency programmes and international fellowships, including the Akademie Schloss Solitude, Stuttgart, Germany, in

2018. Mounier is based in Cairo where she is active in various art collectives in the city, works as a programme manager at al-Mu'assasa al-'Arabiyya li-l-Ta'bir al-Raqami (Arab Digital Expressive Foundation) and contributes to the local photographic culture through exhibitions, curation projects, workshops, lectures, collaborative research and teaching photography. Her diverse visual experiments with female representation through photographic images often includes self-portraiture, as she explores aspects of social coercion, self-censorship, re-enactment roles and performativity. As a photographic artist for over ten years she has produced a creative portfolio of photo-based projects that examine the roles, uses and dissemination of the photographic image by drawing on her lived experience as a woman and mother in Egyptian society. Her expansive approach to photography has involved producing work through modes of collaboration and collective processes, regularly as part of alternative art and educational programmes; informal types of learning spaces which sustain a vibrant cultural ecosystem beyond governmental interference. In her more recent work, Mounier has investigated how the pictorial representation of women in vernacular photographic culture functions in both public settings and private contexts. One of her notable iterations is the project *Was That Really You?* (2016–2022), which looks into the status of the female image in the Arab world. Part of this involved a series of staged self-portraits where she draws on the visual aesthetics of censorship and image manipulation in order to reflect on heteronormativity and gender perception.

In her self-portraiture Mounier reveals the ideological structures in the policing of the female body in both photographic cultures and in the real-life experience of Egypt. Through her meticulous research process, she reviews found images from wide-ranging sources such as amateur archives, family albums, magazines, newspaper, postcards, social media platforms, commercial advertising and stock photography agencies. Her visual research moves between different contexts, often pairing, juxtaposing and reordering the image materials as a way to read into their aesthetics conventions, which she then weaves into the gestures and motifs of her *mise en scène* photographic compositions. She pays particular interest to forms of dramatization of the self, personal expression and self-censorship as she switches between the female roles of image consumer, model and producer. In her most recent series of self-portraits she reflects on aspects of her own gender-based performativity that inevitably arises with having one's image taken, rarely being asked and being looked at no matter how private or intimate the scene may seem. She creatively plays out her own relationship to photography, in front of and behind the camera in which her self-image is regulated by the perceptions of the society that are reflected back when the images are seen in public.

Mounier's staged self-portrait project *Was That Really You?* has been included in the visual art exhibition *Istihdar al-ghiyab* (Retrieving Absence)[9] at the Contemporary Image Collective in June 2022. The portrait series was made over the last few years and is based on Mounier's own family album photographs. As she selects images to develop, she reflects on comments from the family about the snapshots as a way to foreground the subjective construction memory. She writes down these memorial traces to compose a narrative as she stated in an interview, 'I write it like diary, from past conversations and memory' (Artist Interview, 15 May 2022). She edits these memory fragments into a short, concise text that is placed on the photographic surface to act as her own personal narrative history to thread between memory and the image on the visual skin of the photograph. The portrait series in the exhibition consisted of eight framed colour photographs of different restaged family photos accessing her own memories of albums, which refer to vernacular snapshots of her parents and siblings on outings. She appears in all the images taking the protagonist's role, acting out one of her family members or her younger self; she acts as the new narrator in the photographic imagination to take on daydream characters with uncanny, strange qualities. Most of the image works in the series include such a text in Arabic, printed in a light-red colour, which has been placed over the image, and the length of the writing varies from one work to the other. This textual addition has been handwritten by the artist and transferred to silkscreen to be printed onto the photograph. In this way, each photographic edition has singular, analogue quality, because each silkscreen print turns out slightly different each time as the colour, density, thickness of line can vary. Each iteration builds up the expressive properties of text and image and, by using the silkscreen process, this connects with a long-standing tradition in modern art history. Other well-known visual artists working on female Muslim identity, such as the iconic artist Sherin Neshat[10] or Lalla Essaydi,[11] are celebrated for the use of Farsi and Arabic calligraphy in the photographic image. However, they have very different intentions that can arguably over-aestheticize the visual materiality of the photographic image. The calligraphy in Neshat's work and Essaydi's painterly photography successfully utilize the visual qualities of the Arabic language to great effect as the text is layered and re-layered on the female figure; albeit in a fragmented narrative with extracts of text repeated, edited from wide-ranging sources. These highly visual practices use calligraphy in a limited way to often remain unread and can be obstruse with no clear written narrative meaning available for the viewer. As Islamic studies scholar Danielle Widmann Abraham has written for an exhibition publication on Essaydi's work in the United States, 'The women in Essaydi's images are draped with words whose meanings are not transparent' (Abraham 2014: 42). In contrast, Mounier's photographic work deploys the same handwritten touch of Arabic text but differs in approach from these more stylized artworks and contrasts with the flamboyant visuality of Neshat or Essaydi. Rather, in Mounier's work is rooted in an almost anti-aura aesthetic, and another key difference is how the text is meant to be read carefully by the viewer in order to create another, second mental image alongside the visual image composition. The silkscreen Arabic text on top of her photograph can be read as akin to the artistic narrative to introduce a certain tactile quality to the re-enactment of her intimate image.

In Mounier's project *Was That Really You?* the body of work consists of eight different family moments reproduced for the Cairo exhibition through self-portraiture with two from the series most notable in interpretation, composition and concept. The two images in question involve Mounier recreating snapshots of her own father who travelled widely to leave behind a personal collection of artefacts and images of his experiences within and outside of the family circle. There is a sense of absence in the work that has been magnified by the fact he passed away at a young age, subsequently leaving a melancholia legible in the staged photographs. Her autofiction approach draws on the biographical details to compound the visual and textual languages together in a creative portrayal of the father–daughter relationship that can resonate with the public through its broader family values. As Mounier discussed in an interview with the author, this portrait project constitutes elements of performativity of her own personal history:

> Photography helps me to show some things that I wouldn't show in reality. I really enjoy it, like playing this scene. So, posing in front of the camera, just creating photos. But then I feel like that once it's taken, once it's detached like this, it's actually not me in a way. This moment that it's frozen and then I let it go, it's just it's not me. (Artist Interview, 15 May 2022)

The portrait image (Figure 6.1) involves a simple composition: the artist reclines on an anonymous white single bed, as if set in the liminality of a characterless hotel bedroom space. Her re-enactment draws on the original image of her father, taken during a work trip, as she mimics his pose to look into the camera lens to meet the viewer's stare directly. She is dressed in his clothes, black trousers and matching short black jacket with a lined colourful shirt underneath, reminiscent of a 1980s throwback fashion garment. In the composition she is propped up by a pillow resting underneath her shoulders as her left hand appears to support the head in an uncomfortable but still natural-looking pose. The camera shot is vernacular in composition with the frame cropped at the knees and an unlit cigarette is held in her left hand with a gold watch on the arm, which is just about to slip down inside the jacket sleeve, its clock face is half sunken like a sun setting on

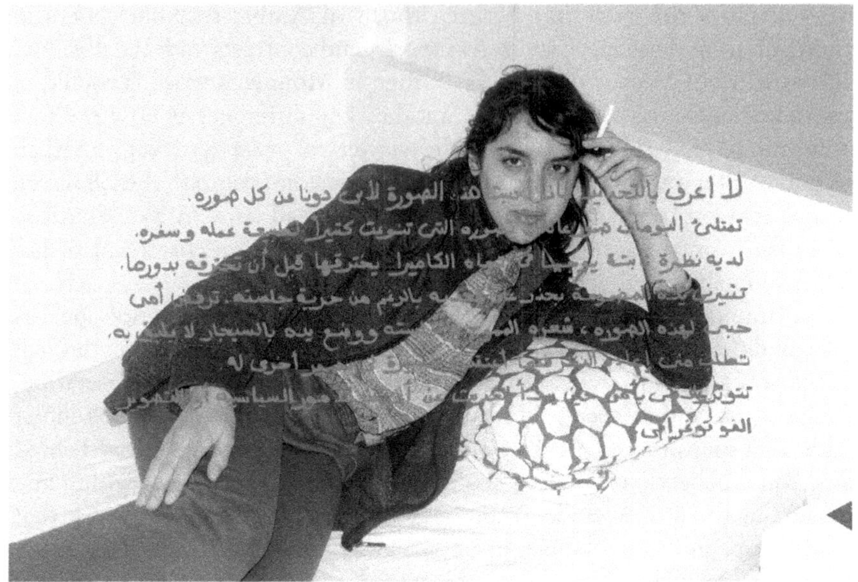

Figure 6.1 Nadia Mounier, *Was That Really You?*, 2022

the horizon. Indeed, the watch is a family heirloom and did belong to her father to be an important motif symbolizing time itself for the viewer, both between the original and the re-enactment time, and as a reminder of the chronotropic effect. In the image Mounier stares back blankly to the viewer, the facial expression unsmiling with a slight hint of recognition in the facial expression. This photographic act is a haunting portrayal of a person who looks confidently at the external world. Mounier is engrossed in this gender of her father as she appears content and self-assured in this role. The block of text on the photograph is in light red with neatly handwritten Arabic and printed across the image surface in seven horizontal lines, interrupting but not preventing the visual aspects of the image to be appreciated; the text is positioned to meet the face from the nose down and not block eye contact. The right hand rests on the knee joint, the pose is curved, as the body rests on the side for comfort. Yet this pose was composed for the staged photograph and only mimics the off guard candid moment that is a key element of snapshot vernacular realism.

The handwritten text across the image surface is a short paragraph acting as another narrative reading of the self-portrait itself.[12] However, the text is Mounier's deep emotional voice and connection to this particular image of her father, in ways echoing *camera lucida*'s memory argument on the subjective potentiality of vernacular photographs; like Barthes the artist does not include the original image for comparison in the artwork. From the text we learn that her affection for the image is not shared by her mother, who is disturbed by it and her daughter's fascination with it, as the artist states in the handwritten text, 'My relationship with my mother tenses up when the conversation turns to politics or photography' (Artist Interview, 15 May 2022). The text reads like an inner voice of the artist as the protagonist, calculating the inevitable tension with her mother against the emotional compulsion to reconnect with an absent father through the re-enactment process. Mounier places herself in an imaginative performance space to play-act being a father while accessing the narrative layers in her own subjective memory. The family relationships can be a way to deepen the discourse on portraiture itself, as she states, 'I think the way that I was raised to like and see photography and visuals really influenced my way of seeing, how I look' (Artist Interview, 15 May 2022). Indeed, her self-portraiture process is a somatic knowledge of the body and family heritage, acted out and performed in the memorial narration that relinks with the past, the what has been, to invoke absence, as the photographic image sits between memory and the self.

A second image (Figure 6.2) from the same portrait series, *Was That Really You?*, sees the artist again in the role of her father, but this time re-creating an earlier vernacular image from his youth before marriage. Mounier became mesmerized by the original image, if not haunted by its interruptive presence in the family album. This portrait is based on an image of her father with a group of his male friends on a visit to Cairo and he is represented as a much younger man before marriage, before he started a family and took up his maritime profession on cargo ships. The artistic re-enactment composition differs from the original in many regards as Mounier poses alone in an empty room, separated from the group of friends, and this time, the setting is the domestic home environment to contrast with the open-air park space of the original image. In this remake the wooden floor is actually plastic, a large green plant in the corner is also fake and Mounier is dressed in white to formulate this interpretation of the original photograph as the motifs combine to replace its details. She reclines on a green mattress, instead of the garden grass, but copies her father's pose accurately and sports neat matching white trousers and shirt with an elegant pink tie; again she looks into the camera lens with a dead-pan look. The green objects, mattress and plant refer to the natural location in the original social image in a public garden, as Mounier inhabits the male persona again fully to most authoritatively take on the character of her father, at a formative time in his life.

The handwritten text uses the same pink ink colour aesthetic and, as before, has been silkscreened onto the image surface by hand; however, the

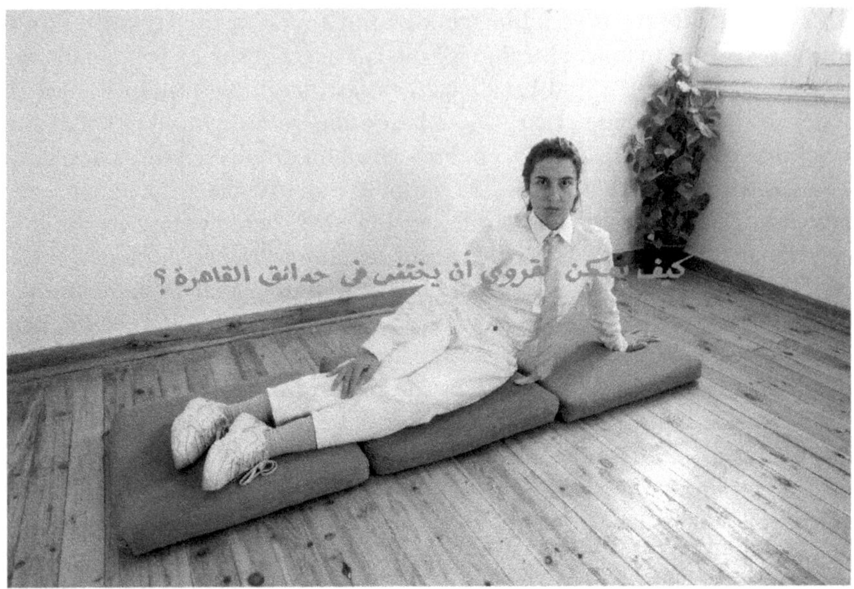

Figure 6.2 Nadia Mounier, *Was That Really You?*, 2022

narrative this time around is reduced to a short single line. The enigmatic Arabic sentence reads *Kayfa yumkin li-qurawi an yakhtafi fi hada'iq al-qahira?* (How can a villager disappear in the gardens of Cairo?) and the text is placed directly in the centre of the composition. This shorter handwriting on the image surface creates a tension in the portrait to reflect an equilibrium between image and text, and allows for a more substantive synergy between the two narrative elements. In the previously mentioned first self-portrait in the series, a longer written text was used, and therein became more independent from and separate to the visual, with its own mental image produced in the mind. Text and image are processed differently as interlinked but separate narratives, one photo based, the other text based. As such, communication is twofold as the viewer takes in the visual image first, and then latterly reads the text. However, in this second staged photo work from the series, Mounier's use of a much shorter text means this self-portrait is taken faster as the visual and textual are processed in one take, with key words standing out in this revisioning of her father's life. This time the text alludes to, in a more poetic fashion and indirect way, the role the metropolis of Cairo plays in the social, political and economics of internal migration within Egypt. The population growth of Egypt has been staggering, in particular since the inception of the Arab republic under Nasser, as the text on the image infers not only the biographical but the possibility of new-found social mobility, the allure of the big city and its dream of Egyptian modernity set against the arcane rigid social structures of rural life. The words 'villager' and 'disappear' are key signifiers in the sentence to the process of personal reinvention and tell us much of the shimmer and lure of modernity under nationalism. Mounier has recast herself in the role of her father at a time of his own personal discovery and the possibility of change in an image of youthful hope. Her father's aspirations framed by the original photograph intersect with Mounier's own autonomy as an artist, exploring her creativity through her autofiction form of photo-narrative biography.

Mounier's self-portrait approach consists of restaged photography, based on vernacular images, along with text narratives composed from the artist's memories, family stories and conversations about her father. The use of image and text on the same pictorial space forms different types of images for the viewer; the photograph has a materiality and the text another through the Arabic-language meaning. These layered self-portraits depend on the act of viewing and reading; for an Arabic speaker this is a decolonial aesthetic gesture, forming a second mental image for the viewer that encodes the visual. This dichotomy of the mental image and the physical is one of the intriguing properties of Mounier's photographic artwork as the external and internal perspectives transform and collide. The nature of such text images appears to 'intersect in the no man's land between semiotics and aesthetics, somewhere in between the conceptual realm of the signs and the aesthetic domain of the senses' (Gori 2017: 41). What images are is less obvious than may seem and can be thought of as a 'family of images' (Mitchell 1986: 17), the image realm where connected material and immaterial entities coexist. Mounier's self-portraits bring together this verbal component with the pictorial in a mental process that was formed in her own autofiction practice and reaches out to the subjectivity of the viewer. Art historian W. T. J. Mitchell[13] has written extensively on how visual culture intersects with philosophy, semiotics and aesthetics in regard to the plurality of what an image can be in his influential *Iconology: Image, Text, Ideology*, where he comments, 'Mental images don't seem to be stable and permanent the way real images are, and they vary from one person to the next' (Mitchell 1986: 14). Mounier has significantly avoided the use of calligraphy as the textual component because of its inherent decorative quality as her decolonial aesthetic requires the viewer to read the text at length. Here the visual and textual are in an equilibrium of meaning through the intersectionality of image types; the visual photography and the mental one created by reading. It may be considered that the family of images can also encounter an image of family as she composes a self-portrait of what can be seen, what is unseen, to balance out the inner life and outer performativity of gender roles with what has been of the photographic medium. As she states in an interview:

> I just think that it's also a recognition of another photo that maybe we have in our minds. I want to look sexy or to be looked at differently. What is in my mind, our minds, as if there is an archive of how a woman should look like in photography. You open a folder in your mind and you bring one out. (Artist Interview, 15 May 2022)

Mounier's work is specific to Egypt in many ways through its exploration of the family, one of the foundational pillars of the culture and, in particular, by focusing on the father figure who is emblematic of nationhood. However, this project work is more than straight photography as the image is not enough alone and as in the case of other image-makers from the Global South, the image surface is not a fixed space but one in motion with aesthetic opportunity (Pinney and Peterson 2003). Through this she shares much with the next body of work in this chapter that also can be understood as an autofiction visual narrative. Ibrahim Ahmed's photomontages are an exploration of the self by using allegorical approaches and moves away from the indexical reading of the medium.

Analogue ruptures and surface tensions

Artist Ibrahim Ahmed (b. 1984) spent his childhood living between Bahrain and Egypt before his family moved to the United States when he was a teenager. In 2014, he made the decision to move to Egypt and to set up a life in the informal neighbourhood of Ard el-Lewa in Giza,[14] on the east side of metropolitan Cairo. Ahmed's creative practice consists of producing artworks in different media as he moves between fabric-based sculpture, painting, video and more recently photomontage. Although these artistic outcomes can differ in material form, medium and scale, there are common concerns and ideas explored through the art practice to address the issues of masculinity, colonial legacies and gender identity in the representation of the self. His extensive exhibition record over the last decade includes solo shows in Tintera, Cairo (2021); Institute for Contemporary Art (ICA), Richmond, Virginia (2021); Sara Zanin Gallery, Rome (2018); Gallery Nosco, Marseille (2018); and Townhouse Gallery, Cairo (2016), among others. His work has been included in group exhibitions, including the Sharjah Art Museum, Dakar Biennial, Havana Biennial, Biennale Internationale de Casablanca and Bamako Encounters African Biennale of Photography. In 2020, he was shortlisted for the Emerging Photographer of the Year Award in Photo London and his work is held in collections such as the Museum of Old and New Art in Hobart, Australia. His studied English literature at Rutgers University, New Jersey, and although his background was not in visual art, he had an informal art education when he worked as an art handler in New York City after graduation.

Somewhat uncharacteristic of his artist counterparts and broader generation, Ahmed made the decision to return to Egypt from the United States and this has influenced the course of his art career as he became linked to, in a deeper sense, the cultural traditions of his homeland. The new-found space he occupies is enriched by everyday life in Ard el-Lewa as his practice inverts the movements of the cultural diaspora and his artworks are embellished rather than inhibited by his surroundings. However, in certain regards, Ahmed does remain an outsider, an Egyptian exile in Cairo; in spite of regular summer family holidays there, his upbringing in Bahrain and particularly the United States mark a gap between him and his homeland. In an interview he refers to the nature of his identity divide as part of his autobiographical narrative:

> Seventeen years in the States, thirteen years in Bahrain, in a British school. And really, I was deeply indoctrinated in a lot of these ideas, colonial indoctrination, in this foreign school was all this stuff. I was completely internalizing Orientalized ideas of myself. (Artist Interview, 25 November 2021)

At its core Ahmed's photography practice involves the playful manipulation and transformation of materials through the everyday influences and encounters which shape life in this working-class area of Giza, where he lives and works. Through art production he reflects on the notions of cultural authenticity, the fluidity of male identity and the reproduction of self, as his creative research links with local histories, everyday objects and materials. The Egyptian state has harassed informal neighbourhoods like Ard el-Lewa, and it can be seen as symptomatic of marginalized communities in Egypt across the Global South.[15] Ahmed has found a home in this local environment and felt a sense of familiarity, in part, because of his own transnational background as someone who grew up outside of his homeland, but does not belong in a complete sense to any particular place. Ahmed first crossed the threshold of Ard el-Lewa when he took up the offer of an artist residency programme in the area in 2014, organized by local artist Hamdy Reda.[16] Through this residency experience Ahmed became so fascinated by the area he was inspired to abandon his other travel plans and relocate to this peripheral edge of the Egyptian megacity.

The personal decision to relocate to Egypt would open up the artist to explore his identity and sense of belonging that has informed his practice since. One of his most visceral cases and intimate artworks is a textile-based sculpture which encapsulates the paradox of his autobiographical position and his current relationship to this locality. The fabric artwork, *Does Anyone Leave Heaven?* (2019) (Figure 6.3), is a large-scale tapestry, ten by four meters, and is made up of the US flags that adorn clothing and other textile products sold in Egypt which the artist noticed in street markets. Ahmed removed this national emblem from the various garments, clothing, bags and miscellaneous items that are, most often, designed to appeal and hail young men. He then set about weaving them together and involved local tailors in the process to produce a cutting visual commentary on cultural imperialism and the ubiquitous nature of this flag across the world. The artwork points towards the symbolic dominance of Western imagery in the Global South and the contemporary allure of emigration out of Egypt, in particular for youth populations. The origin of the artwork and the title came about through conversations with young males in the area who would ask Ahmed about his decision to leave the United States. It seemed incongruous to most of them, who are set on leaving Egypt for North America or Europe, because wealthy Western countries represent to them unbridled personal freedoms or financial opportunities, as the artist states in an interview with the author: 'Cairo is a place to escape and the USA is a place to dream about' (Artist Interview, 15 May 2022). The textile artwork was first installed in a narrow street in the area, hung between houses, and later exhibited widely in international art galleries and institutions. In one particular exhibition outing, as part of the 13th Havana Biennial in Cuba, he was surprised to be asked to alter or remove the artwork altogether because of its material criticism of cultural hegemony. A report in the American monthly women's fashion magazine *Harper's Bazaar* over the controversy cited the co-curator José Fernandez's justification for the exclusion of his work from the event: 'the government cannot be seen actively presenting an artist who is directly criticising the US. We have a complicated relationship with the US, and we can't be seen promoting this sort of work' (Nour El Din 2019). Such state censorship was surprising even for an artist coming from Egypt and the reaction to the tapestry was unusual given the antagonistic history and ideological differences between the Cuban regime and the US government. In the end, the textile artwork was removed by the organizers and as a response Ahmed took dozens of photographs of Cubans wearing the American flag as part of their own clothing or attire; he later included this street photography with the sculpture tapestry in subsequent installations. The censorship reaction of the Cuban state does demonstrate the visceral effect art can have to critique hegemonic structures and an awareness of Western cultural dominance by reusing an ideological part of everyday clothing pervasive across the globe. In an author interview, Ahmed discussed his own difficult relationship to the United States and his life experiences there:

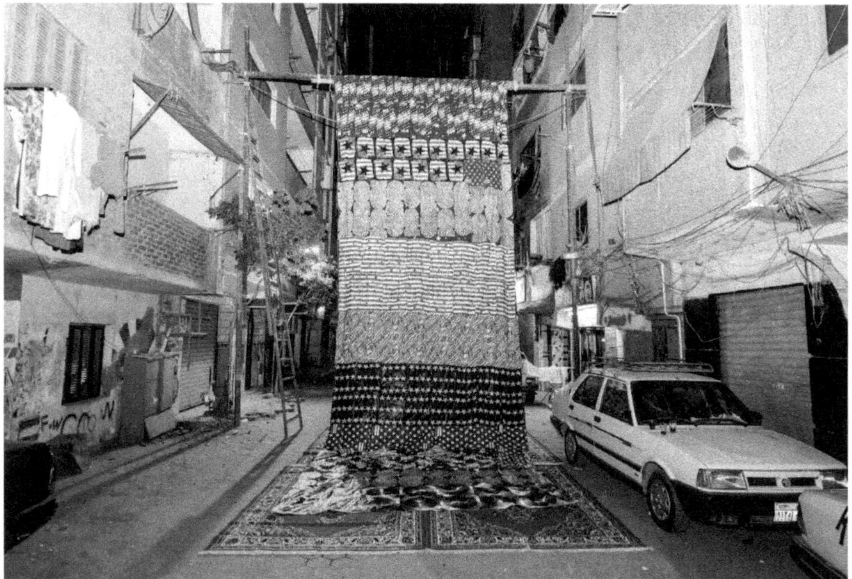

Figure 6.3 Ibrahim Ahmed, *Does Anyone Leave Heaven?*, 2019

I left because of the intensity of racism. I couldn't handle any more. I think being in Egypt again allowed for me to just be. In the context of the United States, if you're not white, it's really hard to just be. (Artist Interview, 15 May 2022)

His use of the photographic medium emerges from his creative background with textiles, sculpture and painting as part of his fine art practice. A photographic image is often presumed to be the end result of a process but in Ahmed's case the photograph is used as a starting point, a material like any other as part of a creative labour that involves cutting, slicing, juxtaposing various images in a montage. Although such types of art practices are seen, in general terms, as within Western avant-garde contexts, the Egyptian artistic movement Jamaʿat al-Fann wa-l-Hurriyya (Art and Liberty Group) (1938–1948) provides another alternative genealogy of decolonial aesthetics. This group's use of photography synergized with the local heritage and traditions to include distortion, double-exposure, photomontage and other creative image approaches to visualizing the inner space of the subconscious. The art historian Amina Diab has written on the group's aesthetic origins:

Art and Liberty's search for an Egyptian soul, in its Pharaonic, Islamic or Coptic heritage, points to the group's peculiar vanguardism – or rather, it's consistent search for local relevance – since avant-garde movements typically express a break with all past traditions. (Diab 2021: 59)

Therefore, image manipulation has a local resonance in the visual traditions of Egyptian art, in both contemporary and historical contexts, as Diab suggests the surreal qualities of Pharaonic imagery (animals on human figures) or the geometric abstraction of Islamic art have reverberated through global visual cultures. Writing for Ibraaz on the Groupe Art et Liberté art curator Alexandra Stock pointed out that art international movements merged with older Egyptian influences, to suggest that 'they forged universalism with Egyptian-ness so as to present themselves as universal precisely because they were local' (Stock 2015). Moreover, it could be argued that the history of art, especially through modernist movements, has been influenced by global aesthetics, such as African masks and Pharaonic visual expression (Drewal 2013). In this light, Ahmed's photomontage work is not an unfounded aesthetic import in Egypt; rather, it is his use of local cultures that is significant in a formal sense. Moreover, a key value lies in the specificity of the modes of production based in Ard el-Lewa and, combined with his own autobiographical narrative, are fused into a unique type of fragments of self-expressive portraiture. Over a period of five years he has produced four interlinked photomontage series which share an overall sense of liminality in the performance of masculinity, as Ahmed explores his own identity by using family images as part of his studio photography. The final photomontages form a fragmented vision of the self and consist of four types of iterations, namely: *To Gaze at a Moving Target* (2022); *Some Parts Seem Forgotten* (2020–2021); *Quickly but Carefully Cross to the Other Side* (2020–2021); *You Can't Recognize What You Don't Know* (2020–2021). Each series ruptures, in different inventive ways, photographic surfaces to disrupt linear time through a refracted lens and these works have featured prominently in two solo exhibitions, *I Never Revealed Myself to Them* (2021) at Tintera, Cairo, and *It Will Always Come Back to You* (2021) at the ICA, Virginia.

The self-portraiture series *You Can't Recognize What You Don't Know* (Figure 6.4) is made up from individually produced analogue black-and-white print photomontages and each work starts out with the artist posing in a photo studio location. The space is reminiscent of the vernacular charm of the portraits by Mali photographer Malick Sidibé; a strong single light is used from above, casting a dark shadow behind the figure, and the backdrop varies from one image to the next as each *mise en scène* includes sparse props on the bare concrete floor. The spotlight comes from above the figure and the harsh textures appear to suggest liminal if not abandoned spaces, trapped if not confined in a windowless chamber. The photo studio appears makeshift, and a local photographer was hired to shoot the self-portraits of Ahmed during his performance. One particularly intriguing photomontage in the series is the image entitled *Figure#85* (Figure 6.5). Here the artist poses with his gaze lowered to look at the floor, as he stands on a cement

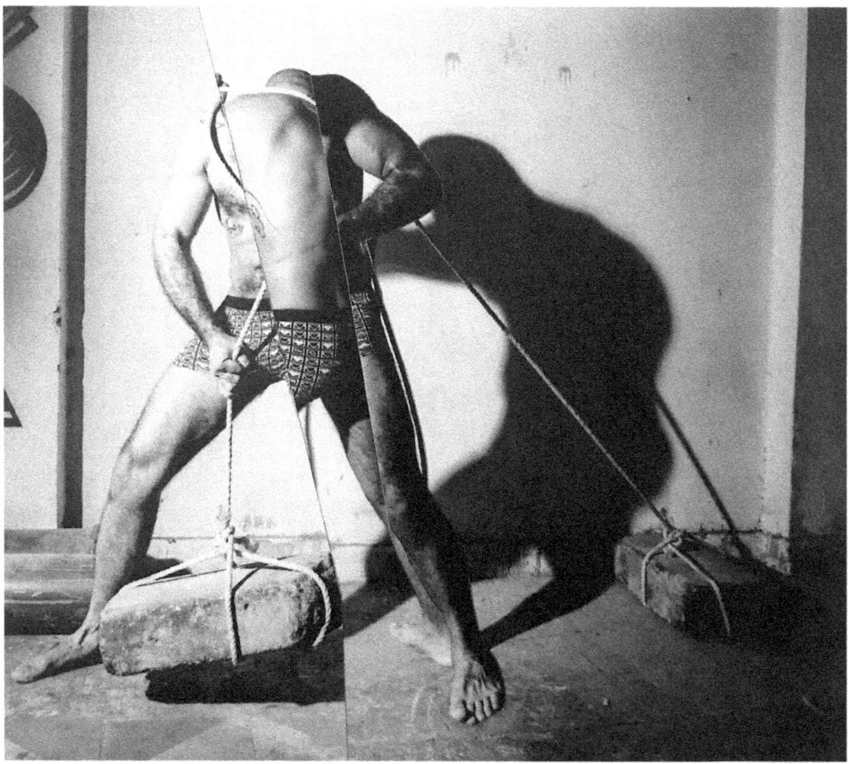

Figure 6.4 Ibrahim Ahmed, *Figure#21, You Can't Recognize What You Don't Know*, 2019–2020

block, holding a rope that is tied around the concrete cube. He appears wearing only male shorts with small 'love' hearts printed in a grid pattern on the underwear garment which he bought in local street markets. He is positioned in the centre of the square format frame and his body is muscular and toned with two tattoos visible on his torso; a five-pointed star on his right shoulder, and midway on his chest on the left side the Arabic word *ruhiyya* (soul) drawing on tattooing traditions of the rural Nile Delta where his family come from. This male figure fills the frame and apart from the concrete block the composite photomontage also includes the motif of five pyramid-like shapes on the white backdrop, some partially cropped in the composition. The studio façade has a bare theatrical feel, in a way reminiscent of the well-known studio photographer Van Leo and other Cairene celebrity photographers; however, this time around the lighting and space lacks their commercial gloss. The raw aesthetic in the self-portrait *Figure#85* is a composite of four poses and the photos reveal the body language based on

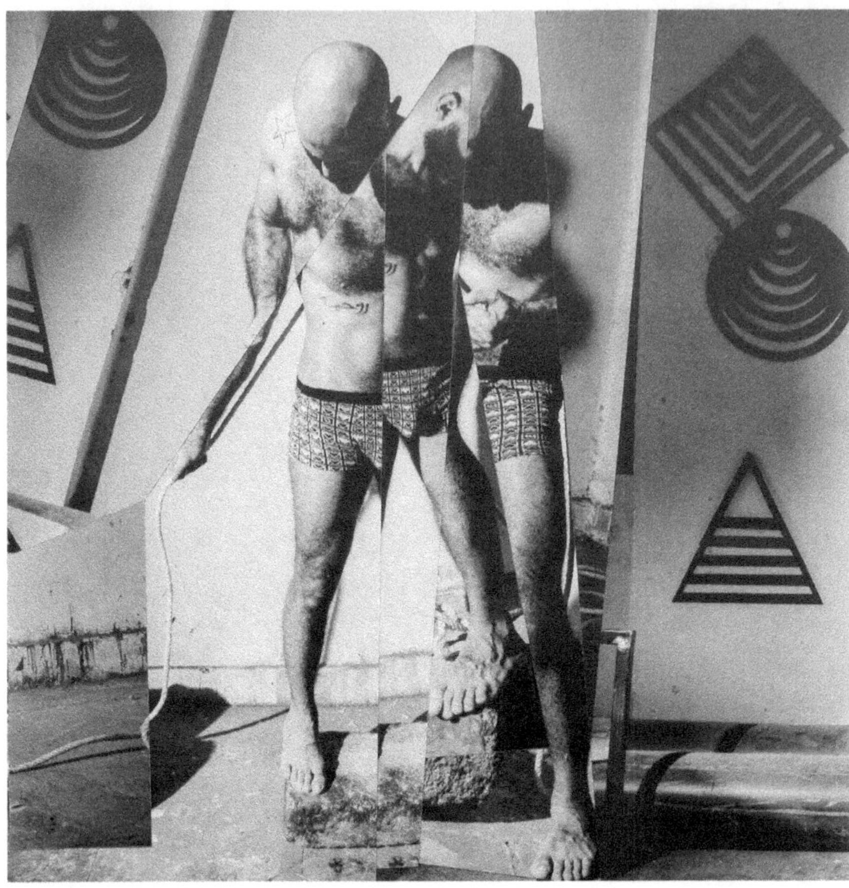

Figure 6.5 Ibrahim Ahmed, *Figure#85, You Can't Recognize What You Don't Know*, 2019–2020

family snapshots of his father taken during gatherings as he copies 'four different directions, facing the camera, right, facing back my back to the camera' (Artist Interview, 15 May 2022). This approach is a formal decision as it enables the photographed male figure to be montaged later into an uncanny, singular sculptural form. In the re-enactment of the father figure through photography Ahmed's photomontages are curiously analogous to Nadia Mounier's self-portraiture work based on her own images of her father. In an interview the writer Sama Waly described his photomontage process for the online culture media site Orient XXI, 'the labour-extensive layering of hundreds of cut-out images to reveal an essence hidden behind the architecture of bodies' (Waly 2022).

Ahmed's photomontages involve two distinct stages: firstly, the studio portraits are taken, then follows an analogue post-production process which involves hand-cutting the black-and-white prints into a single composited portrait. By this process each photomontage is a one-off edition of his work, an analogue image composed of cut-up studio portraits. In the aforementioned *Figure#85*, the male body has been sliced up vertically into four constituent parts. This slicing act transforms the figure into a weird vision of the male body with three legs, three heads and three arm-like shapes, in ways reminiscent of Aristophanes' tale in the *Symposium* of the mythological human soulmate.[17] Similarly, this analogue distortion and fragmentation of the image surface shatters the photographic single-point perspective on the visual plane, as it has multiple viewpoints that are unsettling for the viewer. In the Arab context these human forms can be connected to the local traditions in Egypt of spirits known as jinn,[18] who still influence contemporary beliefs and coexist as part of superstitions woven into everyday life. Each person can have a jinn that exists as a shadow in a parallel reality to affect one's real-life existence. The creative approach in this image breaks with the camera gaze as the ocular enigma of the figure is re-assembled in the mind to imagine what act he engages in. Pulling a rope connected to a large cement block on which the man stands is a futile act if not an absurd one, and a gesture which resonates in the struggle of Sisyphus in Greek mythology or even the existential interdependency of characters Hamm and Clov in Samuel Beckett's play *Endgame*. Art critic Osman Can Yerebakan reads representation in Ahmed's self-portraits as part of the debates on male identity: 'The unending battle reflects the entrapment of masculinity which Ahmed long found himself contained by' (Yerebakan 2021).

However, in this visual composition the cement block can be read as less symbolic because it is a quotidian object used in Ard el-Lewa to stop cars parking on the streets. Such types of large objects (stones, chairs, tins) are commonly used as makeshift traffic cones by unskilled workers who have carved out an income for themselves by controlling parking places in the city. These unofficial car attendants, known as *sayes*, are mostly male but sometimes female, and charge Cairene car owners a small fee for their services. In this sense, the cement object addresses this informal local economy and can be also understood as a manifestation of the relationship between masculinity and car culture in Egypt. Ahmed built up his knowledge of cars to bond with local youths and says, 'the cement slab is from Ard el-Lewa and I am using it to tie into the idea of car culture' (Artist Interview, 15 May 2022). The figure in the photomontages is involved in an action that is not fully visible; what he is doing or attempting to do is not wholly clear. The male remains, on an emotional level, harder to determine as the face is hidden, and his inner state not revealed to the viewer because the focus is directed at the sculptural features of the body. This photomontage is an apotheosis to masculinity; *Figure#85* is a self-reflective portrait that holds an obvious sense of struggle which seems distorted in time and space. In fact, the history of the medium is evoked through the abnormal version of the human body in the early motion studies in photography by pioneers Muybridge or Marey. The eye returns to the somatic motif of male bodies in the reconstruction of masculinity played out in the photography. This theme is included in the catalogue for the solo exhibition at the Tintera photographic gallery who commented on this aspect of his work:

> For Ahmed, this ongoing body of work acts somewhat as a visual diary, with each iteration evolving as he delves deeper into his personal history and the relationship to his own manhood. (Tintera 2021)

The interaction between the artist's own biographical experience of masculinity and the performance of masculinity is key to this photomontage artwork. The performance and indoctrination of body comes about through the artist's relationship to his own father and, as the family moved from one country to the next, his father and nation become intertwined during his childhood. Indeed, the patriarchal nature of the Egyptian state is a part of this self-portraiture, as Ahmed comments, 'The breaking of a man to fit into this role doesn't happen as a man happens as a boy' (Artist Interview, 25 November 2021). His male body is seen in labour, cut adrift, as the biographical narrative of being uprooted between rural Egyptian and Western cultural contexts is played out in the art making. This is manifested in the photomontage process itself that functions like the shifting biographical timeline of Ahmed's life, chopping and changing, and he has set about reconstructing it as a form of visual storytelling; juxtaposing, cutting, slicing up the self to reconfigure the person, in a re-enactment of his lived experience of migration and fractured identity. In addition, photography is related to the biographical narrative as his father purchased privately owned cameras to document the family as they resettled in Bahrain and finally to the United States. Each relocation further reproduced more vernacular family photography to become compressed and skewed into the performativity of masculine identity. The photomontages layer memories, feelings and family images to explore the self, acted out consciously or not in the studio, and the artwork reconstructs his past. As he has said in an interview with the author, 'I think had I not come to Egypt, I wouldn't have been able to make this body of work. I think there was a certain level of aggressive masculinity that was in the States' (Artist Interview, 15 May 2022).

The father–nation fusion in the visceral intensity of masculinity found in Ahmed's photomontage series brings into view the motif of the rural Egyptian body, *fellahin*, through the troubled lens of photography. The colonial history of the medium illustrates the fetishization of the North African body, submissive to the camera gaze and trapped within a visual iconography of colonialism that haunts these complex self-portraits. As Ahmed comments about his father's heritage and physicality, 'My father was a farmer, the farm boy, his body from the rural to the modern man' (Artist Interview, 15 May 2022). In the *Figure#85* image the semi-clad, male figure is both performative of masculinity in the theatrical space, though also bound to a dead weight, tied down, his head lowered in a powerful but somewhat abject pose. Ahmed is aware of this historical gaze on his photo work and elaborates, 'I keep on thinking about the history, black-and-white images, nineteenth-century Egypt and twentieth century. We know nothing about the sitter, fabricated fantasies' (Artist Interview, 15 May 2022). Literary scholar Tarek El-Ariss has researched Arabic literature from the nineteenth century onwards and has written on the impact of colonialism to address how Egyptian and other Arab writers have placed the body as a central motif of the encounters with Orientalism. The photographic historian Stephen Sheehi concludes that 'al-Ariss situates the body of the Arab as a site of cultural conflict and epistemological rupture in these literary works' (Sheehi 2016: 175). With a background in literature Ahmed is fully aware of this hauntology of colonialism that frames his image, and *Figure#85* shows an archetypical lone North African male bound up in struggle, weighed down inside the pictorial plane, as modernity disciplines the body, to connect with nationalist rhetoric. Building on his autobiographical narrative Ahmed sets out to create another visual lexicon through disruption of photographic histories and he makes space for alternative re-imaginings to unlearn the tenets of the masculinity. Waly reviewed the photomontage artworks *You Can't Recognize What You Don't Know* to comment, 'If the question of manhood is intrinsically tied to a nationalist identity, what place is there for those whose identity has been uprooted by the very nationalist project that upholds the notion of masculinity?' (Waly 2022).

Each of these unique photomontages is an analogue iteration of the artist's autofiction narrative and his visual position within Egyptian cultural representation. Having received his higher education in the United States and worked in the contemporary art world in New York, Ahmed is well aware of the debates on contemporary identity politics and his own position within the Western world. His photomontage work has become his own articulation of the desire to delink from cultural hegemony and find his own artistic roots beyond the hierarchy of Western knowledge; he explains this process: 'for me, the most radical act is to really go inward and decolonize your own understanding of the self' (Artist Interview, 15 May 2022). His uprooting from Egypt as a child to British schooling in Bahrain and then life in the United States meant he was bound to an ideology that he had to internalize but which fractured his identity to simplified social codes. The unpaved alleyways of Ard el-Lewa became a decolonized zone, like a *mulid*, where the artist found deeper cultural channels to link into, such as Sufism, as something the Egyptian state cannot fully regulate. As he has commented, 'there is the spiritual practice that I am embodying in my work; it's an undercurrent' (Artist Interview, 15 May 2022). This spiritual genealogy has a particular heritage in the delta area and through his practice Ahmed opens up onto the forces of the marginal rural identity. His photomontage artworks retain visceral power and strange beauty through their resistance to the coercion of Western aesthetics. By this he moves beyond reproducing the status quo of photographic history to disrupt belonging and the uniform imagination of heteronormativity in mainstream Egyptian society. As with the work of Nadia Mounier the index of the photographic image is not enough and Ahmed's photomontage approach transforms what the camera describes to produce a vision of the gendered self. It is this relationship between aesthetic forms and decoloniality that lies at the core of the creative expression of the contemporary generation of photographic artists in Egypt.

Notes

1 The Arab Image Foundation has become internationally and regionally recognized as the leading photographic institution in the Arabic MENA region. In addition to housing and conserving hundreds of thousands of photographs, the Foundation has spearheaded conservation and preservation projects in the Middle East, co-sponsoring workshops to disseminate the knowledge and skills needed to identify, restore and conserve the Arab world's large photographic archive, estimated to be 600,000 visual items in a well-managed archive. For more information, see http://arabimagefoundation.org (accessed 29 September 2023).

2 An example of this cultural framing exhibition is the Victoria & Albert Museum exhibition *Light from the Middle East*, in London, which included the photomontage work of Egyptian Nermine Hammam. The exhibition and book publication explored the various ways that contemporary MENA artists deploy the language and techniques of photography. It presented over twenty-five artists whose multiple viewpoints are appropriate to a region where collisions between personal, social, religious and political life can be emotive and complex. It includes a wide array of work made by the diaspora, ranging from photojournalism to staged and digitally manipulated photographs.

3 There are many notable exceptions to this classification photography work in Egypt. The projects of Heba Khalifa, Rehab Eldahil, Mohamed Mahdy, Roger Anis, Ravy Shaker, among many others, can be seen as key examples of hybrid photographic work that could be best described as conceptual documentary

practices. Such photographers work in editorial and commercial contexts too but also extend their practices to more personal and creative uses of the medium. Their more experimental projects are often supported by cultural intuitions, such the Arab Documentary Photography Program. Some photographers have stretched the documentary genre through staged photographic works; among them Roger Anis's *A Blessed Marriage* (www.rogeranis.photo/albums/a-blessed-marriage, accessed 29 September 2023) and Ravy Shaker's *Letter to Moses* (www.arabdocphotography.org/project/61, accessed 29 September 2023) are impressive bodies of creative visual work. Their output is indicative of mixing styles and approaches when switching between professional editorial commissions and more personal modes of production. In addition, young photographers have studied on scholarships, in particular, the Danish School of Media and Journalism, Aarhus, Denmark, under the supervision of Søren Pagter and Mads Greve.

4 This may give a misleading impression that landscape topics are overlooked and under-represented by local photographers and artists living and working within Egypt. There are many merited projects from Hala Elkoussy, Paul Geday, Myriam Abdelaziz, Anthony Hamboussi and Nabil Boutros, among others, who have produced project work on informal urban development, salt mines, artistic impressions of the picturesque and cityscapes. The point here refers to the haphazard nature and under-development of photography work addressing the topographical vision, akin to Western cultural production.

5 A turning point in the Western history of photography came about in the 1975 exhibition *New Topographics*, at the International Museum of Photography, New York, which visualized a radical new way to depict landscapes. The show marked a move away from more natural vistas and instead represented a postmodern vision of the world. Often shot in black-and-white monochrome these unromanticized views captured stark industrial sites, urban city sprawl and other prosaic scenes normally overlooked by landscape photography. Some of the primary exponents of this vision include Bernd and Hilla Becher, Stephen Shore, Robert Adams and Lewis Baltz.

6 The original essay, *Das Kunstwerk im Zeitalter seiner technischen Reproduzierbarkeit* (The Work of Art in the Age of Its Technological Reproducibility), was published in 1935 and is a cultural criticism which states that the mechanical reproduction in photographic processes devalues the aura or uniqueness of an artwork. This absence of traditional and ritualistic value means the production of art would be inherently based upon the praxis of politics and it was influential on the theory of art in mass culture. This is the problem Benjamin sees in *Neue Sachlichkeit* (matter of factness) art, a genre which embodies Benjamin's objections most clearly. The content of the *Neue Sachlichkeit* consists of depictions of the harsh conditions of workers with a revolutionary character, yet at the same time, it retains the bourgeois productive apparatus and is subsumed by mainstream media cultures.

7 Contemporary research into visual perception has established there is a two-way neural activity moving upstream and downstream involved in the process of

seeing. Studies in human vision have found that the ratio is approximately 50:50 between what the eye takes in and how the brain responds. Therefore, the whole of the mind is active in seeing, not just localized sectors such as the visual cortex, and both cultural and psychological neurodiversity are forming the complex picture in reading a photographic image.

8 The term 'simulacra' has been central to the writings of Jean Baudrillard who was himself a photographer. Because photography in the digital age needs no umbilical connection to the real and it is only a connection to data computer code, in this sense it has arrived at the final phase hyperreal of what Baudrillard described as 'successive four phases of the image, 1) it is the reflection of a profound reality; 2) it masks and denatures a profound reality; 3) it masks the absence of a profound reality; 4) it has no relation to any reality whatever: it is its own pure simulacrum' (Baudrillard 1994: 6). He has written widely on this ontological issue in essays and books and in *The Perfect Crime*, he notes, 'The [analogue] photo is not an image in real time. It retains the moment of the negative, the suspense of the negative, that slight time-lag which allows the image to exist before the world – or the object – disappears into the image, which they could not do in the [digital] computer generated image, where the real has already disappeared. The photo preserves the moment of disappearance and thus the charm of the real, like that of a previous life' (Baudrillard 1996: 86).

9 Curated by the Contemporary Image Collective's Andrea Thal and Ahmed Refaat, the exhibition included work from three diverse local artists: Rawya Sadek, Hagar Ezzeldin and Nadia Mounier. *Istihdar al-ghiyab* (Retrieving Absence) brought together the articulations of three ongoing artistic projects that explore gender identity in Egypt and through multimedia approaches of photography, visual art and installation. The projects were influenced by biographical content, household materials and family albums to evoke the sense of being a woman in their cultural identity.

10 Visual artist Shirin Neshat is best known for films and photographic works which explore the relationship between religious and cultural value systems of Islam. Her work is well known in the contemporary art world as she has defined artistic visions of Muslim women for Western eyes to fuse politics with emotional registers in a classical way. Her *Women of Allah* series, created in the mid-1990s, introduced themes of the discrepancies of public and private identities in both Iranian and Western cultures. The split-screened video *Turbulent* (1998) won her the First International Prize at the Venice Biennale in 1999. Her works are included in the collections of the Tate Gallery in London, the Museum of Modern Art in New York, the Tel Aviv Museum of Art and the Walker Art Center in Minneapolis, among others.

11 Photographic artist Lalla Essaydi looks at how gender is inscribed on the bodies of women in the Arab cultural context. Born in Morocco and living in the United States she draws on Orientalist imagery to produce her artworks that consist of Arabic calligraphy drawn over images of female bodies, referencing the tradition of henna. The images depict women in decorative settings and scenes in a way

that exemplifies society's views of women as primarily destined to be seen and looked at. Her artwork uses photography in a painterly way and it has been widely exhibited and collected in Western art institutions.

12 The handwritten text on the surface of Mounier's self-portrait photograph states in full, 'I can't tell you why I've loved this photo of my father out of all the others. My family albums are filled with different photos of him because of his travels and the nature of his work. He holds a steady gaze towards the camera, fixing it before the exposure. I'm intrigued by his hand resting on his thigh despite his relaxed posture. My mother doesn't like the photo or my love for it; his wavy hair, his sitting position, his hand holding a cigarette is inappropriate for her. She asks me to reconsider and suggests other photos of him. My relationship with my mother tenses up when the conversation turns to politics or photography' (Artist Interview, 15 May 2022).

13 A recent publication dedicated to the theories of Mitchell was edited by Croatian scholar Krešimir Purgar, as it addresses his lifetime of academic work on image theory. The author, Francesco Gori, defines a key part of research: 'Leafing through the history of semiotics and aesthetics, we encounter everywhere the presence of such a third element at the crossroads between iconic and linguistic representation, the senses of hearing and sight, aesthetics and semiotics' (Gori 2017: 44).

14 The persistent urban growth of Cairo shows that, while lacking public services and infrastructures, informal settlements are nonetheless successful in generating dense and affordable housing for working-class communities. However, a governmental policy to legalize these settlements is yet to materialize and their potential is not understood. Ard el-Lewa is located on the east side of the city and land was bought through a local savings-and-credit association called *gamaya* where land could be bought for two Egyptian pounds per square metre (at the time, about $6) with a legal subdivision licence. *Gamaya* is a social and financial way for low-income communities to live in Cairo and it relies on monthly subscriptions from its members. Areas like Ard el-Lewa depend on informal finance solutions for populations without access to banks. Demographic growth and rural migration to Cairo from rural parts of Egypt has soared with the acute need for cheap housing. Public housing and urban infrastructure programmes were put on hold for decades so that state funding could be directed into the military regime.

15 The government has started to demolish informal areas, like Ard el-Lewa, and social housing projects have yet to resolve the problem for more than half of the population. Yahia Shawkat's excellent work *Egypt's Housing Crisis* (2020) is a comprehensive research study, while David Sims has published two notable books on Cairo's urban development; see *Understanding Cairo* (2011) and *Egypt's Desert Dreams* (2018) for detailed analyses of this housing crisis.

16 Artellewa is an art space founded in 2007 and managed by Cairo-based visual artist Hamdy Reda. The space is located in the Ard el-Lewa area, a densely populated informal urban area. This project space creates a dialogue between artists and the local community through exhibitions and events, artists residencies,

site projects, workshops for community and members, as well as supporting emerging artists.

17   In one part of Plato's *Symposium* the Greek theatre writer Aristophanes outlines the fantastical account of the origins of love to explain how originally humans were soulmate creatures with four legs, four arms and two faces on each side of the head. This mythological human had three types of genders, namely, male, female and androgynous. All of these genders had two pairs of genitals but only the androgynous humans had both male and female sex organs. Sexual orientation was fluid as male soulmates were gay, female soulmates were lesbians and the androgynous soulmates were heterosexuals. These humans were famous for their powerful abilities which threatened the gods and Zeus exacted revenge by cutting these soulmate humans in half, thereby creating the longing in the human condition to be reunited with this missing other self.

18   The belief in spirits or jinn is particularly prevalent in Egypt and has its origins in Arabic and Islamic mythology. The spirit entity has been conceptualized as human-like forms that live on earth alongside humans. They are not deemed wholly evil or good – rather, more mischievous – but are said to possess magical powers that make them invisible and, as such, they can shapeshift, which allows them to take the form of animals, usually snakes and serpents, or even humans. Evil, godless, malicious or otherwise, a harmful jinn may influence the world indirectly through sorcerers or possess people or more directly through their own actions. Egyptian anthropologist Hager El Hadidi has written a compelling book on this cultural phenomenon in Cairo, *Zar: Spirit Possession, Music, and Healing Rituals in Egypt* (2016).

Conclusion: Decolonial aesthetic futures

Decolonizing images: A new history of photographic cultures in Egypt has set out to look at the cultural layers present in a diverse collection of visual works produced within Egypt. The ambition of the book is to discover the latent properties of photographic materials created in the local context, as a way to offer an alternative narrative to the dominant history of photography; one not embedded in Western aesthetic values. This contributes to the history of photographies by speculating on what decolonizing images can mean in the context of Egypt's encounter with the medium and tells the story of how photographic images intersected with local values. This book provides a timely opportunity to delink from the cultural hegemony of dominant accounts of the medium and underscores the role photography played in the reproduction of modernity. The visual case studies in the book span a timeline from nineteenth-century colonialism to contemporary fine art practices, as these photographic materials have mediated between the medium and Egypt's visual culture. Such a visual heritage speaks to a psychological space as much as a geographical one which comes through the lived reality of everyday Egypt. In this sense daily life is not the same as in Western societies, as Walter Mignolo points out cultural values are not universal because 'in Tehran, or La Paz ... the issues, problems, and knowledge-making have different needs, genealogies of thoughts, affects, and problems' (Mignolo 2011: xxiv). Therefore, a non-Western experience of modernity can reconsider the photographic image because of the ways in which the visual is treated, imagined and understood over phases of social transformation to suggest other values for photography.

Decoloniality is not a singular entity itself but rather a framework of approaches that seeks to disrupt colonial pasts and rethink the knowledge economy in order to allow breathing space for other cultures formed on the margins to become visible, beyond the orbit of Western thought. Such a reset decentres from hetero/cisnormativity, gender hierarchies and racial privilege underpinned by modernity to allow for the multiplicity of lives of colonized people to appear. The lineage of photographic image works in this book makes visible local knowledge, complete with their own problematics and peculiarities, as a way to offset the stereotypes of Egypt and show how living and the image are not separated but intersect with each other. Decolonizing the image is a way to unlearn the canon of photography and revalue the connections between knowledge production, creative practices, social relationships and political agency. The integration of the photographic image into broader debates can form visual bonds between being and viewing, and create alternative sensibilities which do not seek to partition life from the image, as can occur in Western ontologies. The introduction of photography brought the world into sharp focus as a vision created through Eurocentric eyes. This resulted in a fixed, spatio-temporal relationship as an exterior realm of images became mediated and separate from being. The rupture caused echoes of older discourses, taken up by Māori scholar Linda Tuhiwai Smith in *Decolonizing Methodologies*. For her the decolonial turn is a critical challenge to the fundamental history of Western thought; she refutes contemporary philosophy and states, 'Our colonial experience traps us in the project of modernity. There can be no "postmodern" for us until we have settled some business of the modern' (Smith 2021: 38).

However, criticism of the decolonial has emerged, in particular, from African postcolonial theorists who suggest the term has been overused and needs to be reconsidered if not totally abandoned. One prominent voice is Nigerian scholar Olúfẹmi Táíwò, who suggests the decolonial project has essentially failed in the African context because it stifles discourse to become a universalizing obstacle to genuine scholarship and it is mostly a contemporary academic trend with 'little to contribute to intellectual thought' (Leonard 2022).[1] Other scholars in the field question the overrating of the concept, as Josias Tembo states, 'decolonial theory may engage with African postcolonial theory and postcolonial theory more generally in more productive ways than the present sweeping dismissals' (Tembo 2022: 48). In his paper 'Rethinking the Decolonialization Trope in Philosophy', Táíwò draws critical attention to two exponents of decolonization in Africa, Kenyan author Ngũgĩ wa Thiong'o and Ghanaian philosopher Kwasi Wiredu, as he suggests that it 'obscures more than it discloses' (Táíwò 2019: 140). Part of his argument involves the issue of language and in his analysis of Kenyan and Nigerian literature he discredits authors who write in indigenous languages because their works can become perceived as cultural nationalism and he suggests that the English language has been reclaimed if not refashioned into an authentic expression of African identities. In a less confrontational stance, theorist Achille Mbembe differs somewhat to acclaim the writing of Ngugi wa Thiong'o because it acknowledges the importance of place and the local, and comments that his literature puts 'Africa at the centre of things, not existing as an appendix or a satellite of other countries and literatures, things must be seen from the African perspective' (Mbembe 2016: 35).

Despite the valid concerns expressed by some African postcolonial theorists about the decoloniality project and their undoubtedly persuasive arguments on its shortcomings, decoloniality remains useful when looking at Egypt's visual cultures. In part this comes about because of the unfixed nature of decolonizing knowledge and it is about more than de-Westernization; for instance, rejecting colonial languages, and in the case of photography it can provide an opportunity for a nonconformist imagination and different sensibilities to manifest. In Egypt the visual operates alongside censorship control and in the context of this book, decoloniality is a thinking mode to connect with broad knowledge systems and frameworks to reorientate Western cultural power. The contemporary visual content of this book shares something of 'magical dualism' (Ghazoul 1994) but not in the struggle for prominence between the rational and mystical; rather, as an embodied consciousness and formed as a response to healing colonial wounds. Many of the images discussed in the present work were formed by the encounter between local traditions and photography, to leave a shadowy floating veil hovering over the image. For instance, in Chapter 3 the magazine *al-Musawwar* published an image on the front cover to show a scene from the Tanta *mulid* (Figure 3.2). In this news photograph a Sufi sheikh is depicted in an ecstatic state as the camera lens looks down from high on the religious reverie in a fusion of photography's modern gaze focused on the metaphysical within the mystical dimension of Islamic rituals.

In contrast to many of the narratives advanced by Western photography, Egypt's image materials make a clear distinction between private and public roles, the hidden and visible, the seen and unseen, while operating under fixed codes of religious morals, social dogma and even state censorship. Furthermore, Egypt's experience of liberation struggles has fermented over decades to manifest as what seems from the outside like a uniform imagination, personified by the military state culture. Such a limited vision perpetuates hierarchy and censorship that has been characterized by social inequalities at the expense of more radical autonomous imaginings; most clearly challenged by political activism during the 2011 uprising. The book sets out to argue for decolonial aesthetics through the singular creative origin that is connected to broader properties of the specific situation. As Chapter 6 demonstrated, the subjective expression in the self-portraiture work of Nadia Mounier (Figures 6.1 and 6.2) sees her gender autofiction narratives linking with and formed by local cultural values. Moreover, the photographic object is not enough for her, and more is required of photography because these text-image photo works are specific to the situation but not only specified by it, that is, not wholly determined by the situation. This awareness is conscious, free and intentional in the singular imagination evident in the visual object, and the photographic image can be of something but not only specified by it. Political expression was contested, as Chapter 3 demonstrates, through the visual case study of a group of female protesters in central Cairo (Figure 3.1) and this political agency resurfaced a century later in the video activism of the Mosireen project (Figure 4.1) in Chapter 4. Furthermore, in different ways both of these image works reflect more than their specified historical moments to evolve beyond their initial point of inception and have had much to do with debunking gender roles and nationalist myths.

What lies on the other side of the specific context of historical moments is the singular creative energy, formed by its own genesis, while occurring within the dynamics of a particular situation in history. Singularity should not be misunderstood as a type of universality as it is linked closely to the socio-cultural characteristics of its origin; it is specific to but not specified by its environment alone (Hallward 2002). In the endless indivisibility of any historical event the singular and the specific intersect with each other without fully succumbing to the temptation of either. The photomontages by Ibrahim Ahmed, discussed in Chapter 6, visualize a dissecting of the self with each image, a unique analogue iteration of specific forces and singular energies. In this way, the singular keeps in check and transforms universal tendencies or claims which can be overly determined to lack the awareness of the nuances and sensibilities of a particular cultural case. As Hallward states, 'We learn to think rather than merely recognise or represent, to the degree that we actively transcend the specified or objectified' (Hallward 2002: 48). Decolonizing means transforming what is depicted to move beyond set positions in cultural affairs, be they the rhetoric against reason, critique of universality or contingency conditions. As theorist Aijaz Ahmad reminds us, 'The tendency in cultural criticism is to waiver constantly between the opposing polarities of cultural differentialism and cultural hybridity' (Ahmad 1995: 16). Therefore, the specific is representative in the local setting through social, cultural or historical forces, while the singular retains the individuality in its own creative origin. Moreover, the specific and the singular oppose universality, in the Cartesian sense, as single-point perspective rationality can often push aside knowledge in Global South contexts. Prita Meier comments in her research on the photographic representation of Swahili cultural expression through the depiction of the architecture in Zanzibar. She goes on to suggest that local aesthetics were made auxiliary because 'Africa is always the local and the west the global' (Meier 2013: 98).

In terms of photography decoloniality seeks to disconnect from Western values in order to define the parameters of its own decolonial aesthetics, a fundamental reorientation to detach from the legacy of Orientalism and the global art market. The decolonial artist does not look for art world endorsements but, importantly, to delink does not mean de-Westernization. Rather, it is the approach to use whatever systems are available in a context in order to be visible without compromising one's decolonial principles. In light of this, decolonizing the photographic images of Egypt rests on two primary and interlinked concerns: firstly, that decolonial aesthetics remains recognizable from Western ones and, secondly, the process must be accessible or relevant to a local audience in a specific context. Such principles do not mean decolonial work is devalued by its inclusion in the circuit of exhibitions and biennials across the global art world; in fact, the decolonial is often cited as critical for contemporary art. In addition, the photographic artists featured in Chapter 6, Nadia Mounier and Ibrahim Ahmed, regularly participate in exhibitions, residencies and other international cultural events. In this way, the aim of decolonial aesthetics is more than a question of inclusion or not, because art from the Global South is often mitigated when shown in Western cultural settings. Alternatively, the decolonial option seeks to delink from the legacy of Western aesthetics to produce a reordering of the sensibilities in the shift from 'colonial aesthetics into decolonial aisthesis' (Mignolo 2011: 202). Here Mignolo uses the Greek term *aisthesis*, in a clear division from the eighteenth-century Eurocentricity of aesthetic experience and, in his view, the ethical properties of improving the world is an important criteria for a work of art.[2]

Apart from the aforementioned Western-led global art industry, other cultural hegemonies include non-Western actors, in particular from the Gulf Cooperation Council area that includes six states in the Persian Gulf where well-funded arts institutions appear to support the decolonial agenda but supress basic human rights and freedom of expression.[3] The photographic heritages of Egypt remain wary of the aesthetic traditions formed in the West[4] and are also attentive to the misbegotten soft power of petrodollars in the region. The Global South requires the decolonial cultural worker to close the gap between epistemology, aesthetics and ethics in knowledge production. Decolonizing images can be an option, rather than a discipline for the visual, as it is an interwoven part of knowledge systems that connects visual cultures with the sociological, economic or political to constitute the new possibilities of the photographic image.

The decolonial option, in relation to the heritage of photography in Egypt, can be summarized as the unlearning and detaching from Western hierarchies of knowledge to allow space for other forms of embodied knowledge to be disclosed. Accordingly, this means bringing into view decolonial aesthetic values to the history of photography. The argument of this book exposes Egypt's visual history to a process that defines what are its particular unique properties. Key photographic phases have been developed in this publication to track colonial legacies and, in addition, to consider how the patriarchal nature of nationalism has continued to shape the society. The story of photography in Egypt began with *Le Daguerréotype au harem* (Figure 2.1) when Frenchmen Goupil-Fesquet and Vernet demonstrated the process in the autumn of 1839 to the Ottoman modernizer Muhammad 'Ali. This photographic event is significant because it constitutes two contradictions in the evolution of photography in Egypt. Through the photographic process the camera made public this exterior of the Ottoman fortress while framing the enclosed private harem space that is invisible to the eye. Therefore, the seen and unseen, the index of the building and non-indexical imagination, are both present in this nineteenth-century image. This dualism shapes the chronology of Egypt's visual heritage and subsequent uses of the medium have intersected these specific and singular characters of local visual culture.

Firstly, specificity can be read through the controlling gaze of state as is evident in the lineage from Ottoman to Egyptian rulers because, essentially, little changed in relation to visual literacy. The photographic was often perceived sceptically because the meaning of images is hard to control and the state preferred to censor what it did not fully understand. Even during the optimism of Nasser's anti-colonial rule, the media was nationalized as photography was used as a propaganda tool of the state. For instance, the social documentary photography by Abdul Fattah Eid set out to record the consequences of the High Dam construction in Aswan and the forced migration of Nubians. However, in the photograph examined in Chapter 3 (Figure 3.4), the image displays the intrusive power of Nasserism into the private lives and domestic homes of marginal communities. The dominance of military rule in the twentieth century established a suffocating type of state that propagated a trite visual regime to mix nationalism and censorship in idiosyncratic ways as the spectre of colonialism looked over Nasser's broad shoulders. The specificity of Egypt's photographic history represents struggles between the discernible pillars of the hollowed-out nation consisting of political Islam, military statehood and secular activism to contest the national image. It is this claustrophobic hiatus that triggered a disillusioned generation of Egyptians to revolt in 2011 and Mosireen's video archive, discussed in Chapter 4, holds the collective memory of this remarkable time in Egypt. Furthermore, al-Mahdy's self-portrait (Figure 5.1), covered in Chapter 5, attempted to explode visual censorship in a fluid time in history. Censorship and image politics are two sides of the same specific role for photography in Egypt and speak to the indexical tensions of what is permitted and what is forbidden.

Secondly, singular properties can also be found in the same 1839 daguerreotype framing of 'Ali's harem. The photograph shows two soldiers guarding a doorway entrance to the sultan's hidden pleasures and it is this concealment, a non-indexical quality, that can be found in later forms of photographic expression as the medium took hold. The use of photography as a storytelling device is understood instinctively because of the allegorical and poetic nature of culture and what is beyond the visual object. Furthermore, the division of public versus private, the disclosed and the veiled, has been a reoccurring approach to the medium. The magazines *al-Musawwar* and *al-Ithnayn* both visualized front covers that connect with the local audience through the use of allegorical visual communication. As seen in Chapter 3, the Tanta *mulid* (Figure 3.2) spoke to a mystical spiritual dimension of Islam that is invisible to direct representation, and *al-Ithnayn*'s photomontage text work (Figure 3.3) creatively adapted a Hollywood film poster to draw upon local idioms. These suggestive qualities are important to the cultural mediation of the medium into the cadences of life in Egypt, and in Chapter 6 the artists Ibrahim Ahmed and Nadia Mounier are indicative of a generation who explore contemporary gender identities in an indirect and non-explicit manner; arguably in contrast to Western explicit sensibilities. This form of visual storytelling is based on an oral tradition that took up the ocular within its own terms to delineate the decolonial aesthetics of Egyptian photography. These two apparent opposites, indexical specificity and singular storytelling, are linked to intersect in the image as the hidden metaphysical is linked to censorship and spiritual genealogy counters global modernity. The visual cases studied across this book map out a lineage to explore the properties of Egypt's visual cultures and the attendant theories of decoloniality to propose a non-Western aesthetic sensibility is present.

The vision of Egypt has been fiercely contested and even mythologized along nationalist notions for far too long. Like colonialism, the military state produces its own ghosts as it uses disappearance as a repressive tactic against opponents to haunt the contemporary society and intimidate the population into submission. In recent years many have psychologically withdrawn inwards to exist as apolitical beings while others have emigrated with no intention of returning, gone almost without trace. Sociologist Mona Abaza has defined this present-day depressive national condition as 'a kind of enforced internal exile that has metamorphosed us into obedient but self-absorbed beings' (Abaza 2020: 5).

As digital cultures in 2011 demonstrated, a poignant photographic truth belies any enforced national homogeneity because the meaning of images cannot be anchored down easily or pigeonholed into uncomplicated and undemocratic narratives. The dreams of the 2011 uprising were harshly defeated by the military regime, a patriarchal state born in the non-democratic rule of Nasser with its earlier fascist echoes. An alternative image of Egypt was evident in political Islam which has been dismantled and brutally crushed in the aftermath of the Muslim Brotherhood's removal from power in 2013.

The prominent ideologies of Egypt orbit each other, alongside other lesser influential ones, to contest the collective image of the nation as it faces an uncertain future. The narrative in this book has set out to establish how photography intersects with everyday life and how it is a key cultural force in perception management. As Sara Salem comments, despite the struggle for the majority of the citizens, all hope is not lost:

> This is a world in which we break away from haunted histories of colonialism and anticolonialism; in which we transcend the nation (and all of its own haunted histories); and in which we break free from capitalist modernity. It is a moment in which we rectify the mistakes of anticolonial nationalism and centre all forms of social struggle from the start, from racism to sexism, from homophobia to classism, rather than perpetually relegate them to the future. (Salem 2020: 279)

Arguably for Egypt, decolonizing images can be part of a rethinking of the visual in the twenty-first century to mediate an insecure world under its current oppressive political regime. In time the military matrix will be challenged by the *au courant* generations who experience new political narratives, new technologies and the possibility of creative expression to decolonize the future. This book has explored decolonial aesthetics and cultural knowledge found in Egypt's photographic cultures to help delink from the 'disembodied vision' (Bryson 1983: 95) of the photographic canon and contest its rationality. Therefore, re-imaging photographic legacies and futures involves recognizing other sensibilities to privilege somatic relationships to the image and reconnect the haptic with photographic aesthetics. The ontology of the decolonial image does not emphasize indexical depth; rather, it is concerned with visual bonds in a vertical movement over latent cultural layers and historical narratives. Such subjectivity over rationality may offer hope for some as inner and outer worlds revolve around each other in a decolonial zone. Decolonizing images is an invitation and opportunity to rework the power relationships between the Global North and South while encountering visual cultures that are self-determined within their own local values. The photographic genealogy of Egypt consists of colonialism, state censorship and digital image politics that influenced the vision of a nation to constitute how the singular can transcend the specific in the embodied consciousness of decolonial aesthetic futures.

Notes

1 Ralph Leonard has reviewed the recent book *Against Decolonization: Taking African Agency Seriously* (2022), where Olúfẹ́mi Táíwò questions the usefulness

of the decolonial as a methodology for African intellectual thought in the current setting. He takes the stance that knowledge production or autonomy of thought in Africa could always critique Eurocentric narratives and broaden the intellectual and cultural palate beyond the Western canon without labelling such activity as decolonial. He asserts the term is overused and overly broad in the context of African societies. He disagrees with other African intellectuals about language; for instance, Kenyan author Ngũgĩ wa Thiong'o wrote initially in English but later switched to his indigenous Gikuyu, and represents a decolonial approach to cultural expression. For Táíwò language is one of the concerns at the core of the colonial problem and he holds the view that Nigerians have claimed back the English language for themselves and refashioned it in their own way. In an analysis of Kenyan and Nigerian literature he discredits authors who write in indigenous languages and suggests working in English, akin to debates on Indian literature, happened long before decolonization was a widely applied critical lens.

2 The term derives from the ancient Greek *aisthesis* to mean sensation or perception, in contrast to the intellectual concepts of rational knowledge in European philosophy. Prior to the mid-eighteenth century, aesthetic enquiry was quite different from what it is today, since there was no substantial concept of art as a creative act detached from trades or civic function. Plato questioned the perception of beauty that placed value without proper ethics and practical improvement of the way of life.

3 Six countries make up the Gulf Cooperation Council (Bahrain, Kuwait, Oman, Qatar, Saudi Arabia, United Arab Emirates). The arts in the Gulf area have always been controlled and censored if not carefully curated by these conservative Islamic states. Since their independence from British protectionism in the 1960s–1970s, these Gulf states have worked towards shaping their statehood and invested heavily in infrastructure projects. This included transforming physical landscapes and building new cities to establish nationwide urban planning of buildings, roads and metro systems. In addition, over the last two decades state-of-the-art educational facilities and cultural institutions, museums and galleries have located to the region. The Gulf states' cultural scene today seeks to rival that of the most prestigious international states in global terms of scale, industry and artist attractions, and ultimately market establishment and profits. This has impacted on the cultural scene in Egypt because of the traditional role the country played in the region, specializing in music and film in particular.

4 German philosopher Alexander Gottlieb Baumgarten published the treatise *Aesthetica* in 1750 and the term refers to the feelings and the emotions that can be derived from the senses. Baumgarten highlighted the importance of the senses in knowing and understanding and the term 'aesthetics' is derived from two Greek words *aistheta* and *noeta* meaning a distinction between two operations of the mind perceiving and thinking. Apart from the perplexing issue of how two distinct processes in the mind are related to each other and can be observed, a related issue arises concerning which of the two to privilege. If we derive the *aistheta* (perceiving) over *noeta* (thinking) we privilege sensation; conversely, if we derive *noeta* over *aistheta* we privilege thought. Working in the rationalist

tradition Baumgartner was attempting to relate taste or judgement to an intellectual conception of beauty. Immanuel Kant later modified this interpretation
in his *Critique of Judgment* (1790), to explore the canon of taste and aesthetic
judgement. Therefore, aesthetic experience is born through subjective judgements
that arise to a universal level and, in this way, indicate how aesthetic response
can acquire social meaning. Aesthetics became a branch of philosophy, displacing
Aristotelian poetics, to theorize the beautiful and the sublime, and artistic genius.
That legacy has been transmitted to current discussions on postmodern aesthetics
through figures such as Jacques Rancière or the Altermodern project, a short-lived
attempt to bring politics to postmodern global context as expounded by French
curator Nicolas Bourriaud. Rancière's aesthetic discourse has gained much critical
traction by looking at sensing but from the Western experience only. An issue
remains over his Eurocentric references that rarely include examples from the
Global South, and for Rancière sensibility is not universal but European.

References

Abaza, Mona (2020) *Cairo Collages: Everyday Life Practices after the Event.* Manchester: Manchester University Press.

Abraham, Danielle Widmann (2014) 'At the Threshold of Interpretation: Imaging Muslim Women's Lives'. In Sarah T. Brooks (ed.), *The Photography of Lalla Essaydi: Critiquing and Contextualizing Orientalism* (Harrisonburg: James Madison University), 42–46.

Abu-Lughod, Lila (2015) *Do Muslim Women Need Saving?* Harvard: Harvard University Press.

Adlat (2023) 'Elegance, Fashion and Clothes.' [In Arabic.] https://adlat.net/forumdisplay.php?f=21 (accessed 3 October 2023).

Adorno, Theodor W. (2013) *Aesthetic Theory.* London: Bloomsbury Academic.

Ahmad, Aijaz (1995) 'The Politics of Literary Postcoloniality'. *Race and Class*, 36:3, 13–16. https://doi.org/10.1177/030639689503600.

al-Alwani, Taha Jaber (2001) 'Fatwa concerning the United States Supreme Courtroom Frieze'. *Journal of Law and Religion*, 15:1/2, 1–28.

al-Khatib, Hadi (2017) 'Assad's Crimes Maybe Forgotten as YouTube Censors Content'. The New Arab, 14 September. www.newarab.com/features/assads-crimes-may-be-forgotten-youtube-censors-content (accessed 10 March 2020).

Alloula, Malek (1986) *The Colonial Harem.* Translated by Myrna Godzich and Wlad Godzich. Minneapolis: University of Minnesota Press.

Al-Saidi, Afaf Ahmed Hasan (2014) 'Post-colonialism Literature: The Concept of *Self* and the *Other* in Coetzee's *Waiting for the Barbarians*: An Analytical Approach'. *Journal of Language Teaching and Research*, 5:1, 95–105. https://doi.org/10.4304/jltr.5.1.95-105.

Al-Sumait, Fahed, Nele Lenze and Michael C. Hudson (eds) (2014) *The Arab Uprisings: Catalysts, Dynamics, and Trajectories.* London: Rowan & Littlefield.

Amnesty International (2012) 'Egypt: A Year after "Virginity Tests", Women Victims of Army Violence Still Seek Justice'. 9 March. www.amnesty.org/en/latest/news/2012/03/egypt-year-after-virginity-tests-women-victims-army-violence-still-seek-justice (accessed 8 July 2020).

Anderson, Benedict (2016) *Imagined Communities: Reflection on the Origin and Spread of Nationalism.* London: Verso.

Appadurai, Arjun (1997) 'Disjuncture and Difference in the Global Cultural Economy'. *Theory, Culture & Society*, 7, 295. https://doi.org/10.1177/026327690007002017.

Araki, Nobuyoshi (2007) *Dirty Pretty Things*. New York: Powerhouse Books.

Armbrust, Walter (1996) *Mass Culture and Modernism in Egypt*. Cambridge: Cambridge University Press.

Asad, Amira (2013) 'The Egyptian Feminist Who Was Kidnapped for Posing Nude'. Vice, 14 February. www.vice.com/en/article/8gv3jv/the-egyptian-feminist-who-was-kidnapped-for-posing-nude (accessed 5 October 2023).

Ayalon, Ami (1995) *The Press in the Arab Middle East: A History*. Oxford: Oxford University Press.

Azoulay, Ariella Aisha (2012) *The Civil Contract of Photography*. Princeton, NJ: Zone Books.

Azoulay, Ariella Aisha (2019) *Potential History: Unlearning Imperialism*. London: Verso.

Badger, Gerry, and Martin Parr (2004) *The Photo Book: A History, Volume 1*. London: Phaidon Press.

Baron, Beth (2005) *Egypt as a Woman: Nationalism, Gender and Politics*. Berkeley: University of California Press.

Barouti, Tina (2017) 'Barouti on Sheehi, "The Arab Imago: A Social History of Portrait Photography 1860–1910"'. H-AMCA, January. https://tinyurl.com/395emh5v (accessed 19 June 2021).

Barthes, Roland (1982) *Camera Lucida: Reflections on Photography*. London: Hill and Wang.

Baudrillard, Jean (1994) *Simulacra and Simulation (The Body in Theory: Histories of Cultural Materialism)*. Translated by S. Glaser. Michigan: University of Michigan Press.

Baudrillard, Jean (1996) *The Perfect Crime*. Translated by Chris Turner. London: Verso.

Bayat, Asef (2017) *Revolution without Revolutionaries: Making Sense of the Arab Spring*. Stanford: Stanford University Press.

Bazin, André (2004) *What Is Cinema?* Berkeley: University of California Press.

Behdad, Ali (2013) 'The Oriental Photograph'. In Ali Behdad and Luke Gartlan (eds), *Photography's Orientalism: New Essays on Colonial Representation* (Los Angeles: Getty Research Institute), 11–32.

Behdad, Ali (2016) *Camera Orientalis: Reflections on Photography of the Middle East*. Berkeley: University of California Press.

Bekhrad, Joobin (2014) 'Tehran Bazaar: Contemporary Art in the Time of the Ayatollahs'. *Cairo Review of Global Affairs*, 14, 49–55.

Bendiksen, Jonas (2021) *Book of Veles*. London: GOST books.

Berkley, Angela (2015) 'Snapshot Seeing: Kodak Fiends, Child Photographers, and Henry James's *What Maise Knew*'. *Modern Fiction Studies*, 61:3, 375–403.

Bier, Laura (2020) *Revolutionary Womanhood: Feminism, Modernity, and the State in Nasser's Egypt*. California: Stanford University Press.

Bréhier, Louis (2018) *L'Egypte de 1798 à 1900*. Paris: Combet Books.

Bryson, Norman (1983) *Vision and Painting: The Logic of the Gaze*. New Haven: Yale University Press.

Burckhardt, Titus (1987) *Mirror of the Intellect: Essays on Traditional Science and Sacred Art*. New York: State University of New York Press.

Carville, Justin (2010) 'Intolerable Gaze: The Social Contract of Photography'. *Photography and Culture*, 3:3, 345–350. https://doi.org/10.2752/175145109X 12804957025750.

Chakrabarty, Dipesh (1992) 'Provincializing Europe: Postcoloniality and the Critique of History'. *Cultural Studies*, 6:3, 337–357. https://doi.org/10.1080/ 09502389200490221.

Clifford, James (1988) *The Predicament of Culture: Twentieth-Century Ethnography, Literature and Art*. Harvard: Harvard University Press.

Close, Ronnie (2017) 'Parallax Error: The Aesthetics of Image Censorship'. *Membrana*, 2:2, 74–82. https://doi.org/10.47659/m3.074.art.

Cole, Juan (2008) *Napoleon's Egypt: Invading the Middle East*. New York: Palgrave Macmillan.

Connell, Raewyn (2016) 'Decolonising Knowledge, Democratising Curriculum'. www.uj.ac.za/wp-content/uploads/2021/10/raewyn-connells-paper-on-decolonisation-of-knowledge.pdf (accessed 9 July 2021).

Corbin, Henry (1998) *Alone with the Alone: Creative Imagination in the Sūfism of Ibn 'Arabī*. Princeton, NJ: Princeton University Press.

Cormack, Raphael (2022) *Midnight in Cairo: The female Stars of Egypt's Roaring '20s*. London: Saqi Books.

Dean, Jodi (2014) 'Communicative Capitalism and Class Struggle'. *Journal for Digital Cultures*, 1, 1–16.

de Angelis, Enrico (2020) 'The Controversial Archive: Negotiating Horror Images in Syria'. In Donatella Della Ratta, Kay Dickinson and Sune Haugbolle (eds), *The Arab Archive: Mediated Memories and Digital Flows* (Amsterdam: Institute of Network Cultures), 69–88. https://networkcultures.org/blog/publication/tod35-the-arab-archive-mediated-memories-and-digital-flows/ (accessed 2 October 2023).

de Bellaigue, Christopher (2017) *The Islamic Enlightenment: The Modern Struggle between Reason and Faith*. London: Bodley Head.

Della Ratta, Donatella (2018) *Shooting a Revolution: Visual Media and Warfare in Syria*. London: Pluto Press.

de St. Jorre, John (1999) 'Pioneer Photographer of the Holy Cities'. *Aramco World: Arab and Islamic Cultures and Connections*, 50:1, 36–47.

Devlin, Liam (2019) 'Myth, Montage and Magic Realism: Rethinking the Photograph as a Discursive Document'. *Photographies*, 12:1, 3–18. https://doi.org/10.108 0/17540763.2018.1512518.

Diab, Amina (2021) '"Free Art" and Surrealist Aesthetics: Resituating the Art and the Liberty Group in Egyptian Art History'. *Nka: Journal of Contemporary African Art*, 49, 54–62. https://doi.org/10.1215/10757163-9435667.

Downey, Anthony (ed.) (2014) *Uncommon Grounds: New Media and Critical Practices in North Africa and the Middle East*. London: I.B. Tauris.

Drewal, Henry John (2013) 'Local Transformations, Global Inspirations: The Visual Histories and Cultures of Mami Wata Arts in Africa'. In Gitti Salami and Monica Blackmun Visonà (eds), *A Companion to Modern African Art* (New Jersey: Wiley Blackwell), 21–49.

Edwards, Steve (2006) *Photography: A Very Short Introduction*. Oxford: Oxford University Press.

el-Aswad, el-Sayed (2006) 'Spiritual Genealogy: Sufism and Saintly Places in the Nile Delta'. *International Journal of Middle East Studies*, 38:4, 501–518. https://doi.org/10.1017/S0020743806412447.

El-Bizri, Nader (2005) 'A Philosophical Perspective on Alhazen's Optics'. *Arabic Sciences and Philosophy*, 15:2, 189–218.

El Deeb, Sarah (2017) 'History of Syria's War at Risk as YouTube Reins in Content'. AP News, 13 September. https://apnews.com/article/technology-civil-wars-middle-east-business-online-video-d9f1c4f1bf20445ab06cbdff566a2b70 (accessed 12 August 2021).

El-Gundy, Zeinab (2016) 'Fifth Anniversary of Egypt's 2011 Revolution Marked by Security Concerns'. Ahram Online, 24 January. https://english.ahram.org.eg/News/185752.aspx (accessed 4 October 2023).

El Hadidi, Hager (2016) *Zar: Spirit Possession, Music, and Healing Rituals in Egypt*. Cairo: American University in Cairo Press.

Eltahawy, Mona (2011) 'Egypt's Naked Blogger Is a Bomb Aimed at the Patriarchs in Our Minds'. *Guardian*, 18 November. www.theguardian.com/commentisfree/2011/nov/18/egypt-naked-blogger-aliaa-mahdy (accessed 18 November 2013).

El-Rifae, Yasmin (2022) *Radius: A Story of Feminist Revolution*. London: Verso.

Ersoy, Ahmet A. (2017) 'Review: *Camera Orientalis: Reflections on Photography of the Middle East*, Ali Behdad … *The Arab Imago: A Social History of Portrait Photography, 1980–1910*, Stephen Sheehi'. *History of Photography*, 41:3, 311–315.

Espinosa, Juan García (1979) 'For an Imperfect Cinema'. Translated by Julianne Burton. *Jump Cut*, 20, 24–26. www.ejumpcut.org/archive/onlinessays/JC20folder/ImperfectCinema.html (accessed 2 October 2023).

Farouk, Menna A. (2020) 'Egyptian Court Jails Belly Dancer for "Debauchery" in Social Media Crackdown'. Reuters, 27 June. www.reuters.com/article/us-egypt-women-jailed-trfn-idUSKBN23Y0X7 (accessed 12 December 2020).

Fayed, Ismail (2020) 'On Queerness and the Jargon of Authenticity'. Mada Masr, 22 July. www.madamasr.com/en/2020/07/22/opinion/u/on-queerness-and-the-jargon-of-authenticity (accessed 23 July 2021).

Fernea, Robert A., and Aleya Rouchdy (2010) 'Nubian Culture and Ethnicity'. In Nicholas S. Hopkins and Sohair R. Mehanna (eds), *Nubian Encounters: The Story of the Nubian Ethnological Survey 1961–1964* (Cairo: American University in Cairo Press), 289–300.

Fisher, Mark (2009) *Capitalist Realism: Is There No Alternative?* London: Zero Books.

Flusser, Vilém (2000) *Towards a Philosophy of Photography*. London: Reaktion Books.

Freedom House (2019) 'Freedom on the Net 2019'. https://freedomhouse.org/country/egypt/freedom-net/2019 (accessed 27 September 2023).

Fourier, Jean-Baptiste Joseph (1809) *Préface historique, Description de l'Égypte Imprimerie impériale*. Paris: France.

Gaber, Sherif (2015) 'The Mosireen Collective'. Filming Revolution. https://filmingrevolution.supdigital.org/article/234/sherief_gaber (accessed 28 June 2021).

Gamal El-Din, El-Sayed (2021) 'Egyptian TikTok Influencer Handed 3 Years in Jail for "Violating Society Values"'. Ahram Online, 8 June. https://english.ahram.org.eg/News/413809.aspx (accessed 29 October 2021).

Ghazoul, Ferial (1994) *Mohammad Afifi Matar: Belles étrangères Égypte*. Paris: Ministère de la Culture et de la Francophonie.

Ghoneim, Niveen (2020) '"A Dangerous Precedent": Menna Abdel Aziz v. Egypt's Failing Justice System'. Egyptian Streets, 4 July. https://egyptianstreets.com/2020/07/04/a-dangerous-precedent-menna-abdel-aziz-v-egypts-justice-system/ (accessed 5 October 2023).

Gilroy, Paul (1993) *The Black Atlantic Modernity and Double Consciousness*. London: Verso.

Godlewska, Anne (1995) 'Map, Text and Image: The Mentality of Enlightened Conquerors: A New Look at the *Description de l'Egypte*'. *Transactions of the Institute of British Geographers*, 20:1, 5–28.

Golia, Maria (2009) *Photography and Egypt*. London: Reaktion Books.

Gori, Francesco (2017) 'What Is an Image? W.J.T. Mitchell's Picturing Theory'. In Krešimir Purgar (ed.), *W.J.T. Mitchell's Image Theory: Living Pictures* (New York: Routledge), 40–60.

Gran, Peter (1998) *Islamic Roots of Capitalism: Egypt 1760–1840*. Syracuse: Syracuse University Press.

Grierson, John (1933) 'The Documentary Producer'. *Cinema Quarterly*, 2:1, 7–9.

Grigsby, Darcy Grimaldo (2013) 'Two or Three Dimensions? Scale, Photography, and Egypt's Pyramids'. In Ali Behdad and Luke Gartlan (eds), *Photography's Orientalism: New Essays on Colonial Representation* (Los Angeles: Getty Research Institute), 115–128.

Gruber, Christiane, and Avinoam Shalem (2014) 'Introduction: Images of the Prophet Muhammad in a Global Context'. In Christiane Gruber and Avinoam Shalem (eds), *The Image of the Prophet between Ideal and Ideology: A Scholarly Investigation* (Berlin: De Gruyter), 1–12.

Gruber, Christiane (2019) *The Praiseworthy One: The Prophet Muhammad in Islamic Texts and Images*. Bloomington: Indiana University Press.

Hafez, Sherine (2019) *Women of the Midan: The Untold Stories of Egypt's Revolutionaries*. Bloomington: Indiana University Press.

Hallward, Peter (2002) *Absolutely Postcolonial: Writing between the Singular and the Specific*. Manchester: Manchester University Press.

Hamilton, Omar Robert (2017) *The City Always Wins*. London: Faber & Faber.

Hannoosh, Michèle (2016) 'Horace Vernet's "Orient": Photography and the Eastern Mediterranean in 1839, Part II: The Daguerreotypes and Their Texts'. *The Burlington Magazine*, CLVIII, 430–439.

Haugbolle, Sune (2020) 'Archival Activists and the Hybrid Archives of the Arab Left'. In Donatella Della Ratta, Kay Dickinson and Sune Haugbolle (eds), *The Arab Archive: Mediated Memories and Digital Flows* (Amsterdam: Institute of Network Cultures), 7–19. https://networkcultures.org/blog/publication/tod35-the-arab-archive-mediated-memories-and-digital-flows/ (accessed 2 October 2023).

Hobsbawm, Eric (2010) *The Age of Empire*. London: Abacus Books.

Holert, Tom (2015) 'Coming to Terms: Contemporary Art, Civil Society and Knowledge Politics in the "Middle East"'. In Anthony Downey (ed.), *Dissonant Archives: Contemporary Visual Culture and Contested Narratives in the Middle East* (London: I.B. Tauris), 92–108.

Holzwarth, Hans Werner (ed.) (2009) *100 Contemporary Artists*. Cologne: Taschen.

Hourani, Albert (1983) *Arabic Thought in the Liberal Age, 1798–1939*. Cambridge: Cambridge University Press.

Human Rights Watch (2011) 'Egypt: Don't Cover Up the Military Killing of Copt Protesters'. 25 October. www.hrw.org/news/2011/10/25/egypt-dont-cover-military-killing-copt-protesters (accessed 3 July 2014).

Hunter, G. Frederick (1985) 'Commitment and Autonomy in Art: Antinomies of Frankfurt Esthetic Theory'. *Berkeley Journal of Sociology*, 30, 41–64.

Khatib, Lina (2012) *Image Politics in the Middle East: The Role of the Visual in Political Struggle*. London: I.B. Tauris.

Khorshid, Sara (2021) 'The Unlikely Success of Egypt's 2011 Revolution: A Revived Women's Movement'. Atlantic Council, 27 January. www.atlanticcouncil.org/blogs/menasource/the-unlikely-success-of-egypts-2011-revolution-a-revived-womens-movement (accessed 18 August 2022).

Koetzle, Hans-Michael (2011) *Photographers A–Z*. Cologne: Taschen.

Korany, Bahgat, and Raba El-Mahdi (eds) (2012) *Arab Spring in Egypt: Revolution and Beyond*. Cairo: American University in Cairo Press.

Kraidy, Marwan M. (2017) *The Naked Blogger of Cairo: Creative Insurgency in the Arab World*. Harvard: Harvard University Press.

Latour, Bruno (1993) *We Have Never Been Modern*. Translated by Catherine Porter. Cambridge, MA: Harvard University Press.

Latour, Bruno (2002) 'What Is Iconclash? Or Is There a World beyond the Image Wars?'. In Peter Weibel and Bruno Latour (eds), *Iconoclash: Beyond the Image-Wars in Science, Religion and Art* (Berlin: ZKM; Cambridge, MA: MIT Press), 14–37.

Latour, Bruno (2021) 'Is This a Dress Rehearsal?'. *Critical Inquiry*, 47:S2, 25–27.

Lazarus, Neil (2011) *The Postcolonial Unconscious*. Cambridge: Cambridge University Press.

Leal, Luis (1995) *No Longer Voiceless*. San Diego: Marin Publications.

Lebow, Alisa (2016) 'Seeing Revolution Non-linearly: www.filmingrevolution.org'. *Visual Anthropology*, 29:3, 278–295. https://doi.org/10.1080/08949468.2016.1154751.

Leonard, Ralph (2022) 'Olúfẹ́mi Táíwò's "Against Decolonisation"'. Aero, 17 June. https://areomagazine.com/2022/06/17/olufemi-taiwos-against-decolonisation (accessed 13 August 2022).

MacKenzie, John M. (1995) *Orientalism: History, Theory and the Arts*. Manchester: Manchester University Press.

Manovich, Lev (2001) *The Language of New Media*. Cambridge, MA: MIT Press.

Marks, Laura U. (2014) 'Arab Glitch'. In Anthony Downey (ed.), *Uncommon Grounds: New Media and Critical Practices in North Africa and the Middle East* (London: I.B. Tauris), 257–271.

Marks, Laura U. (2017) 'Poor Images, Ad Hoc Archives, Artists' Rights: The Scrappy Beauties of Handmade Digital Culture'. *International Journal of Communication*, 11, 3899–3916.

Mayeur-Jaouen, Catherine (2019) *The Mulid of al-Sayyid al-Badawi of Tanta: Egypt's Legendary Sufi Festival.* Cairo: American University in Cairo Press.

Mbembe, Achille (2015) 'Decolonizing Knowledge and the Question of the Archive'. Wits Institute for Social and Economic Research (WISER), University of the Witwatersrand, Johannesburg. https://tinyurl.com/2mj8b5xx (accessed 13 August 2022).

Mbembe, Achille (2016) 'Decolonizing the University: New Directions'. *Arts and Humanities in Higher Education*, 15:1, 29–45. https://doi.org/10.1177/1474022215618513.

Meier, Prita (2013) *Swahili Port Cities: The Architecture of Elsewhere.* Bloomington: Indiana University Press.

Michelson, Annette (ed.) (1984) *Kino-Eye: The Writings of Dziga Vertov.* London: Pluto Press.

Mignolo, Walter D. (2011) *The Darker Side of Western Modernity: Global Futures, Decolonial Options.* New York: Duke University Press.

Mitchell, Timothy (1991) *Colonising Egypt.* Berkeley: University of California Press.

Mitchell, W. J. T. (1986) *Iconology: Image, Text, Ideology.* Chicago: University of Chicago Press.

Mitchell, W. J. T. (1992) *The Reconfigured Eye: Visual Truth in the Post-photographic Era.* Cambridge, MA: MIT Press.

Moreh, Shmuel (2004) *Napoleon in Egypt: Al-Jabarti's Chronicle of the French Occupation.* Princeton, NJ: Markus Wiener Publishers.

Mosireen (2014) 'Revolution Triptych'. In Anthony Downey (ed.), *Uncommon Grounds: New Media and Critical Practices in North Africa and the Middle East* (London: I.B. Tauris), 47–52.

Mosireen (2018) 'No Archive Is Innocent'. www.mosireen.com/-no-archive-is-innocent (accessed 26 September 2023).

Mosireen_Soursar (2020) '858: No Archive is Innocent: On the Attempt of Archiving Revolt'. In Donatella Della Ratta, Kay Dickinson and Sune Haugbolle (eds), *The Arab Archive: Mediated Memories and Digital Flows* (Amsterdam: Institute of Network Cultures), 35–40. https://networkcultures.org/blog/publication/tod35-the-arab-archive-mediated-memories-and-digital-flows/ (accessed 2 October 2023).

Mourad, Sara (2013) 'The Naked Bodies of Alia'. Jadaliyya, 1 January. www.jadaliyya.com/Details/27715/The-Naked-Bodies-of-Alia (accessed 25 April 2023).

Nour El Din, Nadine (2019) 'Egyptian Artist Ibrahim Ahmed Speaks Out about His Censored Work at the Havana Biennial'. *Harper's Bazaar*, 16 June. www.harpersbazaararabia.com/culture/art/artists/egyptian-artist-ibrahim-ahmed-speaks-out-about-his-censored-work-at-the-havana-biennial (accessed 16 June 2022).

Özen, Saadet (2017) 'The Visual Making of the Harem'. *Art in Translation*, 9:1, 51–58. https://doi.org/10.1080/17561310.2015.1088220.

Paul, Ian Alan (2015) 'The Revolutionary Practice of Endurance'. Jadaliyya, 25 January. www.jadaliyya.com/Details/31709/The-Revolutionary-Practice-of-Endurance (accessed 18 May 2016).

Paulsen, Kris (2013) 'The Index and the Interface'. *Representations*, 12:1, 83–109. https://doi.org/10.1525/rep.2013.122.1.83.

Perez, Nissan N. (1988) *Focus East: Early Photography of the Near East 1839–1885.* New York: Abrams Books.

Pinney, Christopher (2003) 'Notes from the Surface of the Image: Photography, Postcolonialism, and Vernacular Modernism'. In Christopher Pinney and Nicolas Peterson (eds), *Photography's Other Histories* (New York: Duke University Press), 202–220.

Pinney, Christopher, and Nicolas Peterson (eds) (2003) *Photography's Other Histories*. New York: Duke University Press.

Pratt, Mary Louise (1991) 'Arts of the Contact Zone'. *Profession: Modern Language Association*, 33–40.

Ranciére, Jacques (2011) *The Emancipated Spectator*. Translated by Gregory Elliott. London: Verso.

Rawi, Maysa (2011) '"It Doesn't Matter If You Are Jewish, Arab, Straight or Lesbian": Israeli Women Strip in Support of Nude Egyptian Blogger'. *Daily Mail*, 21 November. www.dailymail.co.uk/femail/article-2064267/Israeli-women-strip-support-nude-Egyptian-blogger-Aliaa-Elmahdy.html (accessed 1 June 2019).

Robinson-Dunn, Diane (2006) *The Harem, Slavery and British Imperial Culture: Anglo-Muslim Relations in the Late Nineteenth Century*. Manchester: Manchester University Press.

Roh, Franz (1995) 'Magic Realism: Post-expressionism (1925)'. In Lois Parkinson Zamora and Wendy B. Faris (eds), *Magical Realism: Theory, History, Community* (New York: Duke University Press), 15–31.

Rose, Gillian (2001) *Visual Methodologies: An Introduction to Researching with Visual Materials*. London: Sage Publications.

Ryzova, Lucie (2014) 'Mourning the Archive: Middle Eastern Photographic Heritage between Neoliberalism and Digital Reproduction'. *Comparative Studies in Society and History*, 56:4, 1027–1061.

Ryzova, Lucie (2015a) 'Nostalgia for the Modern: Archive Fever in Egypt in the Age of Post-photography'. In Costanza Caraffa and Tiziana Serena (eds), *Photo Archives and the Idea of Nation* (Berlin: De Gruyter), 301–318.

Ryzova, Lucie (2015b) 'Boys, Girls, and Kodaks: Peer Albums and Middle-Class Personhood in Mid-Twentieth-Century Egypt'. *Middle East Journal of Culture and Communication*, 8:23, 215–255.

Said, Edward (1994) *Culture and Imperialism*. London: Vintage.

Sakr, Laila Shereen (2023) *Arabic Glitch: Technoculture, Data Bodies, and Archives*. Stanford: Stanford University Press.

Salem, Latifa (1996) *Faruq wa-suqut al-malikiyya fi Misr* [Farouk and the collapse of the monarchy in Egypt]. Cairo: Madbuli.

Salem, Sara (2020) *Anticolonial Afterlives in Egypt: The Politics of Hegemony*. Cambridge: Cambridge University Press.

Seung-hoon, Jeong (2011) 'The Para-indexicality of the Cinema Image'. *Ontologia del cinema*, 46:1, 75–101.

Shalabi, Hiba (2023) 'Honouring Distinguished Women in the Design and Graphics Department for the Month of September 2023'. [In Arabic.] Adlat. https://adlat.net/showthread.php?t=172442 (accessed 3 October 2023).

Shawkat, Yahia (2020) *Egypt's Housing Crisis: The Shaping of Urban Space*. Cairo: American University in Cairo Press.

Sheehi, Stephen (2016) *The Arab Imago: A Social History of Portrait Photography, 1860–1910*. Princeton, NJ: Princeton University Press.

Sims, David (2011) *Understanding Cairo: The Logic of a City Out of Control*. Cairo: American University in Cairo Press.

Sims, David (2018) *Egypt's Desert Dreams: Development or Disaster?* Cairo: American University in Cairo Press.

Smecker, Frank (2014) *Night of the World: Traversing the Ideology of Objectivity*. London: Zero Books.

Smith, Linda Tuhiwai (2021) *Decolonizing Methodologies: Research and Indigenous Peoples*. London: Zed Books.

Snowdon, Peter (2020) *The People Are Not an Image: Vernacular Video after the Arab Spring*. London: Verso.

Sokolowski, Robert (2000) *Introduction to Phenomenology*. Cambridge: Cambridge University Press.

Solon, Olivia (2019) 'Facial Recognition's "Dirty Little Secret": Millions of Online Photos Scraped without Consent'. NBC News, 12 March. www.nbcnews.com/tech/internet/facial-recognition-s-dirty-little-secret-millions-online-photos-scraped-n981921 (accessed 27 September 2023).

Sontag, Susan (2001) *On Photography*. London: Picador.

Spicer, Andrew (2017) 'Iconoclasm'. *Renaissance Quarterly*, 70:3, 1007–1022.

Spivak, Gayatri Chakravorty (1993) *Outside in the Teaching Machine*. New York: Routledge.

Stack, Liam, and David D. Kirkpatrick (2011) 'Nude Blogger Riles Egyptians of All Stripes'. *New York Times*, 17 November. www.nytimes.com/2011/11/18/world/middleeast/aliaa-magda-elmahdy-egypts-nude-blogger-stirs-partisan-waters.html (accessed 4 October 2023).

Steyerl, Hito (2009) 'In Defense of the Poor Image'. *E-Flux*, 10. www.e-flux.com/journal/10/61362/in-defense-of-the-poor-image (accessed 5 September 2017).

Steyerl, Hito (2012) 'The Spam of the Earth: Withdrawal from Representation'. *E-Flux*, 32. www.e-flux.com/journal/32/68260/the-spam-of-the-earth-withdrawal-from-representation (accessed 15 May 2019).

Stock, Alexandra (2015) 'Egyptian Surrealists in Global Perspective: A Report from the AUC'. Ibraaz, 23 December. www.ibraaz.org/news/135 (accessed 23 July 2019).

Stühlinger, Harald R. (2017) 'Editorial'. *Photo Researcher*, 28, 1–3.

Tageldin, Shaden M. (2011) *Disarming Words: Empire and the Seductions of Translation in Egypt*. Berkeley: University of California Press.

Táíwò, Olúfẹmi (2019) 'Rethinking the Decolonialization Trope in Philosophy'. *The Southern Journal of Philosophy*, 57:S1, 135–159.

Tembo, Josias (2022) 'Do African Postcolonial Theories Need an Epistemic Decolonial Turn?'. *Postcolonial Studies*, 25:1, 35–53. https://doi.org/10.1080/13688790.2022.2030582.

Tintera (2021) 'Ibrahim Ahmed'. www.tintera.art/ibrahim-ahmed-1 (accessed 5 October).

Waly, Sama (2022) 'Egyptian Photographer Ibrahim Ahmed Questions Masculinity'. Orient XXI, 28 July. https://orientxxi.info/lu-vu-entendu/egyptian-photographer-ibrahim-ahmed-questions-masculinity,5796 (accessed 20 June 2022).

Warner, Jason (2019) *The Islamic State in Africa: The Emergence, Evolution, and Future of the Next Jihadist Battlefront*. Oxford: Oxford University Press.

Westmoreland, Mark R. (2020) 'Time Capsules of Catastrophic Times'. In Donatella Della Ratta, Kay Dickinson and Sune Haugbolle (eds), *The Arab Archive: Mediated Memories and Digital Flows* (Amsterdam: Institute of Network Cultures), 20–34. https://networkcultures.org/blog/publication/tod35-the-arab-archive-mediated-memories-and-digital-flows/ (accessed 2 October 2023).

Willis, Anne-Marie (1990) 'Digitization and the Living Death of Photography'. In Philip Hayward (ed.), *Culture, Technology & Creativity in the Late Twentieth Century* (London: John Libbey), 197–208.

Wilson-Goldie, Kaelen (2010) 'Photography and Egypt'. *Bidoun*, 19. www.bidoun.org/articles/photography-and-egypt (accessed 29 June 2019).

Winegar, Jessica (2006) *Creative Reckonings: The Politics of Art and Culture in Contemporary Egypt*. Stanford: Stanford University Press.

Woodward, Michelle L. (2003) 'Between Orientalist Clichés and Images of Modernization'. *History of Photography*, 27:4, 363–374. https://doi.org/10.1080/03087298.2003.10441271.

Yerebakan, Osman Can (2021) 'Gently Erotic Photo Collages That Explore Migration and Masculinity'. *AnOther Magazine*, 4 August. www.anothermag.com/art-photography/13488/gently-erotic-photo-collages-that-explore-migration-and-masculinity (accessed 22 June 2022).

Index

EU authorised representative for GPSR:
Easy Access System Europe, Mustamäe tee 50,
10621 Tallinn, Estonia
gpsr.requests@easproject.com